IRAN: RELIGION,

D0109854

IRAN

Religion, Politics and Society

Collected Essays

Nikki R. Keddie

*Professor of History, University of
California, Los Angeles*

FRANK CASS

First published 1980 in Great Britain by
FRANK CASS AND COMPANY LIMITED
Gainsborough House, Gainsborough Road,
London, E11 1RS, England

and in the United States of America by
FRANK CASS AND COMPANY LIMITED
c/o Biblio Distribution Centre
81 Adams Drive, P.O. Box 327, Totowa, N.J. 07511

British Library Cataloguing in Publication Data

Keddie, Nikki Ragozin
  Iran.
  1. Iran – Social conditions
  I. Title
  309.1'55   HN670.2.A8

  ISBN 0–7146–3150–7 (Case)
  ISBN 0–7146–4031–X (Paper)

Typeset by Computacomp (UK) Ltd, Fort William, Scotland
Printed in Great Britain by
Biddles Ltd, Guildford, Surrey

A Claude Cahen et Maxime Rodinson
Les Grands Maîtres

Contents

Acknowledgments

Chapter 1 originally appeared in *Comparative Studies in Society and History*, IV, 3, April 1962. Chapter 2 appeared in *Past and Present*, 34, July 1966. Chapter 5 appeared in *Iranian Studies*, V, 1972. Chapter 6 is reprinted from C. A. O. Van Nieuwenhuijze, ed., *Commoners, Climbers and Notables*, Leiden, Brill, 1977. Chapter 7 first appeared in R. Antoun and I. Harik, eds., *Rural Politics and Social Change in the Middle East*, Bloomington, Indiana University Press, 1972. Thanks to the above for permission to republish.

Parts of Chapter 8 have previously appeared in 'The Midas Touch: Black Gold, Economics and Politics in Iran Today', *Iranian Studies*, X, 4, Autumn 1977, and 'Oil, Economic Policy and Social Conflict in Iran', *Race and Class*, XXI, Summer 1979. Chapters 3 and 4 have not been previously published.

Diacriticals have been omitted in this book.

Introduction

In the years between the publication of the first of the enclosed articles on Iran, 1962, and the most recent, published now for the first time, scholarly and public interest in Iran has increased enormously. Whereas two decades ago one dreaded being asked by an outsider what country one specialized in, knowing that either 'Iran' or 'Persia' could lead to an embarrassed dead silence, based on ignorance, now such dread has an opposite cause – one is sure of being deluged with a spate of questions about Iran's future. The future-minded may find sustenance in the essays within, but they were not written with predictive aims. Rather, the major underlying themes of these articles – the intertwining of religion and politics in modern Iran; the impact of economically powerful Western nations on Iranian society; the patterns of internal social and economic change in the nineteenth and twentieth centuries; the causes and conditions of revolutionary change in Iran; and the political and religious ideologies of modern Iran – are all themes that arose from an analytic approach to history. If these themes, as discussed in individual articles, can help explain some of the apparently startling events of 1978–1979, it is not due to any peculiar past predictive capacity, but rather to a serious effort to understand what forces have been important in Iranian society, even when this importance has not been externally obvious, and not to pay too much attention to the daily or surface events that make up the stuff of much writing about Iran.

In the articles on religion and politics there is a continuum, beginning with 'Religion and Irreligion', through 'The Origins of the Religious-Radical Alliance in Iran', and 'The Roots of the

1

Ulama's Power in Modern Iran' (reprinted in N. Keddie, ed, *Scholars, Saints and Sufis*, but not here), all of which combine considerable primary with secondary reading to come up with new analyses. ('Religious-Radical alliance' almost immediately entered the common scholarly parlance.) These three articles also go together in that they give a brief coverage of the relations of the ulama (religious leaders) to politics from 1500 to 1911 (and even briefly to the present), and also raise the question of some men who presented themselves in religious garb, either figuratively or literally, while in fact holding radical, atheist, or heretical (Azali Babi) views.

Regarding the Babis, discussed in 'Religion and Irreligion in Early Iranian Nationalism,' I have been misunderstood by some who note the space devoted to them and the mention of the Babi background of some late nineteenth and early twentieth century revolutionaries and conclude that I think they were of great importance in leading the constitutional revolution. I never thought so, and the names given in 'Religion and Irreligion' almost exhaust the Babis important in the revolutionary or pre-revolutionary movement; clearly the vast majority of leaders in the revolution were not Babis. The interest of the Babis in the revolution comes not only from their not having been analyzed in this context, but also from comparative history – this is one of several cases in world history where a messianic 'extremist' religious heresy moves, in part, into more secular radicalism and/ or reformism, which suggests ties between messianism and worldly progressivism.

'Religion and Society in Iran' gives a long-term historical survey of the relations among religion, society, and politics from ancient times until now, and discusses more recent developments than do the earlier articles.

The articles on religion and politics, which make up the first group in this collection are based on a varying combination of primary and secondary sources, with the primary being emphasized in both Persian and Western languages. Some of the articles in this section, and certain more monographic ones not reprinted here, were originally written when I planned to write a history of the Iranian Constitutional Revolution, but the sheer ever-growing mass of relevant material on the subject that a conscientious historian would be obliged to read before producing a solid work, and the need to reconstruct from numerous and often contradictory sources a coherent narrative of what was occurring in many cities, discouraged me from regarding this as a feasible task for completion in a limited time period. The project on the revolution, however, did result in three books: *Religion and Rebellion in Iran: The Tobacco Protest of 1891–1892* (London, Frank Cass, 1966); *An Islamic Response to Imperialism: Political and Religious Writings of Sayyid Jamal ad-Din 'al-Afghani'* (Berkeley and Los Angeles, University of California Press, 1968); and *Sayyid Jamal ad-Din 'Al-Afghani:' A Political Biography* (Berkeley and Los Angeles, University of California Press, 1972). None of the articles incorporated in the Afghani biography is included in the two volumes of my articles now published, but an article about him that makes new points is included in the other volume, *The Middle East and Beyond*, as Afghani's life and influence extended far beyond Iran.

As time went on I wrote less intellectual, religio-political, and political history and more social and economic history, as represented in the second section of this volume. This was not an entirely new interest, as my unpublished dissertation was on social history, and an early short monograph, *Historical Obstacles to Agrarian Change in Iran* (Claremont, Calif., 1960) was socio-economic. This work is not included herein, as those of its points that remain valid are incorporated into chapter 7 – 'Stratification, Social Control, and Capitalism in Iranian Villages: Before and After Land Reform' – which also supersedes in part my article on land reform in the *Journal of Contemporary History*, III, 3, 1968. In the field of socio-economic history, research herein is mainly on the twentieth century, based largely on Western-language reports and studies and on reports by and conversations with Iranian experts. Research has concentrated especially in two areas: the agrarian one represented by 'Stratification, Social Control, and Capitalism ...' and the nature of socio-economic change in Iran since 1960, represented in those articles within that cover that period. While in Iran in 1973–1974, after doing a general study of the economy, I launched a specific study of handicrafts and carpets as socio-economic phenomena, and some of this work is reflected in my most recent articles.

The articles in the socio-economic section that cover long periods of time, beginning in 1797 or 1800, cannot reflect detailed research about that entire period, and are rather concerned to put forth general interpretations that will help make sense of the vagaries of modern Iranian history. Such articles are by their nature unusually subject to correction as researchers dig up more primary material and come forth with new interpretations. Nonetheless, it should be clear that history, like other disciplines, progresses not primarily by digging up masses of raw material, but more through putting forth hypotheses based on such material, which can serve as benchmarks for new research.

The field of Iranian studies, including Iranian history, has expanded greatly in the past two decades. Compared to historians of Western countries, trained historians of Iran are still relatively few, but they are far more numerous than they were two decades ago. With this growth it was to be expected that not only important new research, but also disagreements, variant opinions, and revisions of history would arise, although these have not yet reached the intensity and excitement found in major Western controversies. One division rarely sees print in English, although it is important in Iran and may become more so: this is represented by a group of Iranian scholars who, like related nationalists elsewhere in the Third World, reject virtually everything written on their country by Westerners. (This goes in many cases beyond the views expressed in Edward Said's interesting volume *Orientalism*, [New York, 1978] where typical 'Orientalist' attitudes are condemned, but the Hull Group in Great Britain, and Rodinson and Berque in France are praised. To some of the Iranian group, Western writers never seem to merit praise.) Since few of the relevant views of this group are available in English, and it is difficult or impossible to enter into dialog with them, it seems inappropriate here to enter into further discussion of their ideas.

Regarding matters dealt with in the articles found in this book, there have been relevant disagreements in English that either have been published or very probably will be. Many of them are on themes already known in other countries, which is not surprising, as historians of Iran study the history and historiographical arguments of other countries and are influenced by them. Two related themes in economic history came to the fore at a conference at Babolsar, Iran in June, 1978, sponsored by the U.S. Social Science Research Council and Reza Shah Kabir

University (now the University of Northern Iran). Put most simply they are, did peasants get richer or poorer in the nineteenth century; and did merchants gain or suffer from the Western impact? Gad Gilbar of Israel maintained that peasant conditions improved in the nineteenth century and that Iranian merchants were relatively favored in most of this period, and hence able to build up large, often international, businesses. The position he takes on peasant prosperity goes against what I say in Chapter 7; also against very brief remarks by Ann Lambton in *Landlord and Peasant in Persia* (although I do not know to what degree she retains her position after seeing Gilbar's new evidence). Charles Issawi has written that it is probably impossible now to answer the peasant question, and I am somewhat inclined to agree. When one looks at the long and detailed disagreements over whether the French population's position was improving or suffering before the French Revolution, or over similar questions in England before and during the Industrial Revolution, one begins to feel that such discussions are very fruitful in bringing forth new material and refining our viewpoints, but that the statistical material available for the East, even more than for the West, is so weak that we are unlikely to reach a solution agreed on by all. There is also the question of what is meant by economic improvement; Gilbar relied heavily on import and trade statistics, and at one point, when discussing rising peasant consumption of immediately consumed goods mentioned four commodities: opium, tobacco, sugar, and tea. One might argue that their rise, both in itself and in any possible substitution for nutritious items, probably meant a deterioration of peasant intake and diet. Many of Gilbar's points were stronger than this, but more generally convincing were the arguments at the same congress by Vahid Nowshirvani who, while taking a generally 'optimistic' view of peasant improvement, modified it to include decline in certain classes and periods. Very relevant is the most detailed study so far, by Roger Olson, on the impact of foreign trade on agriculture in nineteenth century southern Iran, which suggests that the opium trade contributed to stratification, enriched a few men involved in it, but made life more precarious for many peasants, especially as wheat land was increasingly devoted to opium, all of which findings are consonant with my views. (Olson's article is in M.

Bonine and N. Keddie, eds, *Modern Iran: Continuity and Change*, Albany, N.Y., 1981.)

On the question of merchant improvement, at Babolsar Gilbar brought in important new evidence, but seemed somewhat inclined to accept the British view, based on British documents, that Iranian merchants were favored over foreign ones; whereas most Iranian sources state the opposite.

Another important younger scholar, Willem Floor, not present at the above congress, in his article 'The Merchants (*tujjar*) in Qajar Iran,' (ZDMG, 126, 1, 1976, 101–135), generally supports the Iranian view that Persian merchants were increasingly discriminated against in favor of foreign merchants, particularly just before the 1905–1911 revolution, which increased their discontent then. In an oral comment at the Middle East Studies Association, Ann Arbor, 1978, Floor also said his research led him to believe in general immiseration of Iranians including peasants in this period. It thus seems that a major controversy about the French revolution may be relived on a smaller scale for the Persian constitutional revolution, and one could paraphrase a volume on the French revolution to: 'The Economic Origins of the Persian Revolution: Poverty or Prosperity?' As for the remarks on the subject found in this volume, it is possible that I may have to modify my general view of immiseration on the basis of the newer scholarship (although this is not certain until both sides have published more). Such a modification would, however, retain the view that the Western impact did and does disrupt the lives of many, increases stratification and income gaps, and creates frustrations by partially opening avenues to economic advance but not permitting them to develop fully. Many peasants seem, after 1800, to have lost former rights to the land.

The question of the origins of, and forces behind, the Iranian revolution of 1905–1911 is a related controversy. In recent years some Iranian scholars, including one based in the U.S. and present at the Babolsar congress, Said Arjomand, have questioned the importance given by most scholars to the ulama in the revolution. They have found monarchist and conservative statements by several ulama in the nineteenth and early twentieth centuries and have tended to take these as typical, even though evidence seems lacking that these ulama had as a wide a following among other ulama or the urban public as did those who questioned the powers of the monarch and supported the constitutional movement. This downplaying of the ulama is sometimes related to a greater emphasis on secular intellectuals or on the merchants. The latter emphasis is adumbrated in Gad Gilbar's 'The Big Merchants (*tujjar*) and the Persian Constitutional Revolution of 1906,' (*Asian and African Studies*, 11, 3, 1977, 275–303), and was more forcefully expressed orally by Gilbar at Babolsar, where he noted that the demand for a constitution came from the merchant-guildsmen crowd taking sanctuary at the British Legation, and not from the ulama simultaneously in sanctuary at Qom in 1906. While scholars like myself who have studied the ulama component of the revolutionaries more than the merchant component should welcome this new research into the important role of the merchants (which I did not doubt), we may feel that scholars like Gilbar and Arjomand, whose research and ideas are both original and important, are, however, going too far in playing down the role of the ulama in the constitutional revolution. No scholar, to my knowledge, has claimed that the ulama were nearly unanimous behind the revolution, and my own and others' works point to significant anti-revolutionary ulama in all phases, and particularly after Mohammad Ali Shah's coup d'etat of 1908. It has little meaning, however, to discuss a number of anti-constitutional ulama out of context, or even to note that the ulama did not originate the idea of a constitution; the fact that major leaders of the ulama were in alliance with merchants, guildsmen, secular intellectuals, and others in leading a popular oppositional movement, then demanding a constitution and upholding it once it was granted should remain basic, whatever modifications of our views are brought in by those who study merchants, guildspeople, secular intellectuals, or the anti-constitutional ulama. The leading ulama never had the decisive position of a Khomeini in early 1979, nor did they say, as he does, that the ulama should rule directly, but they were a crucial part of the revolutionary coalition.

In part the above critics are reacting to an Islamic revisionism coming from the opposite side, which may overstress the constitutional commitment of the ulama. The religious opposition in Iran, when it was permitted to publish in the 1960s, not only published works by such well-known Iranian thinkers as Sayyed

Jamal ad-Din 'Afghani,' but also revived far lesser-known figures, particularly a mujtahid who began writing in the early twentieth century, Naini. The interest in Naini in the West was represented by scholars like Hamid Algar ('The Oppositional Role of the Ulama in Twentieth Century Iran,' *Scholars, Saints, and Sufis*, ed. N. Keddie, Berkeley, 1972) and, perhaps less analytically, A.-H. Haeri. Naini attracted interest as the mujtahid who gave by far the best contemporary theoretical justification of constitutionalism from a Shi'i Islamic viewpoint. While one can appreciate the new emphasis on Naini by recent religious opponents of absolute government, and can even agree with Algar that Naini is important as showing that at least some ulama incorporated constitutionalism into a Shi'i belief system, one must also say that there has so far appeared no evidence that Naini was widely followed, or even widely known, at the time of the constitutional revolution. Naini's position is more important for understanding recent years than for the constitutional revolution itself. (The current religio-political leadership, however, opposes the monarchical and Western nature of the Iranian constitution. Ayatollah Khomeini, who in 1978 said that the constitution could serve as a starting point towards an Islamic republic, in his *Hokumat-e Eslami*, 1971, speaks of the constitution as something imposed by the British and copied from the Belgians – the latter is largely true – and says no parliament is needed to pass laws, since all laws are Islamic laws and come from God; parliament should only enforce Islam.) In the past as now the Shi'i ulama displayed a mixture of ideas and motives, and to exaggerate the constitutional or even the revolutionary and anti-royalist nature of the late Qajar ulama is as much a distortion as to deny the importance of anti-government ulama. Above all, the tendency to take the words of one or two ulama as representative of a diverse group at a time when there was no single leader or constitutional doctrine is an essentially polemical procedure that should not be followed by scholars. Individual leaders may be typical or representative of a large group, but this is a point to be demonstrated, not taken for granted.

A recent relevant article about interpretations of Shi'i religion and politics is Joseph Eliash, 'Misconceptions regarding the Juridical Status of the Iranian 'Ulama',' *IJMES*, X, 1 (1979). Eliash says, 'The opinion that Shi'i *mujtahids* are the deputies of the Hidden Imam and that they are authorized to wield his authority in his absence is held by many Shi'i mujtahids and this view is followed by some Western scholars.' Eliash goes on to prove that Shi'i law (elaborated in the early period after the Twelfth Imam's disappearance) gives no basis for this belief, which rests in part on a misinterpretation of one Tradition. There was no designation of the ulama to wield the imams' prerogatives, not even to collect the religious *khums* tax. Eliash denies any doctrinal basis to the ulama's claim to greater political legitimacy than shahs, saying: 'Compared to the Imam, both the Twelver Shi'i ruler and the mujtahid are equally fallible, equally lacking in divine qualities, and equally entitled to none of the Imam's prerogatives.'

While Eliash throws very important light on early, and theoretically fundamental, Shi'i law and tradition, he fails to recognize that religious law and tradition everywhere are less stable in practice than in theory. Growing numbers of ulama in modern times *believed* that they had greater legitimacy even in political matters than temporal rulers; growing numbers of Iranians shared this belief; and many believed the shahs somehow illegitimate and the mujtahids legitimate. The above beliefs can easily be seen as reasonable extensions of earlier Shi'i doctrines, even if the idea of delegation of powers by the imams cannot. Eliash says political claims and powers of the ulama in the past two centuries are owing 'to the social, the political, the military, the economic, and the educational conditions of Iran, not to the Twelver Shi'i doctrines of the Imamate.' While the influences he cites are crucial there was, in effect, *also* a development of Shi'i doctrine, and it is no more legitimate to limit 'true' Shi'i doctrine to its first centuries than it is to judge modern Christian doctrine by the first centuries of Christianity. In both cases, as in other religions, modern thinkers claim to follow their founders, but are moved by a variety of social and intellectual needs to modify doctrines and practices.

Although Eliash's article does not include my works among those criticized, perhaps because I never believed there was a Shi'i doctrine of delegation of the Imams' powers, the article is relevant to some points made within, and hence it is important here to note both the article's significance and that it does not change fundamentally my views on *modern* Shi'ism.

As to the articles within that deal with a long sweep of socio-economic history and with the, primarily socio-economic, background of recent events, while further research will surely modify some of their conclusions, they are recent enough to take into account most of the important scholarly literature. Regarding both socio-economic history and recent years many articles are beginning to appear, and more can also be learned from two recent books in English: Fred Halliday, *Iran: Dictatorship and Development* (Penguin, Harmondsworth, 1979), and Robert Graham, *Iran: The Illusion of Power* (London, Croom Helm, 1978). Although I do not agree with everything in either book, both make major contributions to the understanding of contemporary Iran and their very differences of emphasis both from each other and from what is found within can supplement this volume in building an understanding of the important, unusual, and exciting history of modern and contemporary Iran. Both of these books, as well as my articles within, undermine the popular idea that recent Iran's basic problem was 'over-rapid modernization;' and all of them detail the nature of the late regime's policies that led to massive uprooting, alienation, corruption, income distribution gaps, decisive opposition to governmental and Western policies, and ultimately revolution.

SECTION I

Religion and Politics

SECTION 1

Religion and Politics

1

Religion and Irreligion in Early Iranian Nationalism*

The period 1905–1912 saw a number of nearly simultaneous revolutions or mass movements in Asian countries, which may be considered as the first wave of a revolutionary movement which continues to rock Asia. The Chinese overthrow of the Manchu dynasty, the Young Turk victory, and the Indian mass movement of 1905–1909 are probably the best-known in a series of events which also embraced smaller Asian countries and groups. The main reasons for their simultaneity were probably: the electric effect of the Russo-Japanese War, a startling Asian victory over a Western Power; the Russian Revolution of 1905, an inspiring anti-autocratic struggle which temporarily took Russia away as a bulwark for conservative governments in Asia; the intensification of imperialist pressures on Asia in the late nineteenth and early twentieth centuries, which brought Asian economic and political reactions; and, possibly, the beginnings of economic crisis, which were reflected in Asia. Among these the Russo-Japanese War perhaps deserves to be singled out as the immediate spark, igniting highly inflammatory material in Asia as it did in Russia itself. Not only was Asian pride, hitherto battered by a continuous stream of Western conquests, bolstered by this

* Most of the research for this paper was done on a Social Science Research Council Fellowship for work on a book on the Iranian Revolution 1905–1911, in Iran, England, and the Soviet Union. Thanks go also to Iranian informants, particularly Sayyed Hasan Taqizadeh; to Dr. Abdol Hosein Zarrinkub, who suggested a number of ideas; to the scholars in the U.S. who criticized an earlier draft of the paper; and to Professor Martin Dickson for his painstaking help. Responsibility for views expressed is, of course, the author's. (1979 addendum: much information that could not be footnoted came from the late Sayyed Hasan Taqizadeh.)

13

victory, but the fact that the only Asian constitutional power defeated the only major Western non-constitutional power strengthened the fight for constitutional government as the panacea for internal ills and the 'secret' of Western strength.

It is surprising, in view of current interest in the revolutionary process in Asia, that more adequate individual or comparative studies have not been made of the roots and results of these early movements. Here an analysis will be attempted of unappreciated intellectual background of one of the movements – the Iranian Revolution of 1905–1911. The economic and political background and the revolution itself will be discussed elsewhere.

This revolution aroused world interest when it took place, as seen in such books as E. G. Browne's *The Persian Revolution*, W. Morgan Shuster's *The Strangling of Persia*, and in support from British liberals and Russian Social-Democrats against the policy of their own governments. It still evokes keen interest in Iran, where it is the latest period which can be written about relatively honestly, and where some of its participants and many of their sons and relatives occupy high positions, which often jar strangely with their revolutionary antecedents. The stream of Persian writings of greatly varying merit on the subject shows no sign of diminishing, and someone with the patience to wade through it all could write an *Iran Reviews its Revolutionary Origins*, which would reveal much about contemporary Iranian politics and personalities. The Soviets also continue to show interest in this, as in other aspects of Iranian history, and their scholars have dug into Russian and Caucasian archives and various sources on economic and social history. Soviet works have the most information on the economic roots and class forces of the revolution, and on Russian socialist influence, but often suffer from rigidity of analysis, inability to deal with intellectual history, or interpretations based on current world power lineups.[1] In the West there has been little discussion on the Iranian Revolution and its background since its occurrence, and work on sources does not approach that done in Iran or the Soviet Union.

Even a superficial study of the Iranian Revolution raises at least two questions of a comparative nature. First, why was the Iranian Revolution, in a country which was more backward than China and Turkey, a more profound, radical, and prolonged revolution than were their simultaneous revolts? Second, why did a large part of the Moslem *ulama*, in contrast to the orthodox clergy in almost every other revolution, play a major role in bringing about the Iranian Revolution? And these do not exhaust the questions significant for understanding the Asian revolutionary process. In the following such questions will be raised, and some tentative answers hazarded.

THE BABI EXPERIENCE

The Babi heresy and revolt of the mid-nineteenth century has been studied at length by Gobineau, Nicolas, Browne, and Russian scholars, but its importance in the modern Iranian revolutionary process has not been assessed, nor has it been compared with similar movements elsewhere.[2] Babism was primarily one of a series of radical Shi'a heresies which have arisen in times of social and religious stress. It arose from the Sheikhi movement, originating in the late eighteenth century, which had unorthodox tendencies, but unlike Babism did not present a new prophet or break with Islam. The Sheikhis have not been sufficiently studied to give an adequate résumé of their doctrines. Bausani, an outstanding recent scholar of Iranian religion, says:

> If one could summarize in a few words the complex theological position of the Sheikhis one would say that it is based on two points, one of profound religious charge, the other tending to rationalism: two aspects which remain side by side and sometimes in apparent contrast also in their spiritual successors, the Babis and the Baha'is. The first point is the live sense that the authority of God must always be present and active through an 'intermediary' among men. The first intermediary ... is the prophet Mohammad; after his death it is the series of the twelve *imams*. These having ended with the disappearance of the last, it is absurd, for the Sheikhis, that the community remain – as the Twelver Shi'ites claim – without a head and governed by colleges of *mujtahids*. Such a later intermediary is the *Bab* ..., the 'gate' between man and the world of the *imam*.
>
> The other point is the tendency to symbolic explanation, which sometimes goes beyond realistic symbolism ... to enter into a true rationalist allegory, of the miraculous side of the traditional theological legends.[3]

Sayyed Ali Mohammad (1819–20—1850), born into a merchant

family in Shiraz, after a youth which included trade as well as religious study and meditation, declared himself to be the expected 'Bab' and later a prophet, and drew many Sheikhis and others to follow him in the 1840s. His preaching included strong attacks on the corruption of the clergy, and his growing influence made him a danger. He was imprisoned in 1847, and a series of Babi revolts began in 1848. The Bab and several of his major followers were executed in 1850, and executions and persecutions continued thereafter.

Although Sheikhi doctrine is not well enough known for one to be able to say whether the teachings of the Bab were new on all points, there do seem to be some major departures: (1) The teaching of the Qur'an was declared superseded, and the Bab instituted a new prophetic cycle. (2) The Bab introduced a new law which replaced the Qur'an and Islamic law, rather than simply interpreting these allegorically as most earlier heresies had done; as will be shown, some of the content of this law is historically significant. (3) The Bab had immediate millenarian expectations; and (4) He spoke of progressive cycles of better and better revelations which would go on even in the future.

Despite the deep roots of Babism in Sheikhism, and its resemblance to other Shi'a heresies such as the Isma'ilis and to some ideas of Iranian philosophers like Molla Sadra (d. 1640–41), there are some phenomena which suggest possible ties also between Babism and the early Western impact. One is the new content of Babi thought itself; another the little-studied role of the Azali branch of the Babis in preparing the revolution, as well as the Westernism of the Baha'is, who changed original Babism. Third, it seems more than coincidental that radical messianic movements have arisen in several parts of Asia and Africa shortly after they first felt significant Western economic and political impact.

The major radical heresy of modern Asia, the Taipings of China, shows many points of similarity to the Babis.[4] There are also great differences; notably, the Taipings had very strong Christian elements, while the Babis developed out of indigenous Shi'ism. Also the Taipings are often considered mainly as the leaders of a huge peasant rebellion, while the armed revolts of the Babis against the government seem not as important as their ideological opposition to religious orthodoxy. Yet these differences are not as great as they seem; deeper study shows that the Taipings were as much a Chinese as a Christian heresy and that the Bab was probably influenced by Christian ideas. Nor was the Babi revolt an accident, as some have implied. With the Babis' conviction of divine inspiration, their violent attacks on the clergy and on corruption, their demand to conduct society on new moral and social principles, and their uncompromising willingness to sacrifice themselves for their cause, conflict with the authorities was probably inevitable.

Direct similarities between the Taipings and Babis are numerous. In both cases the movement was started by a young man with a traditional education, living in or near a southern city. Each leader had a mental experience as a very young man which led him to claim divine inspiration, after which each began to preach uncompromisingly against traditional religious practices, corruption, and immorality, and to put forth his revived religion and morality. Both soon gained enthusiastic proselytes and determined enemies, the latter coming especially from ideological representatives of the ruling tradition. Each became increasingly intransigent towards traditional ruling groups as his life went on, and each also made increasingly divine claims for himself as the break with the old order grew.

Not only the leaders, but the Taiping and Babi movements and ideologies, show similarities. Both appeared in periods of economic troubles and general restiveness. Both passed into direct revolt, after some local clashes in the period of confusion and rebelliousness which characterized an interregnum in both countries – in 1848 in Iran, and 1850 in China. Both, like many other messianic movements, wanted to set up the kingdom of God on earth, ruled by peace, justice, and brotherhood, and both were willing to use violence to do this. Both effected a moral revolution in their followers which astonished foreigners, as did the willing self-sacrifice of proselytes and disciples. Although the regulation of social morality is part of both the Confucian and the Islamic tradition, the Taipings and Babis were aberrant both in the new content of their morality and in the rigor with which they enforced it.

Gobineau wrote that the Bab established for Babi society 'a government at once monarchical, theocratic and democratic',[5] and the same could be said of Taiping government. Monarchical rule by the religious leader (though among the Babis this remained theoretical, since the Bab was imprisoned before the revolts and executed during them), disciples who were also governors and generals, equality of all within the faith but intolerance of those outside it, characterized both. Common social practices included some community of property, strict religious regulation of the morality and private lives of followers, and an enhanced position of women. The Taipings declared the end of footbinding, polygamy, and prostitution. A woman was a leading Babi preacher and poet, and the Bab called for an end to women's seclusion, discouraged, though he did not forbid, taking a second wife, and enjoined better treatment of women. Humanitarian morality, new economic principles, and a higher position of women may be modern features of both movements, even though they have partial precedents in earlier heresies and revolts. Both perhaps show proto-nationalist tendencies; among the Babis, Browne's introduction to *Nuqtatu'l Kaf* notes Zoroastrian revivals including a revival of the solar calendar and a Zoroastrian theory of the elements, and among the Taipings there was an appeal to ancient Chinese tradition and to Chinese unity against the foreign Manchus. Both stress national unity, as against the dominant cultural tradition, while as messianic religions they also claim universal validity.

Several reasons may be suggested why the early Western impact encouraged messianic rebellion. This impact both created new economic and political pressures and provided new paths for social change. Western trade, for instance, gave employment in fields traditionally disparaged in most Asian societies. Wars with the West in China, Iran, and elsewhere weakened Asian governments, encouraged decentralization, disaffection, and the corruption and overtaxation found in periods of Asian dynastic disintegration. Western powers also played a contradictory political role, often bolstering governments from which they had won such things as enforced low tariffs and extra-territoriality, while also hoping for reforms which would simplify trade and diplomacy, and so giving some early support to opposition to traditional governments and ideology. Millennial movements might have occurred without the Western impact, but this impact probably hastened their occurrence and accounted for some of their features. The existence of similar developments elsewhere, such as the movement for a *ratu adil* (just prince) in Indonesia, the Ahmadiyya movement in India, and both Islamic Mahdism and Christian messianism in Africa suggests too the causal role of the early Western impact.

As to whether there were new features in Babi thought, this question is more difficult than might first appear. Both Gobineau and Nicolas stress that the Bab, like the Isma'ilis, Sufis, philosophers, and many Shi'ites, in some cases hid his true thoughts in order to make his teachings appear closer to orthodoxy than they really were. This, they say, accounts for the obscurity of the *Bayan*, and, according to Nicolas, for the differences between the Bab's early and late teachings.[6] It would seem reasonable to stress those points at which the Bab's teachings differed from orthodoxy as being the most significant of his true thought. Even with this stress, it is true that most of Babism is traditional, it being the last in a line of militant Iranian heresies ranging from pre-Islamic Mazdakite communism through Isma'ilism and other extreme Shi'a heresies. This aspect of Babism had been discussed well by Browne and Bausani.[7] Number and letter cabalism, the idea of a 'return' of former spirits in new bodies, and esoterism are among its traditional heretical elements.

Apparently new is the economic program, with its high evaluation of trade and traders, emphasis on productive employment and opposition to begging, which traditionally had religious merit, and permission of taking interest. The Bab had none of the asceticism which often went with radical religion. Gobineau also points out: 'What must be noted in the theory of the Bab, is that it is completely removed from the opinion ... according to which matter is responsible for everything evil. Nowhere does the Bab express himself in an unfavorable manner regarding matter.'[8]

The Bab's stand on the position of women has been noted – his call for social contact between the sexes when such an idea was hardly broached by the most enlightened Westernizer and the leading role in his movement of the preacher and poet, Qorrat ol Ain, suggest the newness of his position. Also noted above is proto-nationalism, which had traditional elements, but also may tie in with the modern Iranian nationalism which concentrates on the revival of pre-Islamic culture. The Babis' very violent attacks on the Islamic clergy possibly had both traditional and new features, as did the Bab's humanitarian ethics and stress on the proper and gentle treatment of women and children.

More complex is the question of the Bab's opinion of the nature of his revelation. Orthodox Islam accepts the Judaeo-Christian prophets, but says that Mohammad, bringing essentially the same message in more explicit terms, superseded them and was the last of the prophets. The Bab claimed to be bringing his message in terms according with the greater maturity of mankind, and said there would be a more perfect, or clearer, revelation in the future. He thus suggested two 'modern' notions: first, the 'Protestant' one that the clergy and interpreters have misunderstood the original message of the prophet. Second, the idea of progress: the Bab was convinced that mankind had progressed in maturity and understanding, so he could present a new message in accord with this maturity, and a future prophet would be able to be even more complete. The very act of reopening the cycle of prophets also brought room for new ideas through casting doubt on orthodoxy.

Although there are differences of opinion over the religious content of the Bab's message, it seems clear that it took the direction of interpreting the other-worldly elements of Islam in this-worldly terms. The Bab specifically says that only God can know what exists after death, and interprets Heaven, Hell, and the Day of Judgment allegorically, as referring to states in this world. His emphasis on things of this world distinguishes him from many heretics, and may have led to a more modern outlook among some Babis.

These ideas are all to be found in the writings of the Bab himself. When we come to some of the disciples involved in the revolt, we find stronger notions of political and economic reform. And many later Babis, as shall be shown, became modernists and precursors or leaders of revolution.

The above sketch of new features in Babism suggests some comparisons with Protestant or proto-Protestant heresies of the West. Gobineau suggested this comparison, and noted also the Babi concept of divine grace, conceived of as an innoculation which each soul either has or lacks. This meant an activist predestination not unlike that of the Calvinists. The comparison may extend to the fierce attacks on the corruption of the clergy, claims to have the true interpretation of the scripture, new economic attitudes, strict social and individual morality, and the theocratic ideal. Again it should be noted that differences are also striking, as might be expected in movements arising from different religious traditions and appearing under varying historical circumstances. The comparison is suggestive, however, and should provide a warning against considering the 'modern' features of Babism a result of Western *ideological* influence. The concepts of grace and the rule of saints could hardly have reached the Bab from the West. They may well have arisen in Babi thought as a similar response to social strains not unlike those found in the West in the late Middle Ages and Reformation periods.[9]

The comparison also raises another question often asked by students of modern Asian religious thought. Why did not Asian religions develop a theologically consistent 'Protestantism' in the modern period? The answer, for Iran, at least, seems to lie in the rapid pace of political and ideological change, and in the fact that it took place under foreign pressure. Thus, as shall be shown, many thinkers who were early concerned with religious reform, abandoned inward concern with religion as such, and passed over to more modern Western free thought. Also, the pressing nature of political problems, which involved questions of national survival or revival not faced so acutely by the sixteenth century West, turned the attention of thinkers from religion to politics, so that even apparently religious writings were often directed to political and nationalist goals. H. A. R. Gibb and W. C. Smith have noted the apologetic nature of modern Islamic writings, and it seems safe to state that this is due largely to the non-religious motivations behind them. It is true that religion and politics have always been intertwined in Islam, but their relation among modern writers has often been to *use* religious appeals for secular ends.

The significance of the Babi movement for later Iran, then, was *not* that it brought a religious and moral revival of the country, as many contemporary observers hoped. Its continuing significance was probably more political than religious. The Babis continued to attract some converts and admiration, the latter based largely on the fact that they were the enemies of the disliked government and orthodox clergy. They remained a small group, however, important more as symbols and unrecognized leaders in reform than as a mass religion.

The position of Babis in the growing revolutionary movement in Iran is not widely known, for many reasons. Several years after the execution of the Bab, the majority of the Babis became followers of the Baha'i religion, which changed the original Babi ideas in a universalist, pacifist, and liberal direction. Such attenuation of revolutionary religious sects has several parallels elsewhere in the world. The Baha'is favored Western principles, and comprised one part of the Westernizing movement, but, particularly during the revolution, they specifically renounced participation in politics, and tried to gain tolerance for themselves by proclaiming loyalty to the Shahs. A minority of Babis remained faithful to the Bab's appointed successor, the *Sobhe Azal*, after whom they are called Azalis. The pressure of persecution made them go underground even more than the Baha'is, and they adopted the practice of claiming to be Moslems and even entering the ranks of the Moslem ulama as preachers, teachers, etc. The fact that 'Babi' was used as a scare word to arouse the Islamic masses against all modernist reformers, much as 'Communist' is used in America, led to a denial on all sides that the Babis had any prominence in the revolutionary movement. E. G. Browne, for example, who was in correspondence or personal touch with many leading Azalis, did not mention in *The Persian Revolution* which participants were Azalis, even when they were dead and could not have been hurt personally. In *Materials for the Study of the Babi Religion*, written many years later, however, he notes Azali devotion to the revolution and names as Azalis the great preacher Malek ol Motakallemin and the editor of the best revolutionary newspaper, *Sure Esrafil*, Mirza Jahangir Khan.[10] This corresponds to independent information I have from reliable informants in Iran, and to the above can be added Yahya Dowlatabadi and several less prominent revolutionaries, while the outstanding preacher, Sayyed Jamal ed Din Esfahani, was friendly to the Babis. From the same reliable informants, however, it appears that neither of the great preachers had a religious faith at the end of his life, when both were preaching in the mosques the compatibility of modern reforms with Islam and the Qur'an. Many other revolutionaries, including the early enlighteners and Azalis, Mirza Aqa Khan Kermani and Sheikh

Ahmad Ruhi, went from religious to political concern, as will be shown below. The passage from 'Protestantism' to nineteenth century type free-thought was particularly typical of the Azalis. The fact that they were never able to speak or write their minds completely frankly – either as Babis or as free-thinkers – but in both states had to pretend to be Moslems, has led to misunderstanding in the West. In relation to the Iranian Revolution this misunderstanding has resulted in an overestimation of religious leadership in the revolution, through taking such men as Jamal ed Din Esfahani and Malek ol Motakallemin at their face value.

The Babis, then, passed from a largely traditional religious messianism into two new streams. One comprised the Baha'is, who wanted gradual Westernization from above, but renounced political opposition. (There is a curious coincidence between the Baha'is and the Taipings; the Baha'i goal of 'Great Peace' is literally the same phrase as the Chinese T'ai-p'ing.) The other, the Azalis, continued as a small, underground, and little-known sect, who retained their originators' fierce hatred for the corruption and tyranny of most of the clergy, plus an added hatred of the dynasty which had executed their leaders. Both sects, although intermittently persecuted by central and local authorities, and sometimes executed, continued to attract some proselytes and sympathy. This sympathy was at least as much a sign of widespread hostility to the existing order as it was specifically religious. Azali ideas, such as willingness for self-sacrifice for an ideal, anti-Qajar and anti-clergy attitudes, became transmuted into modern revolutionary tendencies. Browne notes being told that many of the Azalis devoted themselves to the revolutionary cause with the same enthusiasm they had formerly reserved for religious revival.[11]

RELIGION AND IRRELIGION AMONG LATE NINETEENTH CENTURY ENLIGHTENERS

There will be no attempt to restate the intellectual origins of the revolution at any length. These are fairly adequately covered in Browne's *The Persian Revolution* and *Press and Poetry of Modern Persia*. Among the important Persian works, mostly written outside Iran, which helped enlighten Iranians, were *The*

Travelbook of Ibrahim Bek, the writings of Talibof, the newspapers *Akhtar* of Constantinople, *Sorayya* and *Parvaresh* of Cairo, and *Habl ol Matin* of Calcutta. To Browne's accounts should be added an emphasis on the great influence of Russian Transcaucasia in Iran, particularly in Azerbaijan where Turkish was the native tongue. The Azerbaijani enlightener Akhundov (or Akhundzadeh), for example, wrote several works in Persian, and like many North Azerbaijanis took a keen interest in Persian politics. He conducted a correspondence with Malkam Khan and with other Persians, which is collected in Baku and has been partially published. Persian translations of his satiric plays were among the first modern plays in Persian. Like many later Iranian nationalists, he was violently anti-Islamic. Baku manuscripts prove him to be the author of the strongly anti-Islamic and Iranian revivalist *Kamal od Dowleh and Jalal od Dowleh*, wrongly attributed by Browne and most Iranians to Mirza Aqa Khan Kermani.[12] The latter apparently wrote the second volume of this work, which was almost identical in tone and content.

Talibof and other Iranians living in Transcaucasia were among the most active enlighteners of the Iranians; Transcaucasian liberal and revolutionary newspapers and other writings circulated in Iran; and the numerous Iranian workers who went to work in Baku and other Caucasian cities picked up new ideas, including even socialism.[13] As will be developed elsewhere, the profundity and radicalism of the Iranian Revolution in the North can be largely attributed to contacts and influence from the very revolutionary Russian Transcaucacus.

Here there will be discussion of five of the main Iranian enlighteners of the period before 1896, when Naser ed Din Shah was assassinated. Two will be dealt with very briefly, and three 'pan-Islamists' at greater length.

Malkam Khan was an Armenian who spent years in government service in Iran and abroad. He probably founded the first freemason order in Iran, which was suppressed by the Shah, who suspected it of Babi or revolutionary tendencies. He worked for a quarter of a century with encouragement from Akhundov to perfect and publicize a new vocalized Arabic script; in 1889–90 published the Persian newspaper *Qanun* from London, advocating a constitutional reign of law; and also wrote many political tracts which were circulated in Iran. With regard to the religious points to be made below: Malkam was nominally a Moslem of Christian descent, but he worked to spread a 'religion of humanity', which he thought would present Western ideas to Iranians in religious terms that would make them more acceptable, and most reliable informants believe he was a freethinker.[14] The 'religion of humanity' was either closely related to or identical with freemasonry and apparently included among its followers the leading member of the Tehran ulama, Sheikh Hadi Najmabadi.

The example of Najmabadi illustrates the confusion which can result from equating the revolutionary role of the liberal ulama with Islamic influence, and is one of several cases indicating that free thought was more characteristic of thoroughgoing reformers than was orthodoxy. The careful Iranian scholar Mirza Mohammad Qazvini called Najmabadi a freethinker in the following biographical note:

Hajji Shaykh Hadi Najm-abadi was one of the most celebrated of the *ulama* of Tihran and the services which he rendered to the cause of liberty in Persia were almost if not quite equal to those of Sayyid Jamalu'd Din, for he was a *mujtahid* of the first rank and enjoyed the confidence of the gentle and simple. He was absolutely incorruptible ... Every afternoon he used to sit on the ground outside his house ... where he received people of all classes and all faiths, statesmen and scholars, princes and poets, Sunnis, Shi'is, Babis, Armenians, Jews, Ali-Ilahis, etc., with all of whom he discussed all sorts of topics with the utmost freedom. Though a *mujtahid*, he was at heart a freethinker, and used to cast doubts into men's minds and destroy their beliefs in popular superstitions, and he was instrumental in 'awakening' a large proportion of those who afterwards became the champions of Persia's liberties. Sayyid Muhammad Tabataba'i was originally his disciple, but afterwards denounced his opinions as heretical to his father, Sayyid Sadiq, who publicly banned him as an infidel. This denunciation, however, so far from injuring him, actually added to his prestige and increased the number of his admirers.[15]

The three men to be discussed more fully here, the pan-Islamists Sayyed Jamal ed Din Afghani, Mirza Aqa Khan Kermani, and Sheikh Ahmad Ruhi, show even more of the hidden complexities of relations between religion, irreligion, and politics in pre-revolutionary Iran. They also show the serious errors of analysis which can be made by taking the speeches and writings of Asian reformers at their face value, as is too often done in the West.

In Iranian and Islamic history it has been common for philosophers and heterodox religious teachers to hide their true ideas in superficially orthodox writings and oral teachings. Groups like the Sufis and Isma'ilis used various levels of teaching, in which the least initiated were taught something differing little from orthodoxy, while at the highest level the most unorthodox ideas might be taught. Gobineau and Nicolas say that this type of teaching was widespread in Iran in the nineteenth century, and also that the Bab's *Bayan* was deliberately obscure, to be understood only by great effort or with the help of an initiated commentator. Gobineau speaks of the revival and continuation of an Avicennist philosophic tradition, with writings which were externally almost orthodox, but which disciples expounded quite differently to those eager to learn. He notes similar practices among the Sufis of his day, who would pull back from an extreme position if it shocked the listener, but would advance to more outrageous heresies with an apt pupil. Gobineau, despite his errors, shows the nature of Iranian intellectual life, largely because he sees, as one Iranian scholar said, that 'in Iran, things are *never* what they seem'. This cardinal rule for understanding Iran is ignored by some, however aware they are that intellectual life in Iran today is characterized by exactly the opposite ideas from those found in published writings.

In the Islamic world, the need for symbolic interpretation probably first arose from the immutable nature of God's revelation in the Qur'an. The escape from literal honesty may have begun with Orthodox inventions of traditions about the Prophet, which served to meet circumstances he had never foreseen. Among the Orthodox, even the respected theologian al-Ghazali sanctions insincerity and rhetorical arguments to sway the unsophisticated in certain circumstances.

Traditions of ambiguous writing, to be understood only by the 'elite,' usually with the aid of an oral teacher, while the non-adept are expected to remain ignorant of one's true meaning, were strong among the unorthodox, who also indulged in radical symbolic interpretation of scripture. In a schematic way three such unorthodox strains can be distinguished, though they sometimes overlapped or influenced orthodoxy: (1) Those who challenged orthodox religious *and* political authority: mainly the different Shi'a groups and sects. These generally practiced dissimulation and believed in esoteric interpretations of scripture. (2) Those who stressed individual religious experience and were willing to leave political rule to others – broadly, the Sufis. (3) The philosophers, whose reason often led to conflict with orthodoxy, but who favored orthodoxy for the masses partly because, unlike the sects, they did not believe the masses could spark desirable politico-religious change. The philosophers often hoped, rather, to lead rulers to gradual reform, and tended to feel that orthodoxy was expedient to keep the people loyal, disciplined, and obedient. Among unorthodox and orthodox, the ideal of truth might be attached more to good ends than to literal frankness.

Thus, traditions of untruthfulness, ambiguity, and forced interpretation of scripture affected all major groups in Islam, though motives and methods varied. The Isma'ilis generally wanted to have the widest possible political-ideological influence, while the philosophers hoped rather to lead the elite to truth without being persecuted for corrupting the many. In Iran, the combination of Shi'a trends and foreign conquests made traditions of dissimulation particularly strong.[16]

The tradition of writing one way and thinking another carried over into modern times in Iran, and probably in other Islamic countries. Iranian nationalists until at least 1920 had at least two overwhelming reasons to put their writings and speeches in Islamic terms. One was fear of persecution – excommunication, expulsion from a city, and death in case of Babism were possible punishments for suspected heterodoxy. The second, and probably even stronger motivation, was the desire to have wide influence. For the modern reformers, the question of writing deliberately for a small audience does not often arise. Rather, they were concerned with what form of writing and speech might sway politically the clergy and the still largely orthodox or superstitious lower and lower middle classes. In Iran, as will be shown, it was possible to move part of the upper clergy to act against the dynasty, which was regarded as the main enemy by the modernizers. Therefore, for tactical reasons the modernizers made appeals to the clergy, which were written in Islamic terms.

In discussing three radical pan-Islamists, the almost purely political character of their pan-Islam will be indicated. Islam has always had a political side, but these men are notable for their use of orthodox sounding religious appeals as a means to unorthodox secular goals. A distinction should be made between such men and the conservative use made of pan-Islam by Sultan Abdul Hamid and others. To pre-state some conclusions, it seems that reformist pan-Islam was mainly an anti-imperialist doctrine which appealed to Islam, (1) because it was widely believed, (2) in the hope of clerical and official support, (3) to build nationalist pride and refute Western deprecation of Islamic culture, (4) in the hope of reviving the power and dynamism of early Islam, and (5) to distinguish Islamic peoples ideologically from the West they were fighting.[17] These motives may not have been conscious in Afghani, who seems to have believed that reformed Islam *was* the most rational religion, but they were probably more conscious than some of his writings might suggest. Some commentary on the nature of reformist pan-Islam is found in the fact that two of the three major pan-Islamists to be discussed were never Moslems, but first Babis, and later freethinkers. It is true that Babis or deists might consider themselves the truest Moslems, but these men used orthodox terminology and did not make explicit that the 'Islam' which they liked was hardly orthodox.

The question of the true nature of Afghani's private ideas is one which I am far from having solved, but here will be presented some material to open what may have appeared to be a closed matter. The question is important, because if some of Afghani's writings were done on the basis of tactics rather than conviction, they should be criticized on tactical rather than logical or theological grounds. Afghani, particularly in his major work, the *Refutation of the Materialists*, writes as a defender of religion in general and Islam in particular against all doubters, rationalists, and materialists, who are accused of causing the downfall of nations. It must be granted that any statement that Afghani may have been, say, an Islamic Deist, could be attacked with statements in this work. Yet, close analysis of the *Refutation* (which I will publish elsewhere) shows that: (1) the virtues attributed to Islam are almost all secular, such as the encouragement of science, political power, and cohesion; (2) Afghani reflects the ideas and even the terms of the philosophers in appealing to Islam as expedient for social cohesion and stability; and (3) Afghani hints near the end of the work that the Islam he is discussing has little resemblance to the Islam of his own day.

The *Refutation* was written in India to combat the influence of
Sayyed Ahmad Khan and his school. Yet the religious reform
ideas of Afghani and Sayyed Ahmad Khan were almost identical,
and where they differed, as in Afghani's stress on holy war, the
difference was a political one.[18] The real basis of opposition seems
political. Ahmad Khan favored working with the British, and in a
later article Afghani said of him, with a rhetorical inaccuracy
which both orthodox and unorthodox had justified for swaying
the masses:

> Ahmad Khan and his sectarians reject the cloak of religion and ask
> openly for its abandonment, desiring discord among Muslims and
> trying to divide them. They accentuate their error, sowing discord
> between the Hindus and Muslims ... These materialists are not like the
> materialists of Europe. For whoever abandons religion in Western
> countries keeps the love for his country ... But Ahmad Khan and his
> companions, just as they incited others to abandon religion, despised
> the interests of their country and made it easier for souls to submit to
> what the foreigner wanted ... They did not act thus for a considerable
> reward or a great honor, but for a vile scrap of bread, a mean gain ...
>
> These materialists, for the English government, a sort of army in
> India ...[19]

Afghani seems afraid that openly casting doubt on Islam will
weaken Moslem cohesion and encourage admiration of the hated
British. Perhaps the *Refutation* should be read as a political tract,
written to mobilize existing Islamic sentiment against the West.

If we suppose that Afghani was moved mainly by immediate
political aims, the many contradictions in his writings may be
seen as arising from the fact that he appealed for support at
various times to many conflicting groups – the ulama, Islamic
rulers, British and Russian officials, the intelligentsia and masses
of various Eastern countries – and tried to talk in terms that
would move them to act. The terminology of the *Refutation* and
Afghani's high praise and teaching of Islamic philosophy suggest
that he accepted the philosophers' distinction between the
orthodox 'many' and the philosophical 'elite'. This gives ground
for belief that his startling 'Answer to Renan', written in French
for an elite Western audience, and in logical, rather than his more
usual rhetorical, language, may be closer to his true beliefs than
the *Refutation*. Here he does not say that Islam is better than

Christianity but that both, and indeed all religions, are equally bad. Of the Moslem he says:

A true believer must, in fact, turn from the path of studies which have for their object scientific truth ... Yoked like an ox to the plow, to the dogma whose slave he is, he must walk eternally in the same furrow which has been traced for him in advance by the interpreters of the law. Convinced, besides, that his religion contains in itself all morality and all learning, he attaches himself resolutely to it and makes no effort to go beyond ... Wherefore he despises learning ...

It is permissible ... to ask one's self why the Arab civilization, after having thrown such a live light on the world, suddenly became extinguished; why this torch has not been relit since, and why the Arab world still remains buried in profound darkness.

Here the responsibility of the Moslem religion appears complete. It is clear that wherever it became established, this religion tried to stifle science and it was marvelously served in its designs by despotism.

Al-Siouti tells that the Caliph al-Hadi put to death in Baghdad 5000 philosophers in order to destroy sciences in the Moslem countries up to their roots. Admitting that this historian exaggerated the number of victims, it remains nonetheless established that this persecution took place ... I could find in the past of the Christian religion analogous facts. Religions, whatever names they are given, all resemble each other. No agreement and no reconciliation are possible between religion and philosophy. Religion imposes on man its faith and its belief, whereas philosophy frees him of it totally or in part. How could one therefore hope that they would agree with each other? ... Whenever religion will have the upper hand, it will eliminate philosophy; and the contrary happens when it is philosophy which reigns as queen. As long as humanity exists, the struggle will not cease between dogma and free investigation, between religion and philosophy; a desperate struggle in which, I fear, the triumph will not be for free thought, because the masses dislike reason and its teachings are only understood by some intelligences of the elite, and because science, however beautiful it is, does not completely satisfy humanity, which thirsts for the ideal and which likes to exist in dark and distant regions which the philosophers and scholars can neither perceive nor explore.[20]

Assuming Afghani's political goals and Islamic philosophical background, one could say the 'Answer to Renan' gives a clue to why Afghani made such a strong Islamic appeal in the *Refutation* – if one wishes to reach the people one *must* appeal in the name of Islam, because religion is what they want and understand. There is no proof that the 'Answer' reflects Afghani's true views, but since he could have taken various other lines of argument with considerably less danger to himself and his program, it seems harder to see it as a purely expedient work than any other of his writings. It suggests that Afghani's 'Islam' had little resemblance to historic Islam.

There are also scattered published references, in Wilfred Blunt's works, for example, which make it difficult to think of Afghani as the passionate Moslem he appears in some of his writings and speeches. Among unpublished sources, the British Public Records Office has a volume on Afghani which is instructive, and there may be even better material in the India Office. In 1883 Cairo reported the receipt by Sherif Pasha of a letter threatening assassination, almost surely from Afghani, which identifies itself as from the Egyptian Patriotic League and 'states that the members of the League are brothers of the Nihilists and Socialists.' A later enclosure from a certain Syed Hussein in Hyderabad says of Afghani:

> I gathered from his conversation that he was a freethinker of the French type, and a socialist, and that he had been got rid of by the authorities in Egypt for preaching the doctrine of 'liberté, fraternité, égalité' to the students and the masses in that country.

Illustrating Afghani's willingness to change his expressed ideas when it suited him is a letter from him to the British, whom he had repeatedly attacked most violently, at a time when he wanted their protection against the hostile Ottoman Sultan in 1895:

> I am an Afghan (Cabul) and I depend on England. I have passed a great part of my life in the Orient with the single aim of uprooting fanaticism, the most harmful malady of this land, of reforming society and establishing there the benefits of tolerance.

In considering this request, which it later rejected, the Foreign Office asked the India Office for information. The latter sent a printed confidential report from the General Superintendent of the Thagi and Dakaiti Department (!), who had much more detailed and accurate information about Afghani than did the Foreign Office, even though he had spent a very short time in India and was not considered very influential there – a point which indicates the focus of British concern over Moslem agitators. The account of Afghani's life agrees in its externals with other accounts, but makes some special points relevant to his private religious opinions:

> ... While here (in Egypt) he became very friendly with Riaz Pasha and many other Egyptian Freethinkers ... He was in Hyderabad for about 20 months, during his stay he associated chiefly with the rising generation of freethinkers, the followers of Sayed Ahmed of Aligarh. But in spite of all their kindness and hospitality towards him, he published a book in Persian against their doctrines. He seemed to hold strong views on such subjects as 'Revival of Islam' and 'Union is strength.' His story about his expulsion from Egypt was that he was a mason, and that the khedive mistook him for a conspirator.
>
> ... In December 1889 the Sheikh went to Tehran, much to the annoyance of the Shah ... He made a number of converts to his own particular faith which he called 'Naturalism.' Whilst in Persia he thought it proper to conform outwardly to the Shiah faith.[21]

The reference to 'Naturalism' is particularly intriguing, if true, since the word translated 'materialists' in the Persian title of *Refutation of the Materialists* is 'neicheriyyeh', a coinage meaning, literally, naturalism. Although the reference to Sayyed Ahmad Khan's followers at 'freethinkers' is imprecise, Afghani's ties with them are significant.

Other points showing a possible lack of concern in Afghani with Islamic orthodoxy are his collaboration with the Jewish Sanua on his Paris newspaper; and with Babis, agnostics, and atheists in his Constantinople circle; and his closing dealings with various Russians on his visits there, particularly, according to the British Foreign Office, with Pobedonostsev, the Procurator of the Holy Synod, himself no amateur at using religion for political purposes.[22]

Something of the difference in tone between Afghani's public and private statements can also be seen in the letters of Afghani translated in Browne's *The Persian Revolution*. In writing to the great mojtahed, Shirazi, to arouse him against the Shah after the Iranian tobacco concession to an English subject in 1890, Afghani complains of the Iranian prime minister, saying that Naser ed Din Shah

> hath entrusted the reins of government in all things great and small to the hands of a wicked freethinker, a tyrant and usurper, who revileth the Prophets openly, and heedeth not God's Law, who accounteth as

naught the religious authorities, curseth the doctors of the Law,
rejecteth the pious, contemneth honourable Sayyids and treateth
preachers as one would treat the vilest of mankind.

The orthodox tone is typical of Afghani's correspondence with
the Iranian ulama. In a private letter at the end of his life which
may be considered his testament to the Iranians, however, there is
no word of Islam, pan-Islam, the need to defend religion, or the
clergy. Also, Afghani regrets the pan-Islamic tactics which led
him to look to Sultan Abdul Hamid rather than to the people for
support for his program. His concern is clearly for reform, not
religion:

> I rejoice at my captivity and impending death, for my imprisonment is
> for the freeing of my kind, and I shall be slain for the life of my people.
> Only on this account am I grieved, that I have not lived to reap what I
> have sown, and that I have not fully attained to that which I desired.
> The sword of unrighteousness has not suffered me to see the
> awakening of the peoples of the East, and the hand of ignorance has
> not granted me the opportunity to hear the call of Freedom from the
> throats of the nations of the Orient. Would that I had sown all the seed
> of my ideas in the receptive ground of the people's thoughts! Well
> would it have been had I not wasted this fruitful and beneficent seed
> of mine in the salt and sterile soil of the effete Sovereignty!
> ... Strive so far as you can to destroy the foundations of this
> despotism, not to pluck up and cast out its individual agents ...
> Endeavor to remove those obstacles which prevent your friendship
> with other nations.[23]

In the same letter, Afghani says to the Iranians: 'Nature is your
friend, and the Creator of Nature your ally', and this is the only
religious element in the letter. The appeal to nature and its creator
seem significant from one whose major published work was
devoted to an attack on those who made such appeals. Possibly
Afghani may be considered something of an Islamic Deist,
believing that original Islam was more in accord with reason and
nature than were other religions. There was nothing untoward
about his appeal to past secular glories in the name of Islam, given
Islam's political nature. His defense of the clergy, attacks on the
Shah as an unbeliever, and on the rationalism of Sayyed Ahmad
Khan and his school seem to be based on tactics rather than
conviction, however. In any case, the question of Afghani's
private beliefs is one which deserves further study.

Next to Afghani, Mirza Aqa Khan Kermani and his friend Sheikh Ahmad Ruhi were the most important pan-Islamists in the Iranian nationalist movement. Their lives are described in Browne's *The Persian Revolution* and *Materials for the Study of the Babi Religion*, and additional English and Persian material about them can be found in the Brown manuscripts and letters at Cambridge. Browne and others do not seem to have drawn adequate analytical conclusions from what they knew about these two men, however.

They had very similar lives. Both were born in Kerman in the mid-nineteenth century, and as adults went together to Esfahan, Tehran, and Istanbul. Both married daughters of the *Sobhe Azal*, the Azali leader, both were Babis and associates of Afghani, and both were extradited at the demand of the Iranian government after the assassination of Nasar ed Din Shah by a follower of Afghani, and put to death in Tabriz in 1896 along with a third man.

Sheikh Ahmad Ruhi was the son of the *Sheikh ol Olama* Molla Mohammad Ja'far, about whom Browne notes:

> Mulla Muhammad Ja'far was a distinguished theologian and one of the early promotors of the Liberal Movement in Persia, and lived to the age of seventy years. Early in the reign of Nasiru'd Din Shah he was imprisoned on suspicion of being a Babi by Khan Baba Khan the governor of Kerman ...[24]

It seems likely that he was a Babi, since not only Sheikh Ahmad Ruhi, but his older brother Sheikh Hadi *Bahr ol Olum*, was an Azali, the latter being later also a deputy from Kerman in the first *majles*. Molla Mohammad Ja'far and Sheikh Ahmad Ruhi were, like many other Azalis, also members of the Islamic ulama. During his early life in Iran, Sheikh Ahmad Ruhi lectured to Islamic audiences on the exegesis of the Qur'an. In Istanbul he earned his living by language teaching and translated several European works into Persian with the help of another learned Iranian, Mirza Habib. Ruhi is credited with the Persian translation of *Hajji Baba*, which is more devastating than the original, but I am now uncertain whether he, Mirza Habib, or both, actually did the job. Ruhi sent to Browne and was probably the main author of a book explaining Azali doctrine, *Hasht Behesht*, which has only recently and secretly been printed in Iran, along with certain other Azali works.[25] Browne valued this work highly, although he felt it contained some interpretations foreign to the thought of the Bab. Ruhi also wrote other anonymous Azali works.

The content of Ruhi's correspondence with Browne shows his concern to explain Babi doctrine to the Iranians. At the same time his translations involved him in direct Westernization. While covertly working to circulate his Babi works, and while trying to get Browne to publish the anti-clerical Persian *Hajji Baba*, he was joining with Afghani in Islamic appeals to the Shi'a clergy against the Shah. They and Mirza Aqa Khan Kermani wrote letters to the ulama in Iraq and Iran calling for a struggle against Naser ed Din Shah and his concessions to foreign encroachments, letters which were written in the most orthodox terms. And Ruhi had inscribed on his seal, 'I am the propagandist of the Unity of Islam: Ahmad Ruhi is my name.'[26] Toward the end of his life, Ruhi's concerns became more and more political and less religious, and it appears that he lost his religious faith. In the frontispiece photograph of Phillott's edition of the Persian *Hajji Baba* Ruhi is shown leaning on a tablet on which is written in Turkish, 'There is nothing except nature.'

Mirza Aqa Khan Kermani was a poet and prose writer, and an iconoclastic nationalist of the type of the late Ahmad Kasravi, who rejected both Islam and the cultural traditions of Islamic Iran. He is known for a famous preface in which he denounced all the Iranian poets but Firdousi as inculcating a passive, corrupt, and anti-national morality. Though a Babi and later anti-religious, he not only joined in the letter writing to the Shi'a clergy noted above, but also wrote works appealing to Islamic sentiment as against the Shah. In his poem, the *Nameye Bastan*, he excoriates Naser ed Din Shah as an unbeliever:

Did the Shah possess spiritual perception he would have made me
    independent of the world,
And had he any portion in the faith of Islam, he would have made me
    celebrated throughout the world for my good deed.
But since the essence of unbelief was in his blood, his wrath was
    kindled at the unification of Islam.
A farthing is better than such a king, who has neither law, nor faith,
    nor religion![27]

There seems no reason to doubt that Mirza Aqa Khan Kermani

was the author of the '100 letters' volume of the fictitious correspondence, *Kamal od Dowleh and Jalal od Dowleh*, though the earlier volume was written by Akhundov. Of the later volume Browne notes that its main motive is the

> glorification of ancient and the disparagement of modern Persia. The Arabs are denounced as barbarians and Islam, especially the Shi'a doctrine, is sharply criticized, while not only Zoroaster but even the communist Mazdak is applauded ... He praises the open antagonism to Islam of the Carmathians, Ismailis and Assassins but condemns the later *ulama*, philosophers and heresiarchs of Persia, including Mulla Sadra, Shaykh Murtada, Shaykh Ahmad al-Ahsa'i and the Bab, whose ignorance, he says, is such that 'not one of them has hitherto uttered two words calculated to benefit Persia,' while the Sufis and mystics are also held up to contempt as well as poets like Qa'ani. Polygamy is condemned, the miserable position of Persian women deplored, and the Persian character disparaged ...[28]

The reference to the Bab and to the founder of the Sheikhi reformist sect seem particularly significant. The author praises earlier heresies and religious reform movements, but in relation to movements *which still had adherents in Iran*, including the philosophy of Molla Sadra, mysticism, Sheikhism, and Babism, his condemnation is absolute. It seems fair to conclude that this is not only an anti-Islamic, but also an anti-religious book, since it attacks most forms of religious thought which still had currency in Iran, with the 'nationalist' exception of Zoroastrianism. It should be noted that this book has never been allowed publication in Iran, and is still available only in rare manuscript copies. It had wide circulation, however, both before and since the revolution.

When writing anonymously, Mirza Aqa Khan Kermani and Sheikh Ahmad Ruhi presented modernist interpretations of Babism and, later, anti-Islamic and anti-religious ideas. At the same time, in letters and writings under their own names they attacked the Shah and those around him for unbelief and for weakening the land and faith of Islam. They shared the immediate political goal of wanting the overthrow of the Shah, and for this an appeal to the clergy and to Islamic sentiment was helpful. At the same time they had the long-range goal of modernizing and secularizing Iran, for which attacks on Islam and the clergy, which must have represented their more sincere feelings, were necessary.

The comparison between Kasravi and Mirza Aqa Khan Kermani was made above,[29] and those at all familiar with contemporary Iranian intellectuals will surely be struck by their restatement of themes found in Kermani. The glorification of ancient Iran and its religion, the hatred of the Arabs and their identification with Islam and of both with Iran's downfall, and, as in a Kermani passage not quoted here, the strong hostility to the clergy are all notes struck again and again with increasing frequency. Some of these ideas have their roots in Iranian tradition, and it seems clear that anti-Arab and anti-Islamic feeling always represented a strong, if frequently underground, strain of thought in Iran. They are even more closely tied with modern nationalism, however. A desire to find a non-insulting 'secret' of decline plus the modern emphasis on national unity and independence has led many Asian peoples to blame their troubles on foreign conquest. In the Middle East this has the curious circular result that the Iranians have blamed their decline on the Arabs, the Turks on the Arabs and Persians, and the Arabs on the Turks; while the Mongols come in for universal condemnation. In China the Manchus were often blamed. This type of explanation ignores the anti-progressive tendencies inherent in traditional class structure, which was often almost identical to that brought in by the conquerors (or, in the case of Iran, perhaps more inhibiting). The rejection of the living culture of the ruling classes in favor of an idealized version of a culture which is either dead or subterranean and popular is also a feature common to modern nationalism in Asia and elsewhere. The dominant culture is recognized to be a brake on progress, and a new, activist, and *national* culture is called for.

Consideration of the personal opinions of Malkam, Ruhi, Kermani, and possibly Afghani indicates that intellectual development in modern Iran was not marked by a gradual change over generations from old ideas to new ones. Rather, more and more intellectuals have been exposed to Western ideas, and these ideas have tended to change their outlook radically from that of their traditional upbringing. As one elderly Iranian who himself experienced this change described it to me, the modern and scientific ideas of the West penetrated 'like a flash of light', overthrowing the earlier ideas held by him and his associates. Such a process can be documented in the writings of Kasravi, who began as a religious conservative and became an iconoclastic and anti-clerical nationalist. In the nineteenth century few experienced this process of change, but those who did became nationalists of a modern type, with ideas still found in Iranian nationalism – rejection of Islam, anti-clericalism, agnosticism, Westernism, anti-imperialism, glorification of the pre-Islamic past, and hatred of modern Iranian actuality. This is not to say that there have been no changes in the ideas of Iranian nationalists from 1890 to today, but rather that these changes are smaller than would appear merely from a study of acknowledged writings and speeches. Speakers and writers before and during the revolution found it necessary to speak in Islamic terms, but many, even in the ulama, were privately agnostic Westernizers. And, as one who remembers the younger enlightened revolutionaries said privately, 'they were hostile to all religions, but *particularly* to Islam.' The difference between pre-revolutionary and post-revolutionary nationalists lay not so much in their ideas as in the openness with which they expressed their ideas, and their tactical evaluation of what words would be most useful for nationalist and/or reformist goals.

Since the works of early nationalists often expressed not what their authors believed but what they considered tactically useful, it would seem reasonable to criticize them not on logical, but on tactical grounds. Here the criticism will not be that there is something inherently wrong in holding one belief in private and stating another in public, and something cowardly or immoral about men who do such things. The devoted lives and martyred deaths of Ruhi and Kermani should acquit them of the second charge, and it is clear that if they wanted to have effective influence on Iranians at that time, they could not publicly proclaim that they were Azalis or agnostics. The real question seems rather: were pan-Islam and appeals to the clergy effective paths to the modernization and regeneration of Iran which these men wanted?

Insofar as Ruhi, Kermani and Afghani identified pan-Islam with support for Sultan Abdul Hamid it seems clear they were tactically mistaken. For a period the three did work with the Sultan to carry out their plans, and there is a reference to this idea in another part of the Kermani poem quoted above. Their support was based on anti-Qajar feeling and, probably, an anti-imperialist notion that a united Islamic state would be a stronger bulwark against the West than separate states. But in fact the Turkish sultans were representatives of an old ruling group, and Abdul Hamid was hardly a reformist. The sultans had been little more of a bulwark against Western domination than the Qajar shahs. Abdul Hamid was willing to adopt pan-Islamic ideas when they suited his purpose, but, as the reformist pan-Islamists should have known, but discovered only late in life, he was not willing to use them in any reforming way. The early cordial relations between the Sultan and the reforming pan-Islamists were finally broken, and the Sultan allowed Ruhi and Kermani to be extradited and mistreated Afghani at the end of his life. The Afghani letter cited above shows that he then recognized the error of appealing to the Sultan. The legacy of association between pan-Islam and the Sultan and Ottoman imperial designs remained, however.

A question which cannot be so easily answered is whether the above three were right in appealing to the Shi'a clergy against the Qajars. As will be shown, the clergy had reason to be anti-Qajar. The clergy also had popular influence, and the above three were able to arouse them to use it against the Qajars. The tobacco boycott of 1891, for example, is attributed to letters from Afghani to the Shi'a leaders. The higher clergy also played an important role in the revolution, particularly its early stages. Yet the point remains that the clergy were not really reformers, and that encouragement of their leadership perhaps in the long run slowed the process of reform. The writings of Afghani were all too convincing to some Iranians. A policy of encouraging clerical influence with one hand and attacking it with the other seems too confused as to ultimate purpose to be defended as really effective.

Reformist pan-Islam, at least in Ruhi and Kermani, did not ultimately aim at strengthening either the Ottoman rule or the Shi'a clergy. Both these groups were to be used as means to get rid of the Qajars and end Western domination in Iran. In a period when nationalism and reformism were weak, a search for powerful allies by reformists was not surprising. But to hope to achieve the overthrow of tradition with the help of the groups which profited from it the most was possible only for an immature nationalism.

THE ANTI-QAJAR ULAMA

The question remains why some of the highest ulama were against the Qajar dynasty and helped lead pre-revolutionary popular movements as well as the revolution. This needs much more study, but a few tentative answers will be essayed. First, most of the well-educated Iranians were members of the ulama in the nineteenth century, and instead of 'clergy', ulama would perhaps better be translated more literally as 'learned men'. Not only preaching but teaching, justice, and the administration of charitable and religious endowments were in their hands, and they also played an important political role. Although anti-clerical feeling was strong, many in the ulama enjoyed the greatest respect in society, far more than the despised secular administrators. A young boy with a keen mind saw in traditional religious education the main path to upward social mobility. In interviewing men who remembered the revolution I asked them all, 'When you were a boy what did you want to be when you grew up?' An absolute majority answered, 'one of the high ulama', or something with a similar meaning, while none said they wanted to be in the secular government.

Since the ulama comprised the majority of intellectuals in Iran, it is not surprising that new and modernist ideas found exponents in their ranks. Very few of the higher ulama were as liberal as Sheikh Hadi Najmabadi, but some new ideas penetrated even the highest ulama of Najaf, Karbala, and Samarra in Iraq. As to those members of the lower ulama who were Babis or freethinkers, their adherence to the revolutionary cause is not to be wondered at.

The role of the highest ranks of the ulama, especially in Iraq, is not to be explained primarily by any adherence to new ideas, however. Their hostility to the late Qajars had other roots. There has always been potential opposition from the Shi'a ulama to the shah. The latter is, theoretically, regarded as a usurper, legitimate succession having passed down through the house of Ali until the last, or hidden Imam, who will reappear to establish legitimate rule. There was also a practical basis for opposition in both Shi'a and Sunni Islam. The ulama was a power group in competition with secular administrators, and often tried to assert or extend its authority as against them, while secular rulers might try to limit this authority. The conflict was kept to a minimum under the earlier Shi'a dynasty, the Safavids, who, largely for policy reasons, encouraged religious orthodoxy and the orthodox ulama. The less conciliatory and orthodox policies of the Qajars, plus the new location of the Shi'a centers *outside* Iranian territory encouraged conflict. Free from the power of the shah, the highest ulama could move against him. The conflicts between the papacy and Western rulers, as contrasted to the much smoother relations in the Russian, Byzantine, and Ottoman Empires form an analogy.

The nineteenth century Western impact exacerbated potential conflicts. Insofar as the shahs, and particularly Naser ed Din (1848–1896), did Westernize, it meant a decline in clerical power. This decline was noted by contemporary observers. The beginnings of Western education ended the clerical monopoly over education and intellectual life, and introduced challenges to orthodoxy. Administrative and legal reforms lessened the role of the shar'ia courts. Western and unorthodox customs came into some vogue, particularly among the ruling class. All these trends lessened the power of the ulama, who tended to blame the dynasty.

Most important, the very existence of Iran was threatened in the late nineteenth century. From the clerical viewpoint, Western rule would mean an intolerable diminution in the realm of Islam and a further curtailing of the power of the ulama. The numerous concessions granted by the Shah seemed to many but a prelude to foreign rule, and it was particularly on this ground that Afghani was able to arouse the Shi'a leaders against the Shah. Their position outside Iran enabled them to lead opposition in a way not open to the ulama of other Islamic countries. Documents indicate that the Sultan, and possibly the British, encouraged this opposition at least until 1905.[30]

Also, the ulama were to a degree sensitive to public pressure and opinion. The loose hierarchical structure of Iranian Shi'ism meant that the position of an individual member of the ulama depended on popularity as well as learning and influence. The teacher who attracted the most pupils also got the most money and the highest position of respect. Therefore, at a time when the dynasty was generally hated, some of the ulama would go along with, or even give direction to, this sentiment.

Afghani, Kermani, and Ruhi helped arouse this potential opposition of the leading ulama towards nationalist goals, notably in the remarkably effective tobacco boycott of 1891, which culminated in the cancellation of a concession. Another instance of pre-revolutionary collaboration between nationalists and clerical leaders was the movement against using foreign goods, which was effective enough to disturb British consular representatives. This was promoted in Islamic terms, but propagated mainly by the secret freethinker Sayyed Jamal ed Din Esfahani.[31]

Thus was laid the basis for cooperation between radical nationalists and clerical leaders who, whatever their private religious beliefs, looked to reform and revolution to enhance, not weaken, clerical power. The shaky nature of this alliance and the problems it raised were shown up only in the course of the revolution itself.

APPENDIX

BIOGRAPHY OF MIRZA AQA KHAN KERMANI (1853–4—1896)

The following is prefaced to Hasht Behest, *and written by a brother of Sheikh Ahmad Ruhi, Afzal ol Molk Kermani, himself a member of Sayyed Jamal ed Din Afghani's circle. It has points not available in Western languages. The parts in parentheses are summarized, the rest is translated. Afzal ol Molk refers to himself in the third person and under a different name, but I translate this as 'I' to make it less confusing, and also change other name forms at times to make them clearer to the reader. 'The Sayyed' means Afghani.*

(Mirza Aqa Khan was born in a village near Kerman, where his father was a landlord. His genealogy is traced; he was descended from Chenghiz Khan; one great-grandfather was a great Zoroastrian *mobad*; and his mother's family had many prominent members and goes back to an Indian *nawab* who came to Iran as a doctor to a Safavid Shah and married into the Safavid family. This family followed the Ne'matollahi order in religion. Mirza Aqa Khan was outstandingly intelligent as a child, and began to study foreign languages as well as traditional Islamic subjects in Kerman. As a young man he began writing poetry and translations. After quarrels with the government in Kerman he went to Esfahan, and entered the service of Prince Zel os Soltan, where Sheikh Ahmad Ruhi, his friend from Kerman, joined him. They then went to

Tehran, where they gave lessons to the sons of notables. Mirza Aqa
Khan was defrauded of his legacy here. After seven or eight months in
Tehran he went to Istanbul by way of Rasht and Baku. He went to
Cyprus to see the Sobhe Azal [the Babi leader], whose daughters he and
Ruhi married. Both became friendly with Mirza Habib, a learned
Esfahani, and they worked together on *Hajji Baba* and other
translations. Mirza Aqa Khan then became editor of the newspaper
Akhtar and gave Persian and Arabic lessons, and Ruhi also lived off
language teaching. After they had spent four years in Istanbul, Sayyed
Jamal ed Din Afghani came from London on the invitation of the Sultan,
and stayed in his guesthouse.)

The late Mirza Aqa Khan ... reasoned and debated with the late
Sayyed Jamal ed Din, explaining ideas which were unknown to the
latter, such as Sufi ideas and the philosophy of Molla Sadra and Sheikh
Ahmad Ahsa'i who had taught the late Hajj Sayyed Javad Karbala'i,
who was one of the letters of the living of the Bab, and for three years
resided in Kerman. And he worked on *Hasht Behesht* and *Qahvekhaneh-
ye surat* in these days, and had a perfect friendship and correspondence
with Mirza Malkam Khan.

The Ottoman Sultan came to believe in the unity of the different
Islamic groups and asked Sayyed Jamal ed Din to write to the Shi'ite
ulama in Iran and Iraq and call them to unity. The late Sayyed Jamal ed
Din answered that this problem had great importance for Islamic states.
Today the Moslems of the world were more than three hundred million,
and if they believed in unity and brotherhood among themselves no
government or people could prevail over or excel them. He said if he had
the power of the sultanate and the necessary money ... he could
accomplish this great work with the help of a circle of patriotic (*mellat
parast*) intellectuals. The Ottoman Sultan gave guarantees and
obligations for this. The Sayyed formed a society of Iranian and other
Shi'ite men of letters who were in Istanbul. This society was made up of
twelve men: Novvab Vala Hajj Sheikh ol Ra'is, Feizi Efendi Mo'allem
Irani, Reza Pasha Shi'i, Sayyed Borhan ed Din Balkhi, Novvab Hossein
Hindi, Ahmad Mirza (who had just come from Iran to Istanbul), Hajj
Mirza Hasan Khan (the Iranian Consul General), Mirza Aqa Khan
Kermani, Sheikh Ahmad Ruhi, myself (Ruhi's brother), Abdol Karim
Bey and Hamid Bey Javaherizadeh Esfahani. When the Sayyed's group
was formed, he spoke to it as follows: Today the religion of Islam is like
a ship whose captain is Mohammad, peace be with him, and all Moslems
are passengers of this holy ship, and this unhappy ship is caught in a
storm and threatened with sinking, and unbelievers and freethinkers
(*ahl-e zandaqeh*) from every side have pierced this ship. What is the duty
of the passengers of such a ship, threatened with sinking, and its
inhabitants close to perdition? Should they first try to preserve and save

this ship from the storm and from sinking, or instead bring the ship and each other to the verge of ruin through discord, personal motives, and petty disagreements? All with one voice answered that preserving the territory of Islam and saving this holy ship was the religious duty of every Moslem. ...

Then the Sayyed asked all to write to every acquaintance and friend in Iran and the shrines of Iraq, in general, and in particular to the Shi'ite ulama in India, Iran, and Arab lands, Balkh, and Turkestan, about the kindness and benevolence of the great Islamic Sultan toward all Moslems of whatever opinion and group they might be. If the Shi'ite ulama united in this Islamic unity the Sultan would give every one of them, according to his rank, special favor and a monthly salary, and would order Ottoman officials to observe the same good conduct toward Iranians in Mecca and Medina as toward their own people, and in recognition of this great action of the Shi'ite ulama and the state of Iran he would bestow on them the holy cities of Iraq ... (the society agreed) and about 400 letters were written in all directions, and a report of this society was given to the Ottoman Sultan ... After six months about 200 petitions from the Arab and Iranian Shi'ite ulama with some gifts and antiques were sent the Sultan through Sayyed Jamal ed Din. (He translated the petitions into Turkish and took them to the Sultan.) The Ottoman Caliph was so happy to see these letters that he embraced the late Sayyed and kissed his face and said to him: Since some are such fanatical Sunnites and will find a pretext to accuse me of Shi'ism, it is better that we turn over the accomplishment of this holy goal to the Prime Minister and the High Gate.[32] We will have the Sheikh of Islam collaborate with us confidentially. He accepted the royal will in this matter and an imperial command went to the High Gate. I was delegated to go to the holy cities of Iraq to investigate the mentality and affairs of the ulama and give a report to the High Gate ... one of the writings from the holy cities fell into the hands of Mirza Mahmud Khan Qomi, the (Iranian) Consul at Baghdad, who sent it ... enclosed with a petition to the Shah of Iran, Naser ed Din Shah, saying that Sayyed Jamal ed Din Afghani was planning the surrender of Iran to the Ottoman Sultan and was taking most of the ulama with him on the plea of the unity of Islam and soon a big revolt would be set in motion.

Naser ed Din Shah was frightened by this report and immediately telegraphed to Mirza Mahmud Khan Ala ol Molk Tabataba'i who was the ambassador in Istanbul, asking him to accuse in whatever way he could those who were involved in this affair and send them to Iran. Ala ol Molk, because of his enmity and spite towards Hajj Mirza Hasan Khan, the Consul General, and toward Mirza Aqa Khan Kermani ... because of their heedlessness, and their saying and writing [of him as]

'Olaq ol Molk' (Donkey of the Kingdom), and their relations with the
Sayyed ... (was looking for a pretext) and acted with Mahmud Pasha, the
chief of police ... and seduced him with a promise to request for him an
important decoration from the government of Iran. He said: In exchange
for these individuals who are fugitives from Iran and speak for the
perdition of Iran ... I will surrender to you whatever Armenians have
fled or may flee to Iranian territory. Mahmud Pasha ... gave a report to
the Sultan on the big service which the extradition of fugitive Armenians
in Iran would be.

In response, the Sultan issued an order that Iranians were under the
control of their ambassador. To explain, parenthetically we should note:
(1) Sayyed Jamal ed Din, because of Sheikh Abul Huda, a friend of the
Sultan, had resigned from attendance on the Sultan. (2) The Khedive of
Egypt had come to Istanbul, and repeatedly requested the High Gate for
an interview with the Sayyed, but it was not granted. He impetuously
went twice ... for a private interview with the Sayyed and secret spies of
the Sultan reported this. The Sultan was very afraid that the Sayyed had
made an agreement to depose him and a treaty of friendship with the
Khedive. (3) Sayyed Abdullah, from Medina ... was hated by the Sultan,
and when he came to Istanbul in flight he took refuge in the Sayyed's
home ... The Sayyed would not surrender him, and entrusted him to the
Khedive of Egypt, who took him to Egypt. It was in this period that the
Armenian disturbances broke out in parts of the Ottoman territory, and
also the ... Young Turks emerged as patriots desiring law and a
constitutional monarchy. The government assigned 13,000 secret police
for the Armenians and Young Turks ... This affair so broke up relations
among the people of Istanbul and the notables and office holders that
none dared meet together. Among others ten spies had been set to watch
over the movements of Sayyed Jamal ed Din and his friends and
acquaintances. Amidst all this Mirza Reza, who later became the
martyred killer of the Shah, who had banished him from Iran ... arrived
in Istanbul, and since he had known the Sayyed in Tehran through Hajji
Mohammad Hossein Amin Dar oz Zarb, who had been his master, he
hurried to the house of the Sayyed. The Sayyed resorted to saying he had
no confidence in Iranians and would not put up any Iranians in his
house; (but sent him, as he was ill, to a hospital, and gave him money.
Mirza Aqa Khan continued to work on books, until the Ottoman police
jailed him, Sheikh Ahmad Ruhi, and Mirza Hasan Khan. Ruhi, from jail,
asked me to see the Iranian Ambassador, Ala ol Molk, who said the
three were being extradited at the request of the Iranian government. He
complained that Mirza Hasan Khan had written of him as 'Olaq ol Molk'
(Donkey of the Kingdom), but said he knew of no crime by Ruhi. He
wrote a petition for Ruhi's release, noting he was the son of one of the

leading Kerman ulama, and gave it to me, telling me to get to Tehran soon to secure Ruhi's release when he reached Iran. The prisoners were put on a boat very suddenly.)

Sayyed Jamal ed Din, with whom Ruhi and Kermani had broken relations for six months, sent a man to me saying not to fear; an imperial telegram has gone to Trebizond to return them ... I went to the Sayyed who said: The wicked Iranian ambassador had them banished, and I saw the Sultan and told him that people who had done clear services for the Prince of Believers for the unity of Moslems had been sent to Iran by the Iranian Ambassador, on an Ottoman government boat, for life imprisonment or execution. He was very sorry and swore that Nazem Pasha sent a report that three seditious Iranians were constantly causing trouble in Istanbul; the [Shah's] will was expressed that they be sent to Iran, and I gave permission. Now I will telegraph Trebizond to return them honorably. (But Abul Huda and the Chief of Police and the Iranian Ambassador delayed their return. Meanwhile, Mirza Reza returned to Iran with my brother, and I heard of his killing the Shah. I heard from Ruhi that the three prisoners were being taken to Iran.) I hurried to the house of the Sayyed and showed him the telegram and asked him ... to ask the Sultan to keep them in Ottoman territory. The Sayyed with perfect calm, after thinking a little, raised his head and said: Supposing they took my son to be killed, and he could be saved with one word of intercession from me; I would consent to his being killed, but not to the shame of begging from an enemy ... Let them be taken to Iran and killed so that among their people the foundation of nobility and honor will be high.

(I then went to the secretary of the Russian Embassy, who had been Ruhi's student. He brought back the answer that Ruhi and Kermani were Babis, and like Nihilists, and had a hand in the Shah's death. Mohammad Ali Mirza, the crown prince of Iran and governor of Azerbaijan, had the three men killed in Azerbaijan on his own orders, in 1896. Afghani died in 1897.)

NOTES

1. In English, besides the Browne and Shuster books mentioned above, there are several pamphlets by Browne, and his *The Press and Poetry of Modern Persia* (Cambridge, 1914), which includes a chronology of the last years of the Revolution. Among the numerous articles in various languages, Ann K. S. Lambton, 'Secret Societies and the Persian Revolution of 1905–6', *St. Antony's Papers: Number 4* (New York, 1959), deserves note. In Persian the best books are probably those of three scholarly Tabrizi eyewitnesses: Esma'il Amirkhizi, *Qeyam-e Azarbaijan va Satar Khan* (Tabriz, 1960);

Ahmad Kasravi, *Tarikh-e mashruteh-ye Iran*, 4th ed. (Tehran, n.d.);
Sayyed Hasan Taqizadeh, *Tarikh-e avayel-e enqelab-e mashrutiyyat-e Iran*
(Tehran, 1959); and by the son of the (Azali) preacher, Malek ol
Motakallemin: Mahdi Malekzadeh, *Tarikh-e enqelab-e mashrutiyyat-e
Iran*, 7 vols. (Tehran, n.d.). The Soviet work showing the most work on
archives but also with the most distortions is M. S. Ivanov, *Iranskaia
revoliutsiia 1905–1911 godov* (Moscow, 1957). Non-Iranian eyewitness
reports are found in published diplomatic documents; in several numbers
of the *Revue du monde musulman*; in E. de Lorey and D. Sladen, *The Moon
of the Fourteenth Night* (London, 1910); and V. Tria, *Kavkazskie sotsial'-
demokraty v persidskoi revoliutsii* (Paris, 1910).

2. On the Babis, besides conversations with Babis in Iran and a few articles, I
have found useful these works of Edward G. Browne: *Materials for the
Study of the Babi Religion* (Cambridge, 1918); ed. *Nuqtatu'l Kaf*
(Cambridge, 1911); ed. and tr., *The Tarikh-i Jadid or New History of Mirza
Ali Muhammad, the Bab* (Cambridge, 1893); ed. and tr., *A Traveller's
Narrative Written to Illustrate the Episode of the Bab* (Cambridge, 1891); *A
Year Amongst the Persians* (London, 1893). Also Alessandro Bausani, 'Bab'
and 'Babis', *Encyclopedia of Islam* (New ed.), and *Persia Religiosa* (Milan,
1959); de Gobineau, *Religions et philosophies dans l'Asie centrale*, 3d ed.
(Paris, 1957); Nabil i A'zam, *The Dawn Breakers*, tr. and ed. Shoghi Effendi
(New York, 1932); A. L. M. Nicolas, ed. and tr., *Le Béyan arabe* (Paris,
1905); ed. and tr., *Le Béyan persan* (4 vols., Paris, 1911–14); *Seyyed Ali
Mohammed dit le Bab* (Paris, 1905). The Azalis have recently printed the
Bayan, Hasht Behesht and other texts in Iran, but these are unavailable
through standard outlets.

3. Bausani, *Persia Religiosa*, p. 405.

4. On the Taipings I have used: Eugene P. Boardman, 'Christian Influences
on the Ideology of the Taiping Rebellion', *Far Eastern Quarterly*, X (Feb.,
1951), 115–124; Lindesay Brine, *The Taeping Rebellion in China* (London,
1862); Theodore Hamberg, *The Visions of Hung-Siu-Tshuen and Origin of
the Kwang-si Insurrection* (Hong Kong, 1854); Joseph R. Levenson,
'Confucian and Taiping "Heaven": The Political Implications of Clashing
Religious Concepts', paper delivered at the Congress of Orientalists
(Moscow, 1960); Lin-le (Augustus F. Lindley), *Ti-ping Tien-kwoh; The
History of the Ti-ping Revolution* (London, 1866); Thomas Taylor
Meadows, *The Chinese and Their Rebellions* (Stanford, Cal., n.d.); W. H.
Medhurst, ed., *Pamphlets Issued by the Chinese Insurgents at Nanking*
(Shanghai, 1853); George Taylor, 'The Taiping Rebellion, its Economic
Background and Social Theory', *Chinese Social and Political Science
Review*, XVI (1933), 545–614; and Ssu-yu Teng, *New Light on the History
of the Taping Rebellion* (Cambridge, 1950). New translations of Taiping
documents are in W. T. de Bary, W. T. Chan, and B. Watson, *Sources of
Chinese Tradition* (New York, 1960), and more will soon be published at
the University of Washington.

5. Gobineau, *op. cit.*, p. 299.

6. *Ibid.*, pp. 278–279; Nicolas, *Le Béyan persan*, iii–xv.

7. Cf. especially Browne's Introduction to *Nuqtatu'l Kaf.* Bausani, *op. cit.*, in his chapter on the Babis discusses both traditional and original features.

8. Gobineau, *op. cit.*, p. 285. On the economic program of the Babis, Minorsky says: 'It is an interesting fact ... that the new preaching was addressed definitely to the middle classes, to the petty bourgeoisie, the lesser clergy, and the traders. The Bab himself belonged to a family of merchants, and it is curious to find among his demands such trifling details as the legalization of loans at interest, the fixing of the monetary standard, and the inviolability of (commercial) correspondence. − In a recent work the activity of the Bab has been studied with relation to the economic crisis which Persia went through at the beginning of the nineteenth century. Further, the author [M. S. Ivanov] points out the extremely radical character the preaching took after the arrest of the Bab. 'His followers, gathered in Mazandaran, went so far as to suggest the abolition of private property, which was regarded as a usurpation. The shah's government, relying on the great landed nobility, closely connected with the administration, drowned the revolt in blood ...' 'Iran: Opposition, Martyrdom, and Revolt,' *Unity and Variety in Muslim Civilization*, ed. Gustave E. von Grunebaum (Chicago, 1955), p. 198. The combination of bourgeois and communist elements in one revolt is far from unique.

9. The idea that the real attraction of Babism in the late nineteenth century was for those interested in political and social reform is suggested, among other places, in a letter from S. Churchill, Tehran, 1889, in the Browne manuscripts in Cambridge and partially reprinted in Browne, *Materials for the Study of the Babi Religion*, p. 293. On the social causes of late medieval heretical revolts see Norman Cohn, *The Pursuit of the Millenium*, 2d ed. (New York, 1969). The ideologies discussed by Cohn have many similarities to both Babi and Taiping ideas.

10. Browne, *Materials*, p. 221.

11. 'As one of the most prominent and cultivated Azalis admitted to me some six or seven years ago, the ideal of a democratic Persia developing on purely national lines seems to have inspired in the minds of no few leading Azalis the same fiery enthusiasm as did the idea of a reign of the saints on earth in the case of the early Babis.' *Ibid.*, p. xix.

12. Browne's attribution, based probably on a letter (now in the Cambridge Browne collection) from the Babi scribe who sent him the manuscript, is in *Materials*, pp. 221–223. Browne notes the work apparently dates from 1863–4, while elsewhere noting that Mirza Aqa Khan Kermani was born in 1853. The Baku Nezami Museum manuscript collection has several Akhundov autographs of the work and of letters about it, and has published a catalogue in Azerbaijani Turkish of its Akhundov manuscripts. Some of these, including the *Kamal od Dowleh* volume, have been published in Russian in: *M. F. Akhundov: Izbrannye filosofskie proizvedeniia* (Baku, 1953).

13. On influences from Russian Transcaucasia see my translation of Sayyed Hasan Taqizadeh, 'The Background of the Constitutional Movement in Azerbaijan', *The Middle East Journal*, XIV, 4 (Autumn, 1960), especially pp. 459–462, and Kasravi, *op. cit.*, pp. 127, 145–146, 193–195.

14. On Malkam Khan cf. especially Browne, *Persian Revolution*, pp. 35–42 and *passim*; and *Press and Poetry*, pp. 20–21; also *Les comédies de Malkom Khan*, tr. A. Bricteux (Paris, 1933). The Cambridge University Library has Malkam Khan's *Qanun* as well as the other Persian newspapers mentioned in *Press and Poetry* as being in Browne's possession. In Persian see especially Mohammad Mohit Tabataba'i, ed., *Majmu'eh-ye asar-e Mirza Malkam Khan*, Vol. I (Tehran, 1948–49).

15. This is from one of Qazvini's very useful biographical notes in Browne, *The Persian Revolution*, p. 406.

16. On insincerity, symbolism, and esoterism in Islam and Iran, see Bausani, *op. cit.*, Gobineau, *op. cit.*, Minorsky, *op. cit.*; J M. Abd-el-Jalil, 'Autour de la sincerité d'al-Gazzali', *Mélanges Louis Massignon*, I (Damascus, 1956); Browne, *A Year Amongst the Persians*; H. A. R. Gibb, *Mohammedanism* (London, 1949); I. Goldziher, *Études sur la tradition islamique*, tr. Léon Bercher (Paris, 1952); Gustave E. von Grunebaum, *Islam* (Menasha, Wisc., 1955); Marshall G. S. Hodgson, 'Batiniyya', *Encyclopedia of Islam* (New ed.), and *The Order of Assassins* ('s-Gravenhage, 1955); and Nicolas, *Le Béyan persan*. On philosophy *vis-à-vis* orthodoxy see George F. Hourani, 'Ibn Rushd's Defence of Philosophy', *The World of Islam* (London, 1960); Muhsin Mahdi, 'The Editio Princeps of Farabi's Compendium Legum Platonis', *Journal of Near Eastern Studies*, XX, 1 (1961), 1–24, and *Ibn Khaldun's Philosophy of History* (London, 1957), especially the parts on Ibn Khaldun's unacknowledged Averroism; Leo Strauss, *Persecution and the Art of Writing* (Glencoe, Ill., 1952) and Simon van den Bergh, tr. and introd., *Averroes' Tahafut al-Tahafut* (London, 1954). Louis Massignon, *Essai sur les origines du lexique technique de la mystique musulmane*, New ed. (Paris, 1954), pp. 125–126, discusses pressures toward fabrication in religions which believe all creative power resides in God, and the Islamic notion that the truth of a statement may lie in its efficacy for good ends. See also the brilliant C. Cahen, *et al.*, *L'élaboration de l'Islam* (Paris, 1961).

17. On Asian appeal to, and reading modern values into, traditional ideals as an alternative to the ideologies of Western oppressors see Nikki R. Keddie, 'Western Rule versus Western Values: Suggestions for a Comparative Study of Asian Intellectual History', *Diogenes*, 26 (1959), 71–96.

18. Sharif al-Mujahid, 'Sayyid Jamal al-Din al-Afghani: His Role in the Nineteenth Century Muslim Awakening', Unpublished M.A. thesis, McGill Institute of Islamic Studies, Montreal, 1954, Ch. iv, shows the near identity of their religious views. This thesis is very useful, particularly for its long passages translated from Afghani's Arabic and Persian writings. Despite Afghani's importance, no adequate biography or analysis of him exists, and the existing sketches all have important errors or omissions. The best brief biography is probably I. Goldziher, 'Djamal al-Din al-Afghani'. *Encyclopedia of Islam* (1st ed.). See also A. Ahmad, 'Sayid Ahmad Khan, Jamal al-din al-Afghani and Muslim India', *Studia Islamica*, XIII (1960), 55–78.

19. Jamal ad-Din al-Afghani, 'The Materialists in India', *Réfutation des matérialistes*, tr. A. M. Goichon (Paris, 1942), pp. 22–25.

20. 'Réponse de Jamal ad-Din al-Afghani à Renan' (from the *Journal des débats*), *ibid.*, pp. 178–179, 183–185. Al-Mujahid says that Afghani here speaks of the 'Muslim religion', meaning what then existed, but elsewhere of an ideal 'Islam'. The terminological argument is not entirely convincing since Afghani is here writing French and using ordinary French terminology. In any case, it is important that Afghani never made this distinction explicit.

21. The documents quoted are from Great Britain, Public Records Office, F.O. 60/594, 'Persia: Jemal-ed-Din: Proceedings of an Expulsion from Persia 1883–1897'. In order; No. 174, Cairo, May 22, 1883; Enclosure in A. 28877, Hyderabad, June 25, 1883; Enclosure in No. 923, Constantinople, Dec. 12, 1895; 'Memo by the General Superintendent of the Thagi and Dakaiti Department', India Office, March 6, 1896 (printed and marked 'Confidential').

22. *Ibid.*, no. 299, St. Petersburg, August 27, 1887.

23. Both letters translated in Browne, *Persian Revolution*, p. 17; pp. 28–29.

24. *Ibid.*, p. 414.

25. Browne and Phillott, who edited the Persian *Hajji Baba*, call Ruhi its translator, but one of the letters from Ruhi to Browne pasted into Browne, Or. Ms. F 53², 'Hasht Behesht', Vol. II, in the Cambridge Library calls Mirza Habib the translator. Browne may have had grounds to consider Ruhi the translator, but Sayyed Mohammad Ali Jamalzadeh wrote me in 1960 that he had concluded from other evidence that Mirza Habib did the job. A comparison showing up the sharper nature of the translation is in H. Kamshad, 'Creative Writing in Modern Persian Prose', Unpublished Ph.D. dissertation, Cambridge University, 1959, pp. 38–43. Letters in the Browne Cambridge collection, including one reproduced in the printed *Hasht Behesht* (n.p., n.d.), facing p. 1, summarized p. *alef*, suggest Mirza Javad Karbala'i, an early Babi leader, and Mirza Aqa Khan Kermani contributed to *Hasht Behesht*; but its concern to present Babi doctrine is more typical of. Ruhi than Kermani.

26. Nazem ol Eslam Kermani, *Tarikh-e bidari-ye iranian*, 2d ed. (Tehran, 1945–46), p. 8. This work is particularly valuable for its primary material and, as he notes, Browne drew on it in his *Persian Revolution*. On Sultan Abdul Hamid's use of the Afghani circle to attract the Shi'a ulama and the Shah's fear of this, see the Appendix to this chapter.

27. Browne, *Persian Revolution*, p. 413.

28. *Catalogue of Oriental Mss. Belonging to E. G. Browne* (Cambridge, 1932), p. 148.

29. This comparison is suggested in Abdol Hosein Zarrinkub, *Naqd-e adabi* (Tehran, 1959–60), p. 504.

30. Appendix to this article; and Great Britain Public Records Office, F.O. 371/102, Persia 1906, Files 13–460, No. 381: London, Dec. 23, 1905, Hardinge to Grey, Confidential (Report on relinquishing post as Minister to Tehran). After summarizing other elements in the political situation, Hardinge gives reasons for clerical opposition to the government, and then notes that relations between the British government and the Shi'a mojtaheds have been generally good. 'A valuable lever in our possession is

the so-called Oudh bequest, a fund left by the last king of Oudh for religious purposes at Kerbela and Nejef, and administered under the supervision of the British Residency at Baghdad. This enables our Resident, as well as his Vice Consul at Kerbela, who is always an Indian Shiah, to maintain close relations with the great doctors at Nejef, Kerbela ... and Samara, whilst the clergy in Persia itself, who have always candidates for a share in these religious endowments find it to their advantage to be on friendly terms with the British Legation ... in order that the Minister may say a good word for themselves or for their friends at Baghdad.' The fear that Great Britain might arouse the Iraq ulama against the Russophil policy of the government 'has acted within recent years as a wholesome deterrent on Persian statesmen'. The Sultan has also cultivated relations with the mojtaheds as part of his pan-Islamic policy, and old hatreds have lessened 'largely owing to the action of the Sultan, whose Ambassador at Tehran is in very close touch with the leaders of the clerical party, and who himself sends presents to the principal Persian Ulema, and is believed to employ one of the ablest among them as his secret political agent. On several occasions the Mujtaheds have attempted to appeal to the Sultan from the Shah, and to invoke the assistance of Constantinople against measures, such as the Russian Loans or the employment of Belgians in the Persian Administration, which they deemed detrimental to Islam. Several of them have asked my advice as to a closer union between Persia and Turkey against the common enemy in the North, and I have been surprised to hear from Persian pulpits panegyrics, doubtless not very sincere, on the Sultan, who not so long ago would have been deemed, as the successor of Omar, only worthy of curses and execrations.'

31. Sayyed Jamal ed Din Esfahani wrote *Lebas ot taqva* against the use of foreign goods. Parts are quoted in M. Esfahani, 'Sharh-e hal-e marhum Sayyed Jamal ed Din Vaez', *Yaqma*, VII, 12 (1333 [1954–55]), 551, and Sayyed Mohammad Ali Jamalzadeh, 'Tarjomeh-ye hal-e Sayyed Jamal ed Din Va'ez', Part 2, *Yaqma*, VII, 4 (1954–55), 400, from which I translate the book's conclusion: 'Honor would be not to have need of our enemies. Our honor is in this, that science and industries become common in our country. Our honor is in wearing the clothing of virtue. The clothing of virtue is the clothing of zeal and bravery. The clothing of virtue is the clothing of Islam and religion. The clothing of virtue is the clothing whose wearing is the cause of the flourishing of Moslem trade and the stagnation of the bazaars of unbelieving traders. The clothing of honor and manhood ... must be worn so that in both worlds heads can be high and worthy.' Jamalzadeh has written me that the author, his father, was irreligious, which corroborates statements from reliable informants in Iran who knew him. His use of religious beliefs for nationalist purposes is also shown in a letter about him from Dr. Afzal ol Molk, *Yaqma*, VII, 10 (1954–55) which recalls his saying to booksellers, 'still the Qur'an, the Book of God, is printed on foreign paper. These gentlemen are not planning to prepare at least one paper factory so that the word of God should not be printed on foreign paper.' (p. 454.)

On the movement against the tobacco concession see Browne, *Persian*

Revolution; Nazem ol Eslam Kermani, *op. cit.*, Ch. i; and especially the eyewitness diary, Dr. Feuvrier, *Trois ans à la cour de Perse*, New ed. (Paris, 1906), Ch. v, which stresses the startling unanimity and determination of Iranians in this movement. The role of the clergy before the revolution is discussed in G. H. Razi, 'Religion and Politics in Iran: A Study of Social Dynamics', Unpublished Ph.D. dissertation, University of California, Berkeley, 1956, Part III, and in Adolphe Back de Surany, *Essai sur la constitution persane*, Published doctoral thesis (Paris, 1914).

32. *Babi Ali*: The ministerial department of the Prime Minister. It is often translated in the West 'Sublime Porte' and used for the Sultan, whose palace it once denoted. From the 17th or 18th century *Babi Ali* referred to the headquarters of the government, as opposed to the Sultan's court. See J. Deny, 'Babi Ali', *Encyclopedia of Islam* (New ed.); and H. A. R. Gibb and Harold Bowen, *Islamic Society and the West*, Vol. I, Pt. I, 44 n., 113.

2

The Origins of the Religious-Radical
Alliance in Iran*

A recurring feature in Iranian history from 1890 to the present is
the appearance of peculiar alliances between part of the religious
leadership and the liberal or radical nationalist elements of the
country in opposition to the government. Although it is a truism
that politics makes strange bedfellows, the recurrence of liaisons
between these particular incompatible bedfellows perhaps
deserves more than superficial understanding. The alliance
between much of the religious leadership of Iran and the most
advanced and Westernized political activists is virtually without
parallel either in the Islamic or the non-Islamic world. There have
been religious activist and anti-Western organizations such as the
Muslim brotherhood elsewhere, but though their mass following
may have been very similar to that which participated in
movements like the Iranian Constitutional Revolution, the
leadership was generally quite different – representing neither the
higher religious leadership on the one hand nor the convinced
modernizers on the other. Outside the Islamic world as well as
within it, the leadership of established churches has tended to be
ranged with conservative governments rather than against them,
and even when this leadership has opposed established
governments, it has rarely allied with political radicals to achieve

* This chapter is a revised version of a paper delivered before the Iranian
Students' Association Conference on Contemporary Iran, Harvard, 1965. Only
a small amount of the documentation on which its conclusions are based can
conveniently be mentioned in footnotes. Here there will be little mention of
sources in Persian, Arabic, Russian and Turkish or of unpublished documents,
which are used and cited extensively in my *Religion and Rebellion in Iran: The
Tobacco Protest of 1891–92*, and *Sayyid Jamal ad-Din 'al-Afghani': A Political
Biography*.

its ends. It is worth asking, therefore, how this unique situation came about in Iran.

To isolate this problem one must try to determine when the alliance originated as an effective opposition tool. My research on this question indicates that the date of the alliance can be pinpointed fairly accurately to the tobacco protest of 1891–2 which forced the cancellation of a British monopoly concession on all dealings in tobacco. Traces of the alliance may be found earlier, as in the opposition to the notorious Reuter concession of 1872, which sold almost all of Iran's resources for a very low price. Opposition to this concession was led by the *ulama* (religious scholars and functionaries), and such opposition helped bring about the concession's cancellation. At the time of the Reuter concession, however, the leading modernizers were men associated with the government, such as the prime minister, Mirza Hosain Khan *Sepahsalar-e A'zam*, and the Western-educated Minister to London and other capitals, Malkam Khan. These men *favoured* and helped promote the Reuter concession, partly because they thought that British investment might be the only way to modernize Iran and to strengthen the country against Russian advances. By the time of the movement against the tobacco concession, on the other hand, most of the modernizers, including the ubiquitous Malkam Khan, were outside the government, and were allied with the majority of the *ulama* against the Iranian government.[1]

How did the alliance, and also the alienation of the leading *ulama* from the government, come about? The question is a very complex one, but a few causal factors may be noted here. For one thing Twelver Shi'ism, the minority branch of Islam that had been Iran's state religion since about A.D. 1500, contained the ideological basis for hostility to secular authority. According to Twelver Shi'i theory legitimate religious *and* political power passed by heredity from Muhammad through his son-in-law Ali and his descendants, called *imams*, until the twelfth *imam* disappeared. Pending the return of the twelfth, hidden *imam* as the messiah, his will was supposed to be interpreted by the leading religious authorities, or *mojtaheds*, while secular rulers should, strictly, be regarded as usurpers. The Safavid dynasty, which established Twelver Shi'ism as Iran's state religion, had forged a descent from Ali and come to power on a religious platform, thus giving themselves an air of religious legitimacy never matched by the nineteenth-century Qajar dynasty. Even in late Safavid times, according to the informative French traveller, Chardin, there were *mojtaheds* who were bold enough to voice the orthodox Shi'i theory that the temporal rulers were usurpers, and that the leading *mojtaheds* should rule.[2] Such ideas came to the fore more boldly under the unpopular and often rapacious Qajars, who never had the Safavids' religious aura. The *ulama* were greatly helped in their pretensions by the fact that the centre of their spiritual leadership and of much of their wealth was in the nineteenth century outside the borders of Iran – in the main Shi'i shrine cities of Ottoman Iraq – so that the central government had no direct power of coercion over the Shi'i spiritual leaders. Such a situation has often led to greater independence of religious leaders from governments – the contrast between the independent pretensions of the papacy and the relative subservience of the Christian pontiffs of Constantinople or Moscow forms something of a parallel. The *ulama* within Iran were also the only ones who could voice popular grievances with relative impunity; and since they often had strong family and traditional ties to the craft guilds or other groups which felt the pinch of rising taxes, growing oppression, and Western economic incursions, they were often appealed to to voice the grievances of such people to the governing bodies. In addition, the *ulama* had their own reasons for discontent; even such minimal concessions as were made to Westernization by Naser ed-Din Shah (ruled 1848–96), were seen as a threat to Islam, while the fact that the increasing pressures from Great Britain and Russia might end in the overthrow of the only existing Twelver Shi'i state, was seen as a threat both to the true religion and to *ulama* prerogatives. Particularly with the concession-grabbing scramble which began during the Ministry of Sir Henry Drummond Wolff in Iran in 1888–90, the fear that Iran and its economic resources were being rapidly sold to the infidels took hold of the *ulama* and also the merchants and religious masses.[3]

If these points give some explanation of the *ulama* side of the picture, what then can be said of the radicals and modernizers – why did such men as Malkam Khan and even followers of the heretical Azali Babi sect such as Mirza Aqa Khan Kermani and Shaikh Ahmad Ruhi, begin about 1890 to throw their lot in with the *ulama*, whom they had earlier regarded and sometimes castigated in writing as obscurantist enemies to progress? The answer in general terms seems to be that around the late 1880s the Westernizers lost whatever hopes they had had in significant reform being achieved by top governmental men. They saw the religious nature of much of the mass reaction against foreign concessions which they opposed on other grounds, and hoped to make use of this reaction in order to halt the government's sale of Iranian resources to foreigners. In the case of Malkam Khan this is quite clear. Though his Islam was surely nominal, and he was apparently converted back to Christianity at one point in his life, his tactic in his newspaper *Qanun*, which he began publishing in 1890, was to prove the compatibility of modern laws with Islam. Also, though his earlier appeals for reform had been directed mostly privately to governmental leaders and even the Shah, beginning in 1889 with his dismissal as Minister to London, he began to appeal mostly to non-official, including religious, personages. That these appeals in religious terminology on Malkam's part were tactical rather than sincere is indicated quite clearly in a speech to an English audience which Malkam made in 1891. Malkam stated frankly that Iranian reformers had agreed together that the only means of making European reforms acceptable to Persians was to present them in an Islamic guise. After noting the great hostility of Muslims to all things European because of the general Muslim belief that the Europeans were trying to impose Christianity and to harm Islam, Malkam Khan went on:

Then how would you benefit this people, and bring them to adopt the benefits of modern civilization, which they really want as much as you do?

That question has been studied by some of our people who have been educated in Europe, and we have arrived at this conclusion ... except that one thing of polygamy, there is not a single point in which Islam is really in contradiction with your civilising principles. As then Islam, as I have said, is an ocean in which are accumulated all the sciences of the past times of Asia – [There is a wonderfully helpful though negative peculiarity in Islam, there being no established church, especially in Persia, every learned doctor having the power to examine for himself, as the traditions are an ocean] – then for any new law or new principle you wish to promulgate, you can find in that ocean many precepts and maxims which support and confirm what you want to introduce. As to the principles which are found in Europe, which constitute the root of your civilisation, we must get hold of them somehow, no doubt; but instead of taking them from London or Paris, instead of saying this comes from such an ambassador, or that it is advised by such a Government (which will never be accepted), it would be very easy to take the same principle, and to say that it comes from *Islam*, and that this can be soon proved. We have had some experience in this direction. We found that ideas which were by no means accepted when coming from your agents in Europe, were accepted at once with the greatest delight when it was proved that they were latent in Islam. I can assure you that the little progress which we see in Persia and Turkey, especially in Persia, is due to this fact, that some people have taken your European principles, and instead of saying that they came from Europe, from England, France or Germany, have said: 'We have nothing to do with Europeans; these are the true principles of our own religion (and, indeed that is quite true) which have been *taken by Europeans!*' That has had a marvellous effect at once.[4]

The insistence that modern laws *can* be found in Islam appears here rather as a self-protective device than a religious conviction.

More important than Malkam as an architect of the religious-radical alliance was a man with strong personal ties to both the modernizers and some of the *ulama*, Sayyid Jamal ad-Din al-Afghani (1838–97). Here there is space to present only a few points which will be developed in my forthcoming biography of Afghani, which will indicate that the standard biographies, based mostly on Afghani's own word, are almost total distortions of Afghani's life and ideas. During Afghani's stay in India in the 1850s and afterwards, he had the opportunity to observe the fact that it was religious feeling against infidels which could most effectively mobilize mass action against foreigners. The battles of Indian Muslims against the British in the Indian *jehad* movement and the Indian Mutiny were ideal cases in point, and their lesson was reaffirmed by the later Mahdist movement in the Sudan, in which Afghani placed great hopes. Afghani is best known as the leading ideologist of Panislam. It is no accident that the rise of Panislamic sentiment followed exactly the path of Western attacks on Islamic lands. Appearing first in India and in Russian Central Asia after their conquest by England and Russia, Panislamic sentiment became a live issue in the Ottoman Empire after the Russo-Turkish War, the French conquest of Tunisia, and the British occupation of Egypt. In Iran it spread particularly after the rise of Western concessions and growing Western control in the late 1880s and the 1890s. Afghani was as much responding to as initiating a trend; and there is good evidence that he began to present himself as a defender of Islam and Panislam only about 1881, with the writing of the *Refutation of the Materialists*. Before that nearly all contemporary references which connect him with religion tie him with irreligion or heresy, and the *Refutation of the Materialists* is largely a sign of the new guise he wished to present in accord with the growing Islamic reaction against Western incursions. Afghani hoped to make use of this religious sentiment and of the *ulama* to save Islamic lands from further Western conquest.[5]

On his two trips to Iran in the late 1880s Afghani influenced some religious leaders and political and religious radicals, and evidence is strong that he brought the latter over to his tactic of attacking the government's concession-granting policy on essentially religious grounds. When he castigated the government in speeches from his sanctuary at the shrine of Shah Abdol Azim south of Tehran, he did so on the grounds that the Shah was selling Iran to the infidels, and the same approach was taken by his followers who began to distribute leaflets and placards against the government after Afghani was expelled from Iran early in 1891. The tactic of alliance with the religious leaders by the radical and unorthodox, among whom I would include Afghani, had its first major success in the tobacco protest movement, where many of the factors discussed above combined to produce a successful opposition to governmental granting of concessions to foreigners.

The tobacco monopoly was an ideal occasion for such a combination. First of all, it was arguable that such a monopoly was both against Shi'i law and against existing treaties with European Powers guaranteeing freedom of trade. Secondly, infidel handling of an item in daily and intimate use by most adult Iranians was bound to arouse religious scruples. Thirdly, vast numbers of Iranians were involved in the growing and sale, not to mention the smoking, of tobacco, so it was an issue on which nearly all could be aroused. Fourthly, the tobacco monopoly capped a rapid succession of concessions to Britishers which aroused Russian as well as local opposition and brought about Russian aid to the protest movement. Finally, it happened to come just at a time when internal oppression was particularly bad, and when both Malkam Khan and Afghani were in a position to agitate from abroad.

The pattern of the tobacco movement illustrates some of the above points. The earliest opposition leaflets and placards posted by Afghani's followers did not even focus particularly on tobacco, but spoke of the general sale of Iran to foreigners, but as soon as it became clear that the merchants and the *ulama* were concentrating their petitions and demonstrations on the tobacco issue Afghani and his followers echoed this emphasis. When a prominent member of the Shiraz *ulama* was rather foolishly exiled by the government from Iran, he went to see the leader of the Shi'i *ulama*, Hajji Mirza Hasan Shirazi at Samara, and on his way stopped off in Basra to talk to Afghani there. It was this encounter which helped motivate Afghani to write his famous letter to Shirazi, translated in E. G. Browne's *Persian Revolution* — a letter written in the most orthodox Islamic terms, castigating the Shah and his prime minister for selling the abode of Islam to unbelievers. Shortly thereafter Shirazi, who had also been appealed to for action by several of the Iranian *ulama*, wrote to the Shah in slightly milder terms, but making almost exactly the same points which Afghani had made to him. Shirazi noted significantly that this was the *first* time he had ever written to the Shah on a political question. And throughout the tobacco movement the placards issued by even the most radical and unorthodox groups have an impeccable religious tone, while it is the Shah and his followers who are constantly accused of having deviated from Islam.

The success of the tobacco movement in forcing the cancellation of the British concession unquestionably gave new prestige to Afghani's tactics among Iranian modernizers. Thus in 1892 we find Malkam Khan's *Qanun* no longer simply arguing that modern law is compatible with Islam, but actually appealing to the leading *ulama*, and especially those at the shrine cities, to take the initiative in calling together a constituent assembly to depose the oppressors — probably meaning the Shah as well as his prime minister — and to reintroduce a truly Islamic legal system. And the Azali Babi publicists of Istanbul, who had hitherto devoted much of their writings to attacks on the *ulama*, from 1892 on join in Afghani's Istanbul circle and help write letters to the Shi'i *ulama* of Iraq and Iran to join in Sultan Abdul Hamid's and Afghani's Panislamic programme.[6]

In so far as the radical opposition was concerned, the tobacco movement was thus a decisive victory for the tactics of Afghani – tactics which might have developed in any case, but of which he was the prime exponent. What the radical opposition did from now on was more than what Malkam Khan had suggested before the tobacco movement, proving reform to be compatible with Islam. After the tobacco movement the reformers made continual attempts to join with the leading *ulama* in oppositional activity. The movement had demonstrated how the leading *ulama*, from their positions of relative impunity, could mobilize both the resentments and the religious feelings of the masses in a way that the reformers could never hope to duplicate on their own. Profound discontent with economic and administrative oppression, which the people saw had increased *pari passu* with the encroachments of foreigners, meant that popular reaction was bound to take a largely traditionalistic and anti-foreign form.

The most important outcome of the religious-radical alliance was of course the Constitutional Revolution of 1905–1911. Though Afghani and his chief followers were dead long before this, their tactics were taken up by the next generation of advanced modernizers, including Mirza Jahangir Khan, the Azali Babi editor of the leading newspaper, *Sur-e Esrafil*; the free-thinking preacher Jamal ad-din Esfahani; and the Azali Babi member of the Islamic *ulama*, Malek ol-Motakallemin. Careful reading of the works of the latter's son Malekzadeh, also an Azali Babi, indicates how conscious among the modernizers was the tactic of putting their own heterodox religious notions in the background and not doing anything to offend the Islamic *ulama* religiously if possible, in order to bring the influential *ulama* along in the main task of setting up a constitutional government.[7] At the time of the earlier anti-governmental movements, there had been foreign help to the opposition: first, during the tobacco movement, from the Russians and later from the Ottomans. Now in the early twentieth century since the Iranian government had changed from an Anglophil to a Russophil policy, there was some British encouragement to the *ulama* opposition, though this was much less than most Iranians imagined, and ceased to be a British policy when Sir Edward Grey came in late in 1905, obsessed by the need for an Anglo-Russian accord.[8]

If the religious-radical alliance had some immediate successes in the tobacco movement and the Constitutional Revolution, it left a somewhat dubious legacy. Already in the 1890s the growing *ulama* power was being used to oppose any kind of modernization, and not just western encroachments. During the revolution the two-edged nature of this power became even clearer, as most of the *ulama* wanted an increment of their own power, not the introduction of democratic or modern constitutional principles. Both before and during the revolution there were some members of the *ulama* who, because of background or education, were thorough supporters of the popular movement or even of constitutional ideals, but they were always a small minority. Since the traditional religious education was virtually the only education open to Iranians in this period, it is not surprising that we find even radicals in *ulama* clothing – clothing which they were loathe to reject at a time when the mosque formed the best platform from which to get a popular hearing.

The first two important events of the Revolution were the taking of sanctuary, in 1905 in a shrine, and in 1906 in the British Embassy, of thousands of men, mainly tradesmen and *ulama*, who succeeded in forcing the weak and ill Mozaffar ed-Din Shah to grant a constitution and a representative assembly. In this early phase, the Westernizers encouraged *ulama* leadership as the only effective force to arouse mass support. When the first parliament began to draft the constitution, trouble appeared, however. While many of the *ulama* and their followers had expected a return to Islamic law, they were now faced with such un-Islamic proposals as the equality of all religious communities before the law. Some of the *ulama* were placated by a provision that all proposed laws must be approved as consistent with Islam by a committee of five *mojtaheds*, but others, including the most learned *mojtahed* of Tehran, Shaikh Fazlollah Nuri, passed into active opposition. Popular association of the revolution with a return to Islam was widespread, and is illustrated by many incidents, such as that of the barber who put up a sign saying he would henceforth stop the un-Islamic practice of shaving, since Iran now had a constitution.

The Westernizers now had their first chance to be more open about their true aims, as well as an incentive to do so to make the revolution mean more than a victory for reactionary theocracy. While most of them continued to try to placate the *ulama* as much as they could, many began to speak more freely on the meaning of Western constitutionalism and progress. Though in these speeches they usually continued to cite the Koran, many of the upper *ulama* began to see clearly where things were heading, and to attack the Westernizers, often with perhaps accidental accuracy, as Babis, unbelievers, and atheists.

The accession of the new, autocratic Mohammad Ali Shah, and the conclusion of the Anglo-Russian agreement of 1907 dividing Iran into spheres of influence, may have prolonged the tenuous *ulama*-Westernizer alliance, by focusing it against common enemies. Some of the *ulama* leaders continued to back the revolution after Mohammad Ali Shah made a *coup d'état* which dissolved parliament in 1908. During the ensuing fighting in the northern city of Tabriz to restore the constitution, however, radical nationalists found themselves arrayed against the almost universal opposition of the Tabriz *ulama*. And after parliament was re-established by force of arms, the division between even the constitutionalists among the upper *ulama* and the growing body of more progressive Westernizers was sharp. The culmination of the split came when the main *ulama* leader of the revolution, Sayyed Abdollah Behbehani, was assassinated by an anarchist, and the main modernist leader, Sayyed Hasan Taqizadeh, was unjustly held responsible, excommunicated, and forced by *ulama* pressure to leave Iran.

In the cities outside Tehran, where *ulama* conflicts with the civil government had not been so acute, there had been less *ulama* support of the revolution even at first. True, the leading Shi'i *ulama* of Iraq, who were the furthest from the realities of the struggle, backed the revolution throughout, though warning against un-Islamic trends, but even their prestige was not great enough to check the trend towards *ulama* apathy and opposition. *Ulama* defection from the revolution as its anti-Islamic potential became clearer was one of the causes of its ultimate failure, though not as important a cause as the revival of Russian power and the Anglo-Russian toppling of the revolutionary government in 1911.[9]

The Iranian revolution thus showed the common revolutionary phenomenon of the break-up into contending parties after initial victory was gained, but in this case the basic opposition of aim of the two groups of revolutionary leaders could hardly have been more complete. On the whole the modernizers gained more from the revolution than did the *ulama*, whose powers were cut down by the constitutional régime.

The long experience of the revolution, which has been so briefly summarized here, taught many of the modernists and the *ulama* the fragility of their alliance. Nonetheless, the mass following and relative impunity of the leading *ulama* has continued to make them seductive allies for nationalist groups whose leaders have been all too vulnerable to attacks and all too deficient in contact with the common people. Thus, despite the rifts between the *ulama* and the advanced nationalists which appeared so clearly as the Constitutional Revolution developed, there have been several subsequent examples of expedient alliances between radical nationalists and individual *ulama* leaders or religiously-oriented groups which had the protection of such leaders. As in the late nineteenth and early twentieth century there is often a common ground of nationalism and of opposition to foreigners – in the one group mainly on religious grounds, in the other mainly on political or economic ones – and of hostility to governmental policy, though again often from diametrically opposed standpoints.

It would seem that most of the positive results which might accrue to the modernizers and nationalists from an alliance with the *ulama* had been achieved by 1909. In the early days when there were only a handful of modernizing nationalists, an alliance with the most powerful anti-governmental and anti-foreign group was natural enough. The basic incompatibility of the two groups would seem to have been amply indicated by 1910, and one wonders what really positive, and not merely destructive, ends could possibly be achieved by such an alliance in later years.

NOTES

1. On the Reuter Concession see my *Religion and Rebellion*; L. E. Frechtling, 'The Reuter Concession in Persia,' *Asiatic Review* (July 1938), pp. 518–38; George N. Curzon, *Persia and the Persian Question* (London, 1892; Cass,

1966); and F.O. 539/10, 'Correspondence respecting the Reuter and Falkenhagen Concessions 1872–75'. The movements against both concessions are discussed in two forthcoming works: Firuz Kazemzadeh's book on Anglo-Russian relations in Iran and Central Asia; and R. F. Algar's outstanding dissertation, now being prepared for publication, 'The Political and Social Role of the *Olama* in Qajar Iran' (Trinity College, Cambridge Ph.D. thesis, 1965). F. T. Foley, a student at the University of California, Los Angeles, is now completing a thesis on Mirza Hosain Khan and reform in Iran, 1860–1880, that contains detailed information on this period.

2. Jean Chardin, *Voyages de monsieur le chevalier Chardin en Perse et autres lieus de l'Orient* (Amsterdam, 1711), ii, pp. 207–8.

3. See Keddie, *Religion and Rebellion*; and Algar, 'The Political and Social Role of the Olama,' especially ch. xii.

4. Malkom Khan, 'Persian Civilization', *Contemporary Review*, lix (February, 1891), pp. 238–44; the quotation is on pp. 242–3.

5. See Nikki R. Keddie, 'Afghani in Afghanistan', *Middle Eastern Studies*, i (July, 1965), pp. 322–49; the section on Afghani in Keddie, *Religion and Rebellion*; and 'Sayyid Jamal ad-Din's first 27 Years: The Darkest Period', *Middle East Journal*, Autumn 1966, 517–533; and 'The Pan-Islamic Appeal: Afghani and Abdulhamid II', *Middle Eastern Studies*, 1966. Other recent critical research on Afghani is found in two long articles by Elie Kedourie which, along with new material, have now been incorporated into his *Afghani and Abduh: An Essay on Religious Unbelief and Political Activism in Modern Islam* (London, 1966); in Niyazi Berkes, *The Development of Secularism in Turkey* (Montreal, 1964); Sylvia Haim, *Arab Nationalism* (Berkeley, 1962); and Albert Hourani, *Arabic Thought in the Liberal Age* (London, 1962).

6. See Chapter 1. There is additional discussion of the post-1892 developments in the last pages of my *Religion and Rebellion*, in addition to which the following should be consulted on the tobacco movement: Ann K. S. Lambton, 'The Tobacco Regie: Prelude to Revolution', *Studia Islamica*, beginning in No. xxii (1965), pp. 119–57, and Edward G. Browne, *The Persian Revolution of 1905–1909* (Cambridge, 1910), chaps. i–ii. Browne gives much useful documentation on the tobacco movement, Afghani, Malkam Khan, and the Constitutional Revolution though some of his interpretations should now be revised.

7. Mahdi Malekzadeh, *Tarikh-e enqelab-e mashrutiyyat-e Iran* (Tehran, n.d.), vols. i and ii.

8. See my 'British Policy and the Iranian Opposition: 1901–1907', *Jl. of Modern History* 39, 3, 1967, 266–282. On British policy toward Iran see also Kazemzadeh, *op. cit.*; Algar, *op. cit.*; and the detailed treatments by Rose Louise Greaves, *Persia and the Defence of India, 1884–1892* (London, 1959); 'British Policy in Persia, 1892–1903', *Bulletin of the School of Oriental and African Studies*, xxviii (1965), pp. 24–33; xxviii (1965), pp. 284–307.

9. On the Revolution see Browne, *op. cit.* and *The Press and Poetry of Modern Persia*; Algar, *op. cit.*; Kazemzadeh, *op. cit.*; W. Morgan Shuster, *The Strangling of Persia* (New York, 1912); and especially Ann K. S. Lambton,

'Secret Societies and the Persian Revolution', *St. Antony's Papers*, iv
(London, 1958); 'Persian Political Societies, 1906–11', *St. Antony's Papers*,
xvi (London, 1963); and *Dustur*, iv, Iran, *Encyclopedia of Islam²*, ii.

3

Popular Participation in the Persian Revolution of 1905–1911

The Persian Revolution of 1905–1911, which took place in one of the most backward countries of the Middle East at that time, nonetheless has many features that are more similar to the great Western European revolutions than are those of other Middle Eastern revolts, coups, and revolutions of the nineteenth and twentieth centuries. Aside from the Algerian revolution, which was against foreign rulers, Middle Eastern revolts have characteristically been carried out by a relatively small section of the army which has moved secretly and quickly to install a new, military-led regime. Mass revolutions extended in time are virtually unknown in the modern Middle East, although Ataturk's military movement had more of a mass character than most military takeovers. In early twentieth century Iran, however, we find most of the features of a classic great revolution – a political, social, and economic crisis crippling the old regime's ability to rule; a growing agitation against the government, including a successful prior mass movement (against the British tobacco concession in 1891–92); mass demonstrations of such scope that the government has to give in to their demands; counterrevolutionary attempts by the government, which succeeded in the Shah's 1908 coup d'etat; defeat of the government by the common people in arms; and the differentiation of an originally united constitutional movement into conservative and radical parties. The revolutionary struggle also continued for a number of years, rather than being decided by one or two brief crises. How can the truly revolutionary features of the Iranian revolution, including widespread mass participation, the adoption of a liberal modern constitution (not

66

retaining such royal prerogatives as remained in the Ottoman constitution of 1876, revived in 1908), and the presence of really radical forces, be explained?

Paradoxically, the very backwardness of the Iranian governmental structure had a great deal to do with it. Whereas in Egypt and Turkey rulers had been occupied with strengthening the military and administrative structure of the government since the early nineteenth century, in Iran this was not true. Histories of Iran often list the reforms inaugurated especially by crown prince Abbas Mirza early in the century, by Amir Kabir in mid-century, and by Mirza Hosain Khan in the 1870s, but what is really striking about Iranian reform is how slight and abortive it was. In the administrative and legal fields this meant that arbitrary and despotic acts continued to be highly frequent at the same time as more and more people came to realize that a better system of government was possible – a realization coming both from direct and indirect contact with the West and from the Islamic ideals of justice that people heard preached. There was, in particular, a growing imbalance between the outmoded system of arbitrary government and the needs of urban craftsmen and merchants. The latter, increasingly, were involved in foreign or long-distance domestic trade, and felt the growing competition of foreign manufactured goods. They needed a government that would do something to protect commercial and craft interests, instead of which they got rulers who kept raising taxes and/or debasing money in order to pay for the Shah's increasingly extravagant and frequent trips to Europe. The urban bazaar classes also objected to the government's growing subservience to England, and especially Russia, which threatened both their own livelihood and the independence of Iran. These urban classes were thus more advanced than their government was, unlike many other parts of the Middle East, and had a stake in a more economically progressive, administratively rationalizing, and nationalist rule. The Muslim merchant class, in particular, grew in strength and numbers more than it did elsewhere in the Middle East, and merchants demanding bourgeois liberal principles of government were of key importance in the revolution.[1]

The lack of a national army had a great deal to do with rendering a mass revolution possible. Aside from marauding and unreliable tribal contingents, Iran's army existed largely on paper, and mainly for the purpose of providing peculated pay for its officers. Troops were generally unpaid and spent their time making a living in the towns where they were stationed. The small Russian-officered Cossack Brigade in Tehran was the only disciplined modern force. The shahs had been too blind to see their need for a reliable army, and too much beholden to the vested interests of landlords and tribal leaders, who liked the country weak and decentralized and did not want to pay for an army, to do anything to build up a modern armed force. This lack of a modern army may be the main factor differentiating the Persian Revolution from other Middle Eastern revolts. There was no particular importance in Iran to trying to infiltrate such armed forces as did exist in order to plan a revolt. It was quite possible to operate through numbers alone, in the confidence that armed forces would not be called in to shoot down thousands of people, and the hope that soldiers might even refuse to fire on religiously-led crowds. The shahs apparently believed that Great Britain would protect their territorial integrity and were unwilling to push through their occasional abortive military reforms once they met with the opposition of vested interests.

The role of the religious leadership was a major factor in encouraging a mass revolution, and here of course Iran is different not only from the rest of the Middle East but also from Europe. It is a practically unique case of a traditional religious leadership supporting and even leading a modernizing constitutional revolution. Although not all the Shi'i leadership was involved – and as the revolution became more radical, especially in Tabriz, many of the ulama went over to the monarchist side – enough mollas and mojtaheds took part in the revolution to make them a leading factor. Their opposition to the Shah's government was based on several points. (1) Twelver Shi'i theory, which regarded any merely temporal ruler as on a far lower plane than the Twelfth, Hidden Imam, whose will was, according to late Twelver theory, to be interpreted by the mojtaheds. This theory was in abeyance under the Safavids, who had a religious aura and had forged a descent from the early Imams, but it came forth increasingly under the Qajars. (2) The economic and political independence of the ulama allowed them to act against the Shah. They collected religious taxes, owned or supervised vast properties, and had their headquarters in the shrine cities of Ottoman Iraq, beyond the Shah's control. (3) The ulama had close family and organizational ties to the urban classes and guilds, and reflected their economic and political grievances. Their hierarchical position was not generally dependent on royal appointment, but rather on their number of students and followers — hence they tended even more to reflect urban public opinion. The 'official' royally-appointed ulama were much less respected than independent ones. (4) The ulama feared growing foreign encroachments and the possibility of unbelievers taking over Iran. Hence they were a national class. (5) The shahs did nothing effective to try to stop the growing split between the two leading elements of the ruling classes — the government and the ulama. The last premier before the revolution, Ain ad-Dauleh, even cut down on ulama support and pensions, thus increasing ulama hostility.[2]

Also important in the development of a mass movement was the courageous role of conscious revolutionaries. Even before the revolution they had played a notable role — as seen in such men as Sayyed Jamal ad-Din Asadabadi, known as 'al-Afghani,' who spoke of constitutionalism and set up a secret society in Tehran; Mirza Aqa Khan Kermani and Shaikh Ahmad Ruhi, Azali Babis and later freethinkers who worked from Istanbul for the enlightenment of Iran and were extradited and executed in Tabriz after the assassination of Naser ad-Din Shah in 1896; Mirza Reza Kermani who killed the Shah; and many writers whose works were smuggled in from abroad. During the revolution their numbers were legion: some were radicals in the guise of Shi'i ulama and had great influence with their weekly preaching and other public speeches. Such were the two Esfahani radical preachers Sayyed Jamal ad-Din Esfahani and Malek al-Motakallemin. Others were eloquent majles deputies like Sayyed Hasan Taqizadeh. Others were men of the people who led armed revolutionary contingents, notably Sattar Khan and Baqer Khan in Tabriz. Some were newspaper editors and writers, like the Azali Babi, Mirza Jahangir Khan, and still others were underground radical organizers like the Caucasian Haidar Khan Amu Oghli.[3] They shared in common their use of eloquence to enlighten others as to the meaning of constitutionalism, popular rights, and national independence.

Finally, one should not leave out the courage and self-sacrifice of the masses of people who participated in the revolution. Many risked their lives repeatedly against a feared, oppressive government for principles they often only dimly understood. The emphasis given by Ahmad Kasravi in his great book on the Persian Revolution to the role and courage of the common people who participated does not seem at all out of place. It was more often the leaders who betrayed the revolution than the followers.[4]

As a mass movement, as well as in other aspects, the tobacco movement of 1891–92 provided a kind of dress rehearsal for the constitutional revolution. The government's backwardness and complaisance to England and Russia, the lack of an army, the role of the ulama, that of revolutionaries and the common people, all appear in this movement in clear form. It was the first coordinated national movement in Iran – a coordination made possible partly by the heavy use of the telegraph, which was to be even more intensively employed in the constitutional revolution, and partly by the interrelationship of ulama leaders in the various cities. The monopoly tobacco concession to a British subject – the only concession given for a product already widely grown and marketed – affected the livelihood of many, and was seen as one sign of the growing sale of Iran to foreigners. As with the 1905–11 revolution, many merchants were directly affected and involved. Discontent with arbitrary and subservient government was widespread enough to produce flammable material among the urban classes, and a series of mass demonstrations in the major cities escalated into major confrontations in Tabriz and Tehran, ultimately bringing on the total cancellation of the concession in January, 1892. This major victory was not immediately followed up, and the government succeeded in buying off some of its ulama opponents through pensions and cash gifts. None of the basic problems was solved, and the government did not even take the precaution of shoring up its armed forces to meet another such emergency.

In the early years of the twentieth century the crisis grew as the spendthrift Shah, Mozaffar ad-Din (1896–1907), made two large loans from Russia to finance his trips to Europe, a pro-Russian commercial tariff treaty was signed, a group of unpopular Belgians, led by Naus, headed the customs department, food shortages and riots grew, and the government raced toward bankruptcy. A major precipitant of the revolution was the Russo-

Japanese war, which bolstered confidence in the ability of an Asian power to beat a European one – and it was noted that the only Asian constitutional power defeated the only major European non-constitutional one. Even more important was the Russian Revolution of 1905, which showed the hated Russian tsar being shaken by revolution, and removed for a time the threat of Russian intervention. Fear of such intervention had helped deter Iranians from moving in the past against the Qajar government.

One explanation for the profundity of and wide mass participation in the Persian Revolution was the extraordinary concatenation of a series of revolutionary circumstances, rarely found at the same time in other Middle Eastern countries. These included the defection of a major part of the ruling classes – unlike Western European revolutions more the clerical part than a section of the aristocracy; the almost total lack of attention by the government to the needs of merchants and craftsmen; the lack of reform in an outmoded and inequitable financial system, at the same time as government expenses grew greatly, leading to virtual bankruptcy; the failure to build up a rationalized bureaucracy, middle-class legal systems, or a standing army; the impact of Western trade, which undermined traditional handicrafts and began to commercialize agriculture, leading to new class distinctions, increased stratification and tensions; the growth of oppositional propaganda and enlightenment; and the immediate precipitants of new loans and tariffs, an unpopular and reactionary prime minister, Ain ad-Dauleh, a weak Shah who gave in to his own and his courtiers' extravagance, and the Russo-Japanese War and Russian Revolution. There was thus a growing imbalance between a government which had scarcely responded to the new needs created by the Western impact and Western exploitation and the felt needs of two classes in particular – the urban merchants and craftsmen and the ulama.

The lack of a standing army and the leadership of the ulama in particular combined to make a mass movement possible. For the ulama already had the massive following, the impunity, and the traditional role that allowed them to bring together huge crowds inside and outside the mosque, and to preach to them for major political changes. An institution which also greatly helped the mass movement was that of *bast* or sanctuary, which rendered inviolable persons who took refuge in mosques, shrines, foreign legations and certain other places. Although similar practices existed in Western Europe in the Middle Ages, and in some other traditional societies, they were suppressed before the modern period, and it was only in Iran that the institution of sanctuary became of major tactical use in a modern revolution.

Although by 1904–05 there were predictions by some Iranians and foreigners that revolution was on its way, and although a few secret societies existed that were working for fundamental changes, almost nobody would have predicted the kind of mass movement that occurred. A series of incidents, some involving Russian properties, in 1904–05 suggested how high tempers were running. What finally sparked the first act of the revolution, in December, 1905, was an intrinsically trivial incident – but this has been true of other revolts and revolutions.

In that month, the governor of Tehran was trying to control sugar prices, which had risen due to the Russo-Japanese war. He bastinadoed several merchants, including an old and respected sugar merchant, and as a result the traders and merchants closed the bazaar. Many merchants and mollas took *bast* in the Royal Mosque of Tehran, and there the radical preacher, Sayyed Jamal ad-Din Esfahani, spoke out against the aristocracy. He was attacked by the Imam Jom'eh (a royal appointee) who proceeded to have his followers expel the crowd by force. That night and in the following days a crowd of ulama and bazaar people left Tehran for the shrine of Shah Abdol Azim, south of the city. The government tried briefly to stop them by force, but then let them through. The crowd at the shrine grew to 2000 persons, and put forth a series of demands to the government, which are variously reported in different sources. The most important, however, was a demand for a representative House of Justice. The Shah eventually gave in to this and the other chief demands, and the *bastis*, who included the most important mojtaheds of Tehran, returned to Tehran.

The event shows both the readiness of a large sector of the ulama and bazaar population to defy the government, and the unripeness as yet of the revolutionary movement – the House of Justice was nowhere well defined, and there was as yet no demand that the government radically change its nature. There were, however, constitutionalists actively at work to influence the ulama and the people, particularly the bazaar classes.

The Shah did nothing to fulfill his promises, and as radical preachers attacked the government, the premier decided to expel two of them from Tehran. The Shah successfully expelled Sayyed Jamal ad-Din, but a crowd tried to block the removal of Shaikh Mohammad. Despite a warning not to advance, a student, Sayyed Hosain, did advance and was shot. In the ensuing popular battle against the troops Shaikh Mohammad was rescued. The body of the dead sayyed was carried through the streets, and further conflicts took place with the soldiers, in which several people were killed, including another sayyed. A great crowd took refuge in a mosque, and then got permission to leave for the holy city of Qom, where about 100 people went, chiefly ulama. Ain ad-Dauleh ordered the city shops to be opened, and partly in response to this some bazaar men asked the British chargé d'affaires whether they could take refuge in the British Legation. The chargé, Grant-Duff, evidently gave a pro-forma discouraging reply, but did not rule it out, so people began first to trickle, then to stream into Legation grounds, where their number eventually reached about 14,000. The *bastis'* demands now included the dismissal of Ain ad-Dauleh and the granting of parliament, and the Shah had to give in. The Tehran *bastis* were largely fed and organized by large merchants and the guilds, and it was in Tehran among these groups that the demand for a parliament was put forth. Contact with the ulama at Qom was continual, however.

These early phases of the constitutional movement show features common to several of the great revolutions in Europe. First of all, there was a coalition of classes and opinions all united against the autocracy. The more liberal and enlightened part of the population succeeded in impressing on the more ignorant or conservative members of the opposition the notion that a constitution and a parliament were the basic solutions to Iran's problems, and so nearly all the opposition came to unite around this as the central point in their platform. Second, in its first phase and in the achievement of what seemed the crucial victory, the revolution was almost bloodless, and what bloodshed there was came from the governmental side. Finally, there was the beginning of what became a continual movement of radicalization, as the revolution moved from a phase in which leadership was clearly in the hands of the higher ulama who had very moderate demands, to one where a greater and greater role was taken by the popular preachers, members of secret societies, and men of the bazaar, especially merchants.

It is also worthy of note that women participated in the revolution from the very beginning, taking part in demonstrations, and eventually forming their own revolutionary clubs in some cities, and even a women's newspaper in Tehran. Several observers point to this participation as a major step forward in Iran.[5]

The electoral law of September, 1906 is a mixture of modern and traditional features, although radical for Iran. Elections were to be by six classes – Princes and the Qajar Tribe, ulama and students, nobles and notables, merchants, landlords, and trade guilds. Landlords had to have property worth about £200, and those in trade guilds had to own a shop of which the rent corresponded with the average rents of the locality. Women and the great majority of the population were excluded. Nonetheless, the heavy representation of Tehran guilds meant that the first parliament was less landlord-dominated than were subsequent parliaments. In 1909 a new electoral law was passed which ended the six-class system, but left in a lower property qualification. The Fundamental Laws of December, 1906, and the Supplementary Fundamental Laws of October, 1907, which still make up the Persian constitution (as of 1978) are, however, more liberal documents – the latter in particular representing mass pressure on the assembly from the revolutionary clubs and others. Unlike the Ottoman constitution of 1876, which was revised to meet the demands of Abdol Hamid, and unlike some other royally granted constitutions, the Persian constitution does not reserve a series of special powers for the Shah – all crimes, for instance, were to be tried by jury and according to law. This, like many other features of the constitution, was subsequently honored more in the breach than the observance. The only exceptions, and they were important ones, were the Shah's continued control over the army, and the ambiguity in practice about ministerial responsibliity, although the drafters intended that ministers be responsible to a freely elected parliament. The Shah appointed ministers but they were to be responsible to the majles – the majles, however, found itself frequently unable to enforce this responsibility.

The fundamental laws were signed by Mozaffar ad-Din Shah just before he died. His son, the cruel and reactionary

Mohammad Ali Shah, began to plot against the constitution and the majles from the time of his accession in January, 1907. In December, 1907, he gathered together various toughs and royal servants and retainers of all kinds into the Topkhaneh Square, where reactionary mollas preached to them against the so-called infidel and 'Babi' majles. The popular revolutionary clubs, or anjomans, which had proliferated in Iran since the revolution began, came out in force and turned back this major threat to the constitution.

The second attempted coup, in June, 1908, turned out quite differently. The Shah's plans were equally clear – he had retired outside Tehran and gathered his forces. Once again the anjomans, many of whom were armed, were prepared to do battle. But this time they were talked out of it, not only by conservative majles leaders, but also by some radicals, notably Sayyed Hasan Taqizadeh, the very popular, brilliant, and eloquent leader of the Tabriz majles delegation. Taqizadeh had explained that a few days before the Russian and British representatives had privately made clear that if there were any armed action against the Shah, Russian troops would intervene to protect him. Yet it is hard to disagree with Malekzadeh and Kasravi who think Taqizadeh was wrong to force the volunteers to disperse. The Russians might not have intervened, whereas without armed opposition the Shah was able to succeed in his coup, to dissolve the majles, and kill many popular leaders.

A counterexample where cautious advice did not prevail was the city of Tabriz, where, after the whole country and most of Tabriz had given in to the Shah after his coup, a courageous man of the common people, Sattar Khan, refused to surrender. He went around with a small contingent tearing down the white flags of surrender that people had put up, and, along with another man of humble origin, Baqer Khan, led the long resistance of Tabriz to royalist blockade. Armed volunteers, who had been drilling and preparing since the revolution began, made up his forces, as they did those of Rasht, the next city to revolt. In July 1909 the northern volunteers met the Bakhtiari tribal forces and other volunteers from the South, deposed Mohammad Ali Shah in favor of his young son, and restored the constitution. The revolution was victorious until the Russians intervened at the end of 1911 and the beginning of 1912.

Mass popular participation can thus be seen as a crucial element in every major stage of the Persian revolution, from the first two *basts* that brought the constitution, to the defense against a coup, and pressure for a more liberal constitution, to the reestablishment of the constitution after a coup. It may be, as Ervand Abrahamian writes, that popular participation was essentially limited to the urban middle classes,[6] with the lower classes tending to side with reaction, but I am not convinced it is quite that clearcut. The sudden entry of masses of people into a modern type of politics had a decisive effect on the political developments in Iran in the period 1905–1911, and helped provide a political education for the country.

POSTSCRIPT, MAY, 1979

The massive protest movement in Iran during 1978 shows some significant parallels and differences, regarding popular participation as in other matters, to the mass movements of the constitutional revolution. As to differences – clearly the government was far more powerful and modernizing and the army much stronger than in 1905. This strong army kept the Shah from capitulating to opposition demands with the rapidity of the Qajars. Qajar government conceded the main oppositional demands after two almost bloodless protest movements by several thousand people. They had no choice, since their army was not strong enough then or afterwards to suppress the popular movement. Faced with a much larger and more persistent movement, Mohammed Reza Shah felt for months that his armed base and strength were great enough to mix strong repression with partial concessions and to resist demands for return to a constitutional monarchy and free elections, not to mention demands for a referendum on the monarchy or for its abolition.

On the other hand, the basic bazaar-ulama coalition that led the 1905–1911 movement was equally responsible for initiating 1978's events, although in 1978 they could be increasingly joined by students, workers, and the predominantly intellectual and liberal National Front. Ulama leadership in an anti-government coalition is an even more striking and unique phenomenon in 1978 than in 1905–06, and some of its bases are the same. The ulama still enjoy great prestige with the bazaar classes to whom they are still tied and related, and with the urban subproletariat; many ulama still resent the autocratic pretensions and activities of what they regard as illegitimate or marginally legitimate shahs; and it is still difficult for a shah to jail or punish a member of the ulama with the same impunity as a lay person. Even more than in 1905, the ulama are often holdouts against increased external Westernization, which by many people is associated with the Shah, the court, and with unwarranted Western intervention in Iranian political and economic life, an intervention that is in itself an object of protest.

As for the bazaar classes, they feel that their economic position has been undermined by the regime's favoring of big and modern enterprises, both domestic and foreign, which is evinced in the government's tax, loan, tariff, and licensing policies as well as in the workings of high level corruption. From 1905 until now an ideology has been worked out associating liberal constitutionalism with Islam, and since Iran's constitution includes a (never-enforced) provision calling for a committee of mojtaheds to pass on the compatibility with Islam of measures passed by the majles this equation is not especially forced. As the constitution is monarchical and associated with the West, however, Khomeini and his followers wish to replace it with a more 'Islamic' one. Both in 1905 and in 1978 governmental complaisance with Western powers that were seen as hostile to Iran and to the economic interests of the bazaar classes entered heavily into the mass movement. In both periods also the relative independence of the government of Shi'i leaders, their ties to the masses and especially the bazaar classes, and the belief of modern Shi'is that proclamations by mojtaheds take precedence over those by the secular government, have all entered into the strength and popularity of religiously led coalitions.

Today, to be sure, there are far more people who wish to change the government than there are those who are willing to follow the dictates of the ulama. To a degree this split was already operative during the constitutional revolution, and especially during the fighting in Tabriz and the subsequent second majles there was an increasingly open and important split between ulama moderates or conservatives and the liberals or radicals centering in the Democratic Party. As was true during the first phases of the constitutional revolution, however, today's liberals and radicals tried in 1978 not to stress differences and not to attack the positions of Khomeini and others on such things as women's rights and family law reform. On the other side, Khomeini and others toned down their statements on such questions during 1978, although in practice parts of the current movement have made life uncomfortable for some women, some minorities, and some foreign nationals. In early 1979 the divisions among different parts of the revolutionary movement are more marked than they were after 1906, with the left, the secular liberals, and religious forces all split internally into differing groups.

What is striking on a comparative basis is the continual re-formation against apparent odds of a popular mass movement through 1978 despite its frequent violent dispersal. Here again, as in 1905–11, Iran is experiencing a mass movement without parallel in the Middle East, and for this the special role of the Iranian ulama may be largely responsible.

NOTES

1. On the merchants see especially Gad G. Gilbar, 'The Big Merchants (*tujjar*) and the Persian Constitutional Revolution of 1906,' *Asian and African Studies*, 11, 3 (1977), 275–303, and W. M. Floor, 'The Merchants (*tujjar*) in Qajar Iran,' *ZDMG*, 126, 1 (1976), 101–135.
2. On the ulama in Qajar politics see H. Algar, *Religion and State in Iran 1785–1906* (Berkeley, 1969); the papers by H. Algar and N. Keddie in N. Keddie, ed. *Scholars, Saints, and Sufis* (Berkeley, 1972); N. Keddie, *Religion and Rebellion in Iran* (London, Cass, 1966); A. K. S. Lambton, 'The Persian Ulama and Constitutional Reform,' *Le Shi'isme imamite* (Paris, 1970), and the sources they all cite. The relation of Shi'ism and politics continues to be studied by scholars like H. Enayat, M. Bayat-Philipp, S. Arjomand, J. Eliash, and M. Fischer.
3. These men are nearly all discussed in E. G. Browne, *The Persian Revolution of 1905–1909* (Cambridge, 1910, reprinted Cass, London, 1966). Subsequent work on them in Western languages includes Chapter 1 of this volume; N. Keddie, *An Islamic Response to Imperialism* (Berkeley, 1968) and *Sayyid Jamal ad-Din 'al-Afghani'* (Berkeley, 1972); S.M.A. Djamalzadeh, 'Taqizadeh, tel que je l'ai connu,' *A Locust's Leg: Studies in Honour of S. H. Taqizadeh*, ed. W. B. Henning and E. Yarshater (London, 1962) and M. Bayat-Philipp, 'Mirza Aqa Khan Kirmani: Nineteenth Century Persian Revolutionary Thinker' (unpublished Ph.D. Dissertation, UCLA, 1971).
4. Ahmad Kasravi, *Tarikh-e mushruteh-ye Iran* (5th Ed., Tehran, 1961). Sayyed Hasan Taqizadeh's defense of himself against Kasravi's exaggerated

charges in his *Tarikh-e avayel-e enqelab va mashrutiyat-e Iran* (Tehran, 1338/1959–60) does not dispel the impression that Taqizadeh was overcautious, especially as compared to popular leaders like Sattar Khan.

5. The above was written before the elaboration of the role of women, based on numerous sources, in Mangol Bayat-Philipp, 'Women and Revolution in Iran, 1905–1911,' Lois Beck and Nikki Keddie, eds., *Women in the Muslim World* (Cambridge, Mass., 1978).

6. Ervand Abrahamian, 'The Crowd in the Persian Revolution,' *Iranian Studies*, August, 1969, 128–149; despite some doubts on the point mentioned, I find this a highly important article.

4

Religion and Society in Iran*

From pre-Islamic times until today religious belief systems in Iran have been closely tied both to social class and to political movements and strategies supported by different social classes and groups. Although all generalizations about the correspondence between any ideological system and a class or class grouping are naturally subject to numerous individual exceptions, characterization of religious groups according to the classes and groups they particularly represented and appealed to is useful to the understanding of relationships between religion and society.

A knowledge of Iran's socio-religious history is helpful even to those concerned mainly with the present, since many recent trends have roots in the more or less distant past. Many striking themes recur through history, sometimes going back to pre-Islamic times: e.g., the division of religious trends into 'official' and 'popular,' with the latter frequently being 'popular-heretical' and even rebellious; the use of apparently similar religious ideologies, such as Twelver Shi'ism, by very different groups in different circumstances, often with a variation in content; and recurrent popular themes in different religions and sects, such as messianism, martyrdom, and attacks on injustice.

Although the modern period has seen unusually rapid developments in the religious sphere as in others, both historical sources and modern experiences suggest that religious change and variation were always present, and much greater in the past than

* Thanks are due to Mohsen Ashtiany, Mangol Bayat-Philipp, Carlo Caldarola, George Hourani, Maxime Rodinson, William Royce, and Peter von Sivers for their useful comments on earlier drafts of this paper.

most writers realize. For example, all idea of a monolithic 'traditional' Shi'ism in Iran in which only modernists are making changes should be rejected in favor of constantly developing religious ideas and practices, partly in response to a constantly changing socio-political reality. Traditionalists as well as modernists are constantly in flux.

PRE-ISLAMIC IRAN: TO CA. 640

Iran, like some other parts of Western Asia, has been fruitful in the creation of religions and heresies, most with an important socio-political content. Many of them have been influential beyond Iran's borders. Our knowledge of the religions of the pre-Indo-European peoples on the Iranian plateau is limited, and we know slightly more of the polytheism of the early Iranians, whose gods were related to those of their Indian cousins and often to earlier Indo-European gods and goddesses. It is only with the reforms attributed to the Prophet Zoroaster in the first half of the first millenium B.C. and the adoption of a state religion by the two great Iranian empires, the Achemenian (6–4 centuries B.C.) and the Sasanian (3–7 centuries A.D.) that the outlines of Iranian religion, and particularly official religion, are better documented. In addition to the Achemenian official religion and Sasanian Zoroastrianism, which supported both the state and a hierarchical social structure, there were great heresies in this millenium, chiefly the Manichean, whose prophet, Mani, lived 216–277 A.D. and whose influence spread far beyond the borders of Iran, and the Mazdakites of the late fifth century A.D. (The cult of one major Iranian god, Mithra, of Indo-European origin, spread also as far as Britain, carried by the Roman legions.)

The official religion in pre-Islamic times was generally in favor of monarchy, social hierarchy, and a belief in rewards and punishments after death such as would tend to make people obedient to the will of their rulers and priests. The complex eschatology characteristic of Near Eastern religions, with its angels, devil and/or evil spirits, heaven and hell, and day of judgment, was apparently influenced by Zoroastrian trends. Zoroastrianism also has the special feature of a good god and an evil one. In Zoroastrianism as in other religions, this system has a social role: oppression in this world can be explained as a trial;

good people, like the good god, may be apparently defeated by the
evil, but can be consoled by the eventual triumph of virtue;
priests and, with the state cult, also rulers, are closer to god than
are ordinary mortals, and hence are to be obeyed; and already,
long before Zoroastrianism became the Sasanian state cult,
society, like the angelic heavens, is naturally hierarchical. The
architecture and iconography of the Achemenian royal palace
city of Persepolis was both a glorification of the submission of all
the peoples of the Persian Empire to the Emperor and an
identification of the Emperor, frequently shown overcoming
large beasts barehanded, with the divine. Achemenian
inscriptions similarly relate emperor to god and to moral
principles. Under the Sasanians Zoroastrianism, which may
originally have had more egalitarian elements, became adapted to
this king-centered ideal, with a priestly cult in addition.

Both the Achemenian state cult and the growing priest-
centered cult of the Zoroastrians were this-worldly in that they
emphasized agricultural and other labor, and approved conduct in
this world as the basis for the good and religious life. This kind of
cult was naturally attractive to dominant groups and classes, and
could gain its widest general appeal in periods of imperial
expansion and prosperity. In a time of difficulty, however, an
important oppositional movement, Manicheanism, arose in Iraq,
an area which was a central part of the Iranian empire and was
highly Persianized.

Manicheanism was founded by the Iranian Mani (d. 277 A.D.)
who deliberately drew on several different religions and heresies
in order to found a religion of wide appeal. Although he retained
the dualistic struggle of good versus evil found in Zoroastrianism,
he drew rather on previous popular and feared gnostic heresies
like the Jewish Essenes in identifying matter with evil and spirit
with good (matter is not evil in Zoroastrianism). Like the earlier
gnostic heresies that influenced him, and like later ones influenced
by Manicheanism – such as the Paulicians, the Bogomils, and the
Cathars – Mani had two main classes of followers: the elite, who
in theory at least did not indulge in sexual intercourse and
otherwise avoided pleasures of the material world; and the
ordinary followers, who were not held to such strict standards.
Manichean pessimism about the world even put into doubt the
outcome of the struggle between good and evil, although it seems

likely that many Manicheans, like many Calvinists, were less pessimistic than the official doctrine of their founder. Socially, Manicheanism seems to have appealed to those alienated from states in decline, which included not only lower class groups but also middle class and intellectual ones. It formed a point of identification with a group and with a more intellectual, if hardly more consoling, religion than the official one, and was often persecuted in Iran as elsewhere in both pre-Islamic and Islamic times. Under Islam the term for Manichean, *zindiq*, came to be a general term for heretic, and Manicheans are heard of particularly among the intellectual and bureaucratic classes. Persecution of them was far less violent than in the Christian West, but sufficed to bring their disappearance in the Muslim Middle East already in medieval Islamic times.

The second major pre-Islamic heresy with social content was Mazdakism, founded by Mazdak in the Sasanian Empire in the late fifth century A.D. Apparently an offshoot of Manicheanism, Mazdakism kept elements of the good-evil and matter-spirit dualism, but was distinguished by an advocacy of communism of property (to a degree that is still in question). Like earlier and later heresies, Mazdak's was also accused of advocating the communism of women, and it is hard to judge the truth of this charge. In most cases this seems to have been primarily one of the worst calumnies the enemies of a heresy can imagine, given the belief of most 'civilized' societies in private property in women. The charge had a slender base in the tendency of many heresies to attack polygamy (mainly an upper class institution) and even to some degree the subjection of women.

As the appeal of Mazdakism spread among the lower and non-official classes its danger was felt by the Sasanians, however much they might be in competition for power with the Zoroastrian priests, and Mazdakism was violently suppressed. Insofar as it remained alive at all, it passed underground and into later Islamic heresies. The spread of Mazdakism is taken as a sign of a wide-scale social disaffection in the Sasanian Empire in the late fifth century and afterwards that was one reason for the relatively easy seventh century victory of the Arab Islamic conquerors. The Sasanians had a rigidified class system, probably somewhat related in origins and structure to the Indian caste system, in which the Zoroastrian priestly class and the bureaucrats and royalty were on top and enjoyed increasing wealth and privileges, while much of the population suffered. Class rigidification went along with a rigidification of cult and religion and persecution of religious deviation. It seems possible that Zoroastrianism was not very deeply held as a personal faith by those outside the priestly class. The stratification of religion and society, along with economic problems furthered by continual wars with the Eastern Roman Empire, produced a situation of decline, economic difficulties, and alienation that rendered Iran, like much of the Byzantine Empire, ripe for Arab conquest.

The above brief summary does little justice to the doctrinal richness and originality of religious movements in pre-Islamic Iran, whose influence on Judaism, Christianity, and hence early Islam, as well as on Western Mithraism and heresies, has hardly begun to be appreciated. In social terms, it may be said that the Mazdakism of the Achemenids and the Zoroastrianism of the Sasanians were religions that generally preached hierarchy, social morality, obedience to priestly and state authority, and hard work in this world. As such they were appropriate ideological buttresses for large hierarchical empires, and could prove satisfactory on a personal level as long as the empires remained large and flourishing. It seems that popular religious trends are poorly documented. In periods between empires or of military, economic, and other problems, however, many Iranians turned to religions or movements that offered personal consolation and/or identification with groups not headed by the official priesthood or bureaucracy, and which either rejected the world as intrinsically corrupt or tried to rebuild it by such a radical means as the institution of communism. While some modern Iranian secular nationalist intellectuals find in Zoroastrianism all the modern and democratic virtues they would like to associate with Iran before it was 'ruined' by Arab conquest, a more dispassionate study would see in Zoroastrianism, particularly the priest-dominated form that characterized the late Sasanian period, a much more mixed phenomenon – one with a great intellectual and spiritual heritage but one that was becoming socially more limited and less viable over time. Modern Iranian radicals often identify with Mazdakism, as an original indigenous communism.[1]

ISLAMIC IRAN BEFORE MODERN TIMES (640–1796)

The most recent of the world's major religions, Islam, arose in early seventh century Arabian cities and soon brought under its sway the desert bedouins. Shortly after Mohammad's death in 632 the Muslim Arabs began a career of rapid conquest, aided by their religion, by economic forces, by the superior mobility of their camels and cavalry, and by religious and social disaffection and weakness in the Byzantine and Iranian empires. While part of the Byzantine Empire remained independent, Iran was rather quickly conquered and the Iranian Empire incorporated into the Arab-Muslim-ruled empire.

This conquest was radically to change the religious history of Iran, although the dichotomy noted above between official religions and oppositional, often heretical ones, continued, and both categories, especially the second, show in Islamic times some influence of earlier Iranian religious movements.

Since old myths die hard it is worth repeating some points known to specialists in Islam: Islam in its first phases did not seek converts, much less offer conquered peoples a choice between conversions and the sword. The Quran had spoken of tolerating 'people of the book' (i.e., those with a scripture), and these at first comprised Christians, Jews, and the so-called Sabeans (Mandeans). After a short period of uncertainty, the Zoroastrians were also characterized as people of the book (the Avesta) and generally, although not altogether, tolerated. The Islamic taxation system rested heavily on the taxes paid by these 'protected' people of the book and not by Muslims. When protected peoples began to request conversion to Islam they at first could do it only by affiliation to an Arab tribe as 'clients.' When the number of converts became great, tax income began to fail, and the caliph had to rule that converts would continue to pay the old amounts. Converts continued for a time to pay higher taxes than Arab Muslims, but there was a rising tide of conversions that came to embrace the great majority of the population in Iran as elsewhere. In Iran, although some of the first converts seem to have been landlords and bureaucrats who could benefit directly and substantially, conversion eventually spread to all classes.

Among the appeals of Islam, in addition to tax saving and the positions and prestige made possible by belonging to the religion of the rulers, were the simplicity of conversion and of belief demanded, and the theoretical equality of believers, as contrasted to the priestly and ceremonial nature of Zoroastrianism. Also, the Zoroastrian church was so tied up with the Sasanian state that it lost both property and prestige with the fall of the Sasanians, and Iranian Zoroastrians had no centers abroad to look to for guidance as did many Near Eastern Christians.

Iranian religious ideas – Zoroastrian, Manichean, and other – entered the mainstream of Islam with the conversion of Iranians, as did Christian and Jewish religious ideas (besides those already present in original Islam) with the conversion of Christians and Jews. These non-Islamic religious trends were particularly influential in the minority branch of Islam known as Shi'ism. Shi'ism was originally a political movement of the believers in the claims to the caliphate of Mohammad's cousin and son-in-law Ali. Shi'ism became permeated by originally non-Islamic *religious* ideas in Iraq, including ideas both of Iranian and non-Iranian origin. The Shi'a came to believe that Ali's descendants were infallible leaders, called *imams*, who had a hereditary title to religio-political rule of the Muslim world. The resistance and martyrdom of Ali's second son, Husain, at the hands of the Umayyad caliphs, became a central Shi'i event. Husain's supposed marriage to a Sasanian princess tied the imams to the Iranian imperial tradition. Early Shi'i movements were nearly all rebellious, 'extremist,' to use the Muslim terminology, and messianic. They expressed the discontent of urban masses in particular, as is suggested by the tag-line for the *mahdi* (messiah): 'He who will fill the earth with justice and equity as it is now filled with injustice and oppression.'

Many non-ruling class Iranians were among those who increasingly opposed the first caliphal dynasty, the Umayyads (661–749) who were, among other misdeeds, accused of discriminating against converts to Islam and in favor of Muslim Arabs. An organized opposition to the Umayyads was formed that comprised many radical Shi'is, both Iranian and non-Iranian, as well as non-Shi'is of both Arab and Iranian origin especially in Khorasan, the Iranian northeast. This opposition movement was largely organized as a military force in Khorasan by the Iranian leader Abu Muslim, around whom extremist religious cults grew up after his death and probably during his lifetime. Armies from

Khorasan overthrew the Umayyads in 749 and set up the Abbasid caliphate, who soon cut their ties to Shi'ism and executed Abu Muslim as too dangerous and popular. After his death various extremist popular religious movements in Iran gave him a divine or semi-divine character. Recent research suggests that at this time only a minority of Iranians were Muslims, and these movements and those that followed included pre-Islamic elements.

Popular religious discontent in Iran was not halted by the coming of the Abbasids. Instead there were a number of extensive revolts in the immediately following centuries that expressed continued mass discontent by peasants and/or townspeople. These revolts often combined Shi'i views with older Mazdakite, Manichean, or Zoroastrian notions, and demonstrate that Muslim conversion had not been so absolute as is sometimes thought. Nevertheless, the ruling classes eventually suppressed the revolts, and the Abbasids, who had early turned against their more enthusiastic Shi'i followers, succeeded in imposing orthodoxy in most of their empire, Iran included. The identification of religion, state, and law, already strong with the Prophet Mohammad but somewhat weakened under the legally and administratively pragmatic Umayyads, took on its classic shape under the Abbasids. Both because of this identification and because of the centrality of belief in most people's lives, opposition, and particularly popular opposition, nearly always took on a religious form, and usually a Shi'i or semi-Shi'i one.

In the Abbasid period (749–1258) some distinctions among Shi'i groups that last until today took shape. These distinctions are often referred to by a number referring to the number in descent from Ali of an imam to whom each group gives particular importance. The Fivers or Zaidis were the most moderate and the closest to Sunnism, but were rarely of importance in Iran. The Seveners or Ismailis were the most 'extreme,' and often took the form of revolutionary movements, such as the semi-communist Carmathians or the conspirators who set up the Fatimid caliphate first in North Africa and then in Egypt as a rival to the Abbasids. The Ismailis were from the first represented in Iran, and the great eleventh century thinker Nasir-i Khosrau was an Ismaili, as was probably the father of Avicenna, whose work shows Ismaili influence. As noted below, the notorious 'Assassins' were Ismailis.

The Shi'is most important to Iran were the Twelvers, or

Imamis, who were considered intermediary between the other two, although evidence now indicates that in the Abbasid period they were predominantly very moderate. The twelfth imam was supposed to have gone into 'occultation' over 1,000 years ago, from which he will return as *mahdi* (messiah) at the end of time. It has been suggested that this 'occultation' of the infant and never seen imam was deliberately arranged in order *not* to have a rival to the Abbasids. Another indication of the moderation of Abbasid Twelvers was the fact that an Abbasid caliph tried to name an imam, Ali ar-Rida (the Imam Reza of Iran's most important shrine in Mashhad) as his own successor, which would have been impossible had this line of Shi'is been considered an oppositional group. In a general way studies indicate that Imami Shi'is included a large number of the urban-dwelling upper and upper middle classes, whose Shi'ism was a non-revolutionary taste that they were concerned to render as little threatening as possible, while the Ismailis were often revolutionary and rebellious, and drew much support from the discontented classes in society. For much of the Abbasid period it would seem that a logical dividing line between religious groups, particularly from a sociological and political standpoint, lies rather between the Ismailis on one side and the other groups on the other than between all Shi'is and all Sunnis, which is the formal division usually made.

This difference between types of Shi'ism is well indicated by the very different histories of two Shi'i groups that held some power in Abbasid Iran after its tenth century breakdown into autonomous states – the Twelver Buyid dynasty and the Ismaili Assassins. The Buyids, who ruled Western Iran and Iraq, including for a time the Abbasid capital of Baghdad, from 945 to 1055, never tried to set up a Twelver Shi'i state or install Shi'i law, but on the contrary supported the religious claims of the Abbasid caliph, whom they could have deposed. Very different were the Assassins (a pejorative name used here for convenient recognition, but never historically used for the Iranian branch of this Ismaili group – deriving in Syria from their supposed use of hashish). The Assassins set up enclaves in Iran and elsewhere where they were subject to the orders of their imam (whose claim to descent from the early imams was more than dubious), and where Ismaili laws and principles were generally applied. Specific to the Assassins and arousing horror then as now was their practice of assassination of prominent persons. As the late Marshall Hodgson noted, however, people are inclined to accept as inevitable the mass slaughter of wars, which rarely touches the powerful and prominent, but reject as horrible a method of warfare that kills a very few prominent men.[2] The long life of the Assassin enclaves suggests the considerable popularity of their revolutionary and often messianic program for restructuring the world, and they were only suppressed by the powerful Mongol invaders in the early thirteenth century.

Contrary to much Iranian and Western mythology, if one studies the whole span of Iranian Islamic history, one can easily ascertain that Shi'ism is not especially Iranian, although it contains Iranian elements among others. Before 1500 there were many more Shi'i movements and states outside Iran than in it, and Iran was far more often ruled by Sunnis, whose ideas were followed by most Iranians, than by Shi'is. The emphasis above on Shi'ism was not meant to suggest the contrary, but merely to stress a trend that since 1500 has become dominant in Iran. The autonomous states that arose in different parts of Iran under the Abbasids were nearly all Sunni, and the Seljuk Turkish Empire that began in the mid eleventh century was not only Sunni but militantly so.

The famous Iranian prime minister of the eleventh century Seljuks, Nizam al-Mulk, was partly responsible for introducing a widespread system of religious education that became the only organized system of education within the empire and its successors. This meant that not only those whose positions required religious training – the jurists, educators, guardians of trust properties, and clerical figures who together comprised the ulama – but also secular officials and intellectuals were likely to get a religious education. Together with the 'feudal' fragmentation of rule that followed the eleventh century Turkish invasions of Iran and the concomitant economic decline, which was increased by the thirteenth century Mongol invasions, this total subordination of education to religious orthodoxy helps explain a decline in intellectual creativity and freedom that begins about the eleventh century. At this time Nasir-i Khusrau writes complaining of the rise in persecution of philosophic thought that he has witnessed, and great caution in expressing such thought was evinced by Avicenna and later philosophers.[3]

Although the system of 'Nizamiyya' madrasas and their growing control over education are usually seen as great achievements of Nizam al-Mulk, they may also be seen as largely successful efforts at thought control. The *Book of Government* attributed to Nizam al-Mulk, and in any case representing Seljuk policy, clearly states the tie between orthodoxy and loyalty to the state, and between heterodox movements, many of which it traces back to Mazdak, and rebellious disloyalty.[4] It is not surprising that Nizam al-Mulk, as an effective champion of orthodoxy and loyalty and of the uprooting of the unorthodox and disloyal, should have perhaps been killed by the Assassins.

A similar policy of promoting Sunnism was followed by the series of dynasties of Turkish tribal origin that continued to rule different parts of Iran. Within Iran, however, various Shi'i or semi Shi'i movements grew up after the thirteenth century Mongol invasion and rule, and although these were, with the continued violent suppression of Ismailism, formally Twelver, some of them (probably influenced by the Ismailis) incorporated various 'extremist' elements. Among these religious movements were the Hurufis, who revived and developed a letter-number symbolism and influenced the Bektashi dervishes of the Ottoman Empire – ironically the sect of the Janissaries.

Ultimately the most important Shi'izing group was the Safavid Sufi (mystic) order, begun as a Sunni order under the Mongols. In the fifteenth century the hereditary chiefs of this order, Junaid and his son Haidar, travelled among the armed tribes of Eastern Anatolia, and it seems that Junaid adopted Shi'ism as well as a policy of conquest largely through contact with these tribes. These policies were continued by Haidar, who also adopted the headdress that made his followers known as Qizilbash or 'redheads,' a name still used for this religious group in Turkey. Tribal followers protected Haidar's young sons after he was killed in battle. One son, Ismail, started fighting in his early teens, and his enthusiastic following enabled him to take Iran's leading city, Tabriz, in 1501. He then ordered the compulsory cursing of the first three Sunni caliphs from all mosques, and in further conquest of Iran continued forcibly to demand this allegiance to Shi'ism.

The religion of Junaid, Haidar, Ismail, and their tribal followers was not the moderate Twelver Shi'ism of Abbasid times. It was, rather, tied to more popular extremist heresies like the Nusairis or Alavis, earlier Anatolian rebels, and the Hurufis. Messianic and incarnationist, it had socially egalitarian elements, and we have contemporary references to the Qizilbash 'among whom there is neither mine nor thine.' Like many other 'extremist' leaders, Junaid, Haidar, and Ismail were considered divine. Ismaili and other popular religious notions found expression in the Safavid movement.

Probably Ismail did not know his religion differed from learned Twelver Shi'ism, which was scarcely then to be found in Iran. A chronicler tells us that only one Shi'i text could be found in Ismail's capital, Tabriz. Ismail met the problem of teaching Shi'ism by importing Shi'i scholars from Arabic speaking lands. In addition to educating Iranians, this helped Ismail and his successors turn away from extremism and toward a traditional law and order. Like such dynasties as the Abbasids and the Fatimids, the Safavids came to power with the support of religious radicals but turned their backs on them and followed a conservative socio-religious policy. Ismail and his successors gave most important offices to the old Persian ruling class and fewer offices than they thought they deserved to Qizilbash leaders. A new learned Shi'i orthodoxy was encouraged, and those who stuck to extremist notions were persecuted. This change is symbolized in the word *Sufi* – at first a respectful term for Safavid followers, it became a negative term inviting punishment in later Safavid times, when Sufism was persecuted.

Ismail began a policy of forceful conversion to Shi'ism, partly to distinguish Iran from the Ottoman enemy, but conversion was in fact gradual. The Safavids had a degree of control over religion unusual for either Shi'i or Sunni rulers, due to several factors: (1) The Safavids could assert their own divinity, or at least charisma, coming in part from a forged descent from the imams; (2) The foreign origin of the early religious scholars, who were imported by the Shahs, made them dependent on the Shahs; (3) The Safavid government hierarchy included appointed religious officials; only later did 'independent' ulama become important.

A Shi'i school system, suppression of Sufis and Sunnis, and considerable thought control produced much ideological-religious unity. Under the late Safavids, some of whom were weak and impious, however, some religious leaders, or *mujtahids*, claimed that the people should follow them, and not the Shahs. By now there were financially independent mujtahids who strengthened their position by appealing to one side of Shi'i doctrine. If the absence of an imam was used under the Safavids to justify acquiescence in temporal rule, it was now said by many that in the imam's absence those most learned in Muslim law and doctrine should be followed in religious and temporal matters. In socio-political terms this doctrine, which became stronger after the Safavids, laid the foundation for a Muslim institution with some analogies to the medieval Roman Catholic church, with a claim to lead secular rulers and the people on non-'religious' matters, while the state was to be regarded as a subordinate body that should take its guidance from the religious institution. Naturally, neither the Safavids nor later rulers acted according to this interpretation but the populace increasingly did, and tended to support the religious institution against generally unpopular secular governments – a situation that has echoes down to the present.[5]

The eighteenth century saw political turmoil: Afghans overthrew the Safavids in 1722, but Iran was reunited in the 1730s by the conquering warrior who became Nadir Shah, who had an original religious policy, aimed at weakening Shi'i power and at promoting his own rule in Sunni lands outside Iran. He suppressed the dominant Shi'ism and confiscated *vaqfs* (religious mortmains). He tried to make of Shi'ism a fifth school of orthodox Islam – a proposal rejected by Sunni rulers. After Nadir's death and the rapid disintegration of his empire Shi'ism was quickly restored, as it had struck deep roots. Even religious properties were built up again in the century after Nadir.

In the second half of the eighteenth century the popular Zand dynasty centering in the south was Shi'i, as were the unpopular Qajars, who reunited Iran in the late eighteenth century. That century saw developments of socio-political significance within Shi'ism. There was a doctrinal struggle between the Akhbaris, who thought that the Koran and Shi'i Traditions sufficed to guide believers, and the Mujtahidis or Usulis, who said that each believer must choose a living mujtahid whose dicta he was bound to follow. The Mujtahidis finally won, and this reinforced the power of the mujtahids, giving them a force unequalled in Sunni lands, where the ulama had no such power to interpret basic doctrine. Also in the eighteenth century most of the leading ulama moved from Iran to the Shi'i shrine cities in Iraq, where Shi'i leadership has remained until recently. This, together with the independent wealth of these ulama, meant they were not dependent on rulers – again unlike the ulama of Istanbul, Cairo, etc. The eighteenth century also saw the development of a new school of Twelver Shi'ism, Shaikhism, which included a more philosophical element than was common in Shi'ism and tried to establish a closer link between humanity and the Hidden Imam.[6]

Looking over Iran from the rise of Islam through the eighteenth century, one can note that the conversion of the great majority of Iranians to Islam meant that they followed a more egalitarian and less priest-ridden religion than before, and one that favored social mobility rather than the near caste system of the late Zoroastrians. Indeed, social mobility in Islamic Iran as in most Muslim countries appears to have been quite high for a pre-industrial country, as the relatively egalitarian Muslim inheritance laws, and the absence of a hereditary aristocracy or other hereditary classes, along with the possibility of promotion in the religious institution through free education and a reputation for learning and sanctity, opened the doors to mobility. Social divisions were reflected in religion in the Islamic period – in the early centuries rebellious heretical movements were mainly characteristic of the popular classes, and it was chiefly these classes who later turned to the less revolutionary but still suspect Sufi orders. But Sufis could be fairly orthodox, as was notably the case of the bazaar classes. In Islamic times orthodoxy was promoted by the state – sometimes rather vigorously as with the Seljuqs and Safavids. By the late Safavid period, however, there begins a split between ulama leadership and the rulers which makes Iran unique in modern times. The population, and particularly the artisans and traders of the bazaars, tended increasingly to follow the ulama in their conflicts with the government, and even sometimes to precipitate such conflicts because of their growing grievances against the government, particularly with nineteenth and twentieth century government complaisance toward Western economic and political might, which often hurt the interests of traders and artisans.

MODERN IRAN: THE QAJAR PERIOD (1796–1921)

This period was characterized by a growing split between religious and temporal authorities, by the emergence of a socio-political leadership among the ulama, and the creation of mass oppositional movements with a religious component. While religio-political opposition movements are frequent in Islam, modern Iran is special in that it was not only radical religious movements that were oppositional, but the recognized leaders of the ruling religion – a situation rare not only in Islam, but elsewhere. In addition to the background of this development discussed above, further causes include the Qajars' adoption of some Westernizing reforms, which threatened ulama power; the growth of Western influence, which threatened the Islamic state of Iran; and the decentralized weakness of the government, which kept it from controlling the ulama as did such governments as those of Egypt and the Ottoman Empire.

In the first part of the nineteenth century ulama political activity appears mainly 'reactionary' or xenophobic, and includes opposition to the Westernizing military reforms of Crown Prince Abbas Mirza, pressure to start a second war against Russia in 1826, and incitement of the crowd that murdered the Russian envoy Griboyedov and his mission in 1829. After later and lesser incidents, leading ulama participated in a movement that brought the downfall of the reforming prime minister Mirza Husain Khan in 1872, mainly because he had negotiated the infamous Reuter concession which granted exploitation rights to most of Iran's resources to a British subject.[7]

The only major event aligning the ulama *with* the government was a radical religious movement that, as was true of many radical messianic movements in Asia and Africa, arose shortly after the early Western impact and expressed, in part, the socio-economic dislocations caused by that impact. This was the Babi movement, which arose at mid-century as a radical outgrowth of the Shaikhi school. By most, the Shaikhis were considered Shi'is, and they were vague when they spoke of the presence of a *Bab*, or gate, to the Hidden Imam. The young Sayyid Ali Mohammad, a Shaikhi from a Shiraz merchant family, changed things in 1844 by announcing that he was that *Bab* or gate. Finding mounting support particularly among the bazaar classes and some lower ulama, he was denounced by the orthodox ulama, and imprisoned by the authorities. Faced with ulama opposition, the Bab increased his distance from orthodoxy, claiming to be a new prophet with a new dispensation, written down in his scripture, the *Bayan*. Babism, while containing features of past Shi'i extremism, also had social features that were in part new. It went beyond past sects in its call for women's equality by discouraging polygamy and encouraging a woman preacher and poet, who is said to have preached unveiled. Babism also had some new economic attitudes, encouraging trade and permitting the taking of interest, and seeing begging and idleness as reprehensible. While most such ideas appealed to the bazaar classes, during the Babi revolts one group even adopted a communistic doctrine. The Babis also had a new progressive view on revelation which had only a few Islamic precedents among radical Ismailis. Like the Muslims they believed in prophets before Muhammad, but they did not think that each prophet brought essentially the same revelation. Rather, each one brought a more advanced revelation, abrogating the last one, in accord with the growing maturity of humanity. Uniquely, the Bab even said that his revelation would be superseded by a future prophet.

The persecuted Babis soon became rebellious and when Mohammad Shah died in 1848 the interval during which Nasir ad-Din Shah travelled from Tabriz to Tehran was taken to launch revolts. Although briefly successful in a few areas, they were put down by the new chief Minister, Amir Kabir, and the Bab was executed. Persecution of Babis became more severe after a few Babis made an attempt on the Shah's life in 1852, and after that many Babis moved to the Ottoman Empire, while those who stayed in Iran adopted the old Shi'i practice of precautionary hiding of their religion. In the 1860s the majority of Babis chose to follow the new dispensation of the Baha'ullah, who claimed to be the new prophet predicted by the Bab. His followers took the name of Bahais, and had a syncretic, liberal, westernized religion that spread outside Iran. The Bahais in Iran tended to be middle class and intellectual groups, often with Western ties. They abstained from politics, unlike the Babi minority who were involved in the opposition to the Qajars that culminated in the revolution of 1905–1911.[8] (A few persons of Bahai origin were politically influential before 1979, but they could not hold official positions and technically remain Bahais.)

If the Babi movement had given one kind of ideological direction to the growing discontent of the bazaar classes, a different direction was seen in protest against the monopoly concession for the purchase, sale, and export of Iranian tobacco given to a British subject in 1890. The middle classes and the ulama had already evinced discontent with the growing control of Iran by the British and Russians, including their economic power. The tobacco concession was particularly damaging to merchants as, unlike most other concessions, it covered a product already widely exploited, and threatened the livelihood of tobacco wholesalers, exporters, and retailers.

When foreigners arrived to buy up the tobacco crop in 1891, ulama-led protests developed in the major cities. The ulama had family and other ties to the merchants and guilds, and were largely dependent on popularity for their status. They were less vulnerable than others to government reprisal, and were seen as natural leaders. When a Shiraz mujtahid was expelled in 1891 for acts against the company, he went to Ottoman Iraq, where he first saw the Iranian born pan-Islamic and anti-colonial activist, Jamal ad-Din 'al-Afghani,' who had himself been expelled from Iran for propaganda against concessions to Westerners. The Shiraz mujtahid also saw in Iraq the leader of all the Shi'i ulama, Hajj Mirza Hasan Shirazi, and Afghani wrote a famous letter to Shirazi urging him to act. Major movements broke out in several cities; and in Tabriz the concession had to be suspended. Late in 1891 Shirazi issued a decree saying that the use of tobacco was against the will of the Twelfth Imam, and there followed a universal boycott of tobacco. Nasir ad-Din was forced to cancel first the internal concession and then after new disturbances, the export concession. The ulama, united partly by telegraphic communication, saw the extent of their political power.[9]

Although the government bought off some ulama opposition, at the end of 1905 the ulama became leaders, along with bazaaris and intellectuals, in what became the constitutional revolution, which gave Iran the constitution that was in effect until 1979. Although some ulama were anti-constitutional, a remarkable number favored the revolution, including most of the leading ulama in Iraq and two of Tehran's leading mujtahids, Tabataba'i and Behbehani. In addition to such men, who got written into the constitution a committee to pass on the compatibility of all laws with Shi'ism, there were lower ulama of a more radical bent. Since nearly all education was still religious, and since the *minbar* (pulpit) was the best forum, radical intellectuals entered the lower ulama. Among them were the freethinking Sayyid Jamal ad-Din Isfahani and the Azali Babi, and possibly later freethinker, Malik al-Mutakallimin. (Both were killed by Mohammad Ali Shah after his coup of 1908 that ended the first constitutional period.)

In the period 1905–1908 liberal and ulama leaders worked together well in the mass protests that brought the grant of a constitution and parliament, and basic differences often led to compromise. With the 1908 coup, however, and the armed resistance that began in Tabriz, there was a more frequent division between conservative ulama and radicals. When revolutionary forces converged on Tehran and deposed the Shah in 1909, the new parliament was more sharply divided into 'moderates,' with a heavy ulama component, and the more secular Democratic Party. The assassination of Behbehani by a terrorist and the subsequent expulsion of the liberal Democrat Taqizadeh showed this split, which became aggravated in subsequent decades despite temporary religious-radical alliances.[10]

The constitutional revolution was a high point of ulama participation in politics. In evaluating the social role of religion through 1911 one may note that the ideological supremacy of the ulama was rarely contested except in the exceptional Babi period, and that a socio-ideological leadership made of the ulama increasingly the representatives of popular grievances, especially those of the urban guildspeople. The government was generally unpopular in Qajar times, and had very little ideological hegemony, while the ulama were generally respected and the religion they represented was widely and deeply believed.

The government introduced the barest minimum of Western education and did not encourage students to go abroad, so that education continued to be almost universally religious education, which strengthened the ideological control of the ulama. Since there was no formal state-appointed or even ulama-appointed hierarchy, and position depended largely on having a large following, the ulama had to be responsive to popular desires and grievances. In addition, the ulama often had family ties to merchants and guildspeople that made them sensitive to their demands and desires.

The strength of the ulama in Qajar times was increased by the lack of effective centralizing reforms, which meant that the Qajars could not control the provinces effectively. No railroads were built, almost no roads, and there was very little expansion, rationalization, or modernization of the governmental bureaucracy. In areas directly controlled by the ulama there was no serious reform – education and justice remained in their hands, as did the charitable works that would later become social services. In part ulama protests helped forestall such reforms, but in part reform was also held back by the weakness of the Qajar Shahs, by Russo-British policies, and by Iran's difficult geographical conditions and ecology when compared to such reforming Mediterranean states as the Ottoman Empire, Egypt, and Tunisia. Iran lacked even the usual first step of significant army reform, and it was partly because of this that ulama-led crowds, usually unarmed, could fight successfully against the royal government in 1905–1906, whereas in Egypt and the Ottoman Empire revolt was synonymous with heavy army participation. (Iran's 1978–79 revolution, however, showed that a largely religiously led movement could stand up even to a strongly armed state.)

The Qajar ulama were perhaps a uniquely powerful Islamic religious class, but their power was partly based on factors that were undermined by modernization and centralization. Already during the 1905 revolution the ideological hegemony of the ulama was partly broken when Western secular notions of constitutionalism, parliaments, elections, and governmental and fiscal reforms were introduced, and more people than ever before were educated by newspapers and orators to be cognizant of such new concepts. Western democracy and even socialism were ideas spread abroad for the first time, and such secular concepts were to have increasing influence among some of the classes that had followed the ulama.

RELIGION UNDER THE PAHLAVIS (1921–1979)

Some anti-British action by the ulama during and after World War I and some religious content in the local democratic revolts in Azerbaijan and Gilan after World War I showed the continued activist role of religion. So too did ulama opposition to the scheme of the powerful new prime minister, Reza Khan, in 1924, to turn Iran into a republic headed by himself. The model of Ataturk, which Reza Khan wished to follow, was opposed by the ulama leadership, who saw Ataturk as the abolisher of the caliphate and the scourge of organized Islam. Ulama opposition helped change Reza Khan's mind, and he instead retained the monarchy, substituting the newly named Pahlavi dynasty for the Qajars in 1925. This was a pyrrhic victory for the ulama, as Reza Shah decreased their power, partly by creating institutions replacing those they controlled – especially modern schools and courts. The centralization of Iran through roads, a railway, and armed forces made it difficult for the ulama or dissidents to act effectively against the center. In social terms, there was some limitation of the role of Islam to the 'private' sphere. In addition, the gap between the secularized middle and upper classes who received a Westernized education and ceased to follow most of the prescriptions of Islam on the one hand, and the bazaar and popular classes who continued in most of their old beliefs and practices on the other, grew in importance. Modern education was one dividing line in this 'two culture' dichotomy – and another was having or not having a good place in the modern sector of the dual economy or society – in the government, the educational system, or in modern business. Religiousness or 'tradition' thus became the hallmarks of certain classes in society, and this situation largely continues until today. The 'traditional' popular classes followed only under duress the 'anti-religious' changes in the civil law, or the forced unveiling of women. (Iran's is the only non-Communist government to have abolished the veil, in 1936.)

The modernizing classes tended to adopt a trend in Iranian nationalism that had begun in the late nineteenth century – the glorification of pre-Islamic Iran and of Zoroastrianism, with the Arab Muslim invaders seen as causing Iran's decline. Iranian Zoroastrians were granted new respect, and Zoroastrian and pre-Islamic motifs entered scholarship, literature, and government pronouncements and architecture. This type of nationalism, which has its parallels in many societies, widened the cultural breach between the devout popular classes and the Westernizing nationalists.[11]

The loosening of despotism after Anglo-Russian policy forced the abdication of Reza Shah in 1941 and brought a resurgence of dissident groups including the tribes, leftists, liberals, and the ulama and religious elements. Religious laymen and some of the ulama reentered politics, notably Ayatollah Kashani. (An ayatollah is a high mujtahid; both groups have grown so that in practice only ayatollahs now hold the power once held by mujtahids, and the term 'mujtahid' is now rarely heard.) Kashani and his group were for a time members of the coalition that comprised the National Front, headed by Mosaddeq, who came to power and nationalized Iranian oil in 1951 and was overthrown with covert U.S. aid in 1953. Religious nationalists like Kashani were, like their 1905–11 predecessors, against Western power in Iran, and could cooperate with secular nationalists. Kashani broke with Mosaddeq, however, and went into opposition. More extreme than Kashani, though at times protected by him, were the band of Fidaiyyan-i Islam, who assassinated leaders considered pro-Western and/or anti-religious. Their main victims were Ahmad Kasravi, an intellectual critical of Shi'ism, and General Razmara, a minister considered too friendly to the West. Many conservative ulama increasingly opposed Mosaddeq, however, and helped lead the crowds whose demonstrations contributed to his downfall. On balance, it may be said that both secular nationalists of the new culture and bazaar opponents of Western competition belonged to the Mosaddeq coalition. The period after 1941 was notable for some Muslim 'revival' after the suppression under Reza Shah, including the readoption of a partial veil, or *chadur*, by the popular classes, and the reentry of religion into politics.

Since Safavid times the Shi'i ulama have been divided between those with government ties or appointments – notably the *imam jum'ehs* of each big city – and those more independent of the government. The former are generally looked down on by their own colleagues and by most believers. The leader of the independent ulama, Ayatollah Burujirdi, lived in Qom until his death in 1961, and Qom has become the center of Iranian Shi'ism since his time, overshadowing the shrine cities of Iraq. Since Burujirdi's death in 1961 and the subsequent consensus against having a single religious leader, the independent ulama have revived their oppositional role. Opposition focused on the growing power of the government, perceived as tyrannical, and on governmental measures seen as anti-Islamic.

A series of reforms in 1962–63 included land reform and votes for women. Although there is disagreement over whether the chief oppositional ulama opposed land reform, as the government claims without documents, some of their followers did, and much of the religious opposition opposed votes for women. It is less known that ulama opposition was also largely based on different issues that the government did not mention. One was Iran's de facto relations with Israel, including supplying Israel with oil, and another was U.S. power in Iran, including an agreement with the U.S. restoring extraterritorial jurisdiction for the U.S. military and their families. Coupled with these was a general complaint against growing tyranny. In June 1963 there were widespread anti-government riots led by the ulama and in 1964 came the exile of the most outstpoken anti-government mujtahid, Ayatollah Khomeini, and they were suppressed with considerable bloodshed.[12] Khomeini continued for years to publish from Iraq, and to broadcast into Iran. His writings show Khomeini to be a fundamentalist on some matters, such as the Family Protection Law of 1967, which went a long way toward equalizing family rights for women and was opposed by Khomeini. On other questions he is innovative, as in his argument that Islam is opposed to monarchy – a stronger point than was made by his Shi'i predecessors, but one that finds some support both in the elective traditions of the 'orthodox' Sunni caliphate and in Twelver belief in the imams and the absence of legitimate rule pending the return of the Twelfth Imam. Khomeini's view that monarchy is unislamic gained wide support among religious opponents of Mohammed Reza Shah. Religious centers like Qom remained centers of student and ulama opposition to the government, sometimes, even before 1978, breaking into open demonstrations, which like most strikes and demonstrations until 1978 got no press coverage.

Unlike the situation in the Reza Shah period, many students of secular subjects and intellectuals with secular educations demonstrated an upsurge in religious interest and orientation in the 1960s and 1970s. In the case of students this can partly be attributed to the ever-growing numbers of university students, which meant that many more students come from religious bazaar, petty bourgeois, or small town backgrounds than ever before. Partly, however, the phenomenon was one of opposition, with students often seeing the Islamic opposition as the only sizable and potentially effective one in Iran, and hence identifying with it. As in the past, the association of government oppression with government ties to the West and of grievances with the phenomena of modernization made many students and intellectuals idealize Islam as an alternative approach and seek in it a comprehensive basis for a more just and independent society.

The tendency for religion to be concentrated among the traditional popular classes has not been overridden by the above counter-tendency, however. Gobineau already noted religious skepticism among nineteenth century educated Persians, and by now many in the modernized middle and upper classes, including many who call themselves Muslim, flout Islamic rules, never go to a mosque, and follow an almost wholly Western life style. The bazaar bourgeoisie and petty bourgeoisie, who are still strong although in relative decline, and the masses, remain overwhelmingly Islamic, and there is a major conflict in life styles: in these classes the women wear the chadur, now increasingly spreading to villages too; marriages are arranged; major religious rules are followed; and religious leaders are influential.

It may be noted that for the above classes religion fulfills important functions: in popular milieux, it helps explain injustices and illnesses that are otherwise inexplicable and uncontrollable; provides reassurance that proper conduct will be rewarded in the next world; gives rules and ceremonies for marriage, birth and death rites, inheritance, and many other major aspects of life; and also provides the occasion for periodic festivals, ceremonies, and group meetings. The very legalism and structured nature of orthodox Islam that create some difficulties in adaptation to rapidly changing modern conditions, make it a religion highly suitable for giving a sense of place and order to groups that still live under quite traditional forms of social organization. At the same time, Western educated groups have increasingly found new interpretations of Islam to meet new needs.

The royal government tried, with very partial success, to identify itself with Islam; compromising on a few points, stressing its ties with complaisant ulama, and teaching its monarchist version of Islam in the schools. A few intellectuals before 1979 wrote and taught that Shi'ism is a supporter of monarchy and otherwise tried to promote the unity of state and religion. An originally Western intellectual trend that ties Zoroastrianism and other pre-Islamic religious trends to Iranian Shi'ism and Sufism was also promoted by government-favored intellectuals. The government also made some not entirely successful attempts to set up a 'religion corps' to teach religion in the villages – parallel to the literacy and the development corps.

Despite heavy pressures and incentives, including jailing of religious as of other opponents, and despite the known differences between the religious opposition and their secular allies, religious opposition to the government, of both a quietist and activist nature, became a major trend in the 1960s and 1970s.

The 1960s also saw the development of groups, of a type that still exist, of guerillas or terrorists with partly religious ideologies. Among these was one, the Devotees of the Iranian People (the Mujahidin), who appealed both to socialism and Islam, and hence were dubbed 'Islamic Marxists' by the government. They were responsible for a number of assassinations, chiefly of U.S. military advisers. In 1975 part of them turned to what they considered pure Marxism, ignoring the fact that terrorism was opposed by Marx, but the religious majority won out and predominate now. The other major guerilla group are the Marxist Fedaiyyin. A number of Iranian students and others in Iran and abroad continue to try to combine Islam and Marxism.

Despite the rapid twentieth century secularization and modernization of Iranian life, oppositional ulama and lay Muslims have kept the respect not only of the religious classes, but also of many non-religious groups who admire their independence of the government. Shi'ism and its leaders retain an important symbolic significance even for many who have lost their belief. The 'back to Islam' trends, particularly in law and personal habits, recently seen in countries like Pakistan, Libya and Egypt, which represent in part a reaction of the popular classes against the secularizing upper classes, indicate that secularizing changes are not always permanent and undirectional. Iran's 1979 government appears, as of today (March 1979), to be part of this Islamic movement, though it is impossible to say how long this will last. This Islamic and anti-Western trend is strengthened by the presence of secularized lay intellectuals among those who attack the secularization and Westernization of Iran and call for the reestablishment of an Islamic society, as they interpret it. Although Al-i Ahmad's *Gharbzadigi* ('Westoxication') was not at all a religious essay, similar attacks on imitation of things Western were taken up by the new group of lay religious thinkers who surfaced in the 1960s. These men, associated with reformist mosques and schools that were opened, and later closed by the government, in the 1960s, in addition to opposing the government, tried to set up the basis for a reformed Islamic society, based on their interpretations of Islam. Although the leaders of this trend were sometimes jailed, the writings of one, Ali Shariati (d. 1977), were also used in the newspapers by the government, probably because of their anti-Communist content. The main thrust of Shariati's interpretation of Shi'ism is activist and progressive, however, and his vast following undoubtedly contributed ideologically to the 1978–79 revolution.[13] There thus exist several competing interpretations of Shi'i Islam, but since mujtahids have often differed in their views, this is not an entirely new situation. Recent events have shown up differences among ayatollahs, like the fundamentalist Khomeini, the moderate Shariatmadari and the liberal-progressive Taliqani.

ISLAM AND SOCIAL GROUPS TODAY

Aside from the political considerations that form such a key aspect of the relations between Iranian religion and society, mention should be made of aspects of belief and practice of different social groups. Iranian Muslims of the traditional and traditionally oriented classes – especially the bazaar, the villagers, and recent migrants from village to town – tend to identify Islam with 'the way things have always been,' or tradition. They tend to consider veiling and other traditional practices regarding women, Islamic marriage law and customs, and family practices, as centrally Islamic and right, and this has been part of the basis for widespread failure to observe reform laws in this area – a phenomenon also found in other Muslim countries. Observing these laws would also mean that dominant men would have to give up some prerogatives to dominated women, and if they are not forced or persuaded to do so they are unlikely to want to comply, unless women learn to stand up for their new legal rights. Practices do change, but far more slowly than laws, and change is not inevitably in one direction.

On these and other matters it may be noted that Islam, both Shi'i and Sunni, has shown itself to be the most tenacious of traditions and religions in clinging to people's allegiance and to areas that the non-Muslim world, East as well as West, has largely secularized. This is particularly true of the domain of marriage and family law, many provisions of which are found in the Koran and hence considered divinely revealed. The permission of polygamy up to four wives, and free divorce by the husband but not the wife are Koranic, as are inheritance laws that give daughters half as much property as sons. In Iran and other Muslim countries, female inheritance, which often limits male and family prerogatives, as daughters marry out and with their property become members of another family, is often circumvented, especially in rural areas, by various legal fictions that demonstrate the possibility of overriding Koranic provisions when it is in the interest of dominant groups to do so. Islamic law gives child custody to the father at an age that varies by sex and legal school. Shi'i law has the special feature of temporary marriage, whereby for a financial consideration (male dowries being characteristic of Muslim marriages) a man marries a temporary wife for a time specified in the contract. Although often a form of legalized prostitution, flourishing particularly in pilgrimage cities, this institution might serve a variety of other purposes, and, if the marriage was contracted for 99 years, divorce might be made impossible, and marriage be firmer than was a normal marriage.[14]

As in many other aspects of life before the modern period all classes were theoretically subject to essentially the same rules, although it has been noted that the urban wife tended to be veiled and to inherit, while the rural and tribal wife was unveiled and tended not to inherit. With the spread of Western economic and political influence, of Western education, and of Western laws in other spheres, the Western-educated classes tended in marriage as in other matters more and more to conform to Western ways, but this was not true of the popular classes. As the twentieth century progressed, and particularly under the Pahlavis, polygamy was abandoned by the upper classes even while it remained legal. Large harems had been limited to the upper classes, and particularly the royal family. After the Qajars they went quickly out of fashion. The degree of personal choice in a marriage partner was positively correlated with position in the class hierarchy, as well as with passing decades. As upper class women and others with a Western education began to work in large numbers in recent decades, their family life took on more and more the character of that of their Western counterparts. This change in family patterns, like many related changes, seems to have taken place without great trauma for the classes affected, who were willing in various spheres to adopt Western ways, which accorded better with their position in the economy and society, and did not consider that this had much to do with their private religious beliefs, which were usually 'modernized' in any case.

Among the popular classes in both city and countryside, however, there was no such dramatic change in economic or political roles, and no such transformation of education and ideology as among the Western-educated classes. Therefore, they tended to stick to their religious and other customs, which were quite functional for the life they knew. The complex of marriage and family practices, some of which were based in religious law, helped insure the size, power, and continuity of the family, as well as the control of older generations over younger ones and of men over women. Family alliance needs were predominant in the choosing of mates by the parents, and, as in most traditional societies, there was no idea of a love match, or even of too much contact between husband and wife. Polygamy was limited to special needs or desires, and at most usually involved bigamy among the popular classes.

The fact that family law and practice are embedded in the Koran and in some of the central institutions of popular life, plus the fact that family law favors men, who are dominant in society and disfavors women, who are weak, accounts for much of the hesitation of even reformist Muslim governments to tamper with this sphere. (Egypt, for example, has been discussing family reform legislation fairly constantly since World War II, but has done almost nothing, and Algeria is similar.) Reza Shah took the radical step of unveiling, but did not significantly reform family law.

In the post-war period it has been, on the whole, those Muslim governments who have had an upper or modernized middle class, pro-Western orientation of 'conservative reform', that have passed more reformist legislation regarding women, marriage, and the family – such as Iran, Kuwait, and Tunisia – while the more petty bourgeois 'radical' regimes like those of Algeria and Egypt have been left behind. This seeming paradox finds a partial explanation in what has been said above – it has been the upper, Western-oriented and educated classes who have been open to rapid Westernization regarding women, marriage, and the family, while the traditionalist popular classes have been more conservative, largely due to their contrasting experience with and attitudes toward the West. Recently Iraq is a socialist *and* reforming exception to the above trend, while Marxist South Yemen has mobilized and educated popular class women, as might be expected of a really radical Marxist state.

The Iranian Family Protection Law of 1967, rewritten in 1975, has been the focus of conflict, often unreported, between religious and secular, between upper and popular class groups, and between some men and women. The law itself was a compromise between what was wanted by those who believed in women's equality and more traditional reformers. Polygamy was not completely outlawed, but was limited to certain circumstances, and if done against the will of the first wife became the grounds for a divorce complaint by her. Children were to be put in the custody of whichever parent the court judged fittest. Divorce became more equal and had to be granted by a secular court. The traditional ulama opposed this law as unislamic, and in many areas among the popular classes its provisions are still not carried out, as the force of custom and 'religion' against a woman suing for divorce, for example, or getting child custody, are still too great for its provisions to be met. There were efforts by the official Iranian Women's Organization to teach women their rights, but unsurprisingly these do not yet meet the need, and it seems likely that struggles will continue. (As of March, 1979, the status of the Family Protection Law is unclear, and secular divorce proceedings have been suspended.)

Even among those who consider themselves Muslims, religious beliefs and practices have always varied, in large measure along class lines, and these variations are probably greater today than before. While the educated Muslim tends to follow a rationalized Islam largely if indirectly influenced by Western ideas and by the ideas of Muslim reformers of various countries in the last centuries, including Iranian reformers, the popular classes tend if anything to follow religious practices and beliefs that are less rationalized, if often functional, that what is found in the Koran and learned Traditions. Belief in jinns, spirits, and witchcraft is widespread.

A major feature in the religious and social life of rural and urban masses are pilgrimages either to large urban shrines of imams or the direct families of imams or to smaller, often rural, shrines of supposed descendants of imams. These range from the major urban shrines in Mashad, Qom, Rayy, and Shiraz, among others, to the small shrines found throughout the countryside.

Also important in the life of the popular classes are the ceremonies surrounding the major religious holidays, which in Iranian Shi'ism mostly commemorate the deaths of imams. Ceremonies commemorating Mohammad and Ali are important, but even more celebrated are the ten days of mourning for the martyrdom of Ali's son Hosain, including mourning processions, which now rarely include the traditional self-flagellation, and often culminating in one or more passion plays, or *taziyehs*, which center around the events surrounding the death of Hosain and his followers in battle against the Umayyads. During the mourning processions and the plays spectators typically become very emotionally involved, and this religious theatre is really also a rite or ceremonial in which audience attitude and reaction is much more a part of the totality than in the secular theatre of the West. The changing attitude of the secular authorities toward popular religious custom is suggested in their varying treatment of the taziyeh. Although its origins are disputed and go back many centuries, religious theatre as such probably began shortly before the Qajars, and it was sponsored by Qajar rulers and princes, in part as a means to gain religious and general popularity. Under Reza Shah it was widely suppressed, and the self-flagellating processions even more so. After the war suppression was sporadic and both made a comeback (along with other traditional practices like veiling). In 1976, the festival of arts in Shiraz centered on presentation of taziyehs, along with an academic conference about them. In their original form the taziyehs are widely varied by locality – some small and modest, while others occupy terrains that are as large as football fields and feature realistic combats of mounted warriors.

Other still popular religious ceremonies include *rauzeh-khans*, in which a preacher recites a story of martyrdom of an imam, and *sufrehs* for women, held in the home and involving the eating of a special meal, again generally in commemoration of a martyr, and a sermon by a preacher, often female.

Iranian religion through the ages has been characterized as one of 'opposition, martyrdom, and revolt,' and all three themes have appeared prominently in this exposition, but martyrdom and its social role have thus far been explicated the least. Without going into martyrdom in pre-Islamic Iranian religions or in Sunni movements, one may note that in Shi'ism martyrdom is a central theme, with the martyrdom of Ali and especially Hosain particularly stressed. It is widely believed among Shi'is that all the imams were martyrs, even though this is not in accord with the facts. The martyrdom of Hosain in particular plays some of the role of that of Christ in Christianity, with Hosain often appealed to as an intercessor with God regarding the afterlife or other matters. In addition, the sufferings of Hosain and his party, including his young sons, are a point of identification particularly for the popular classes who undergo many inexplicable sufferings, including the sudden death of young children. Finally, the drama of Hosain's battle against the Umayyads has repeatedly and often explicitly been given politico-social significance by the religious classes: Hosain becomes the archetype of current groups fighting for justice, and the Umayyads of the unjust monarchs or others who oppose them. This comparison was often made during the constitutional revolution, and it has been repeated more recently.[15]

A feature of Shi'i Islam only recently studied is the presence of women preachers or mullas, who teach and preach to girls and women as male mullas do to men. Several women both past and present have studied with male mujtahids and received from them attestations that their learning is great enough to be equal to the mujtahids. Most religious authorities do not consider these women mujtahids, as they consider being of the male sex a prerequisite of being a mujtahid. Nonetheless, by some they have been considered mujtahids worthy of being followed, and several have written treatises and gained some renown.[16] More common is the ordinary woman mulla, who especially in pre-Pahlavi times had greater access to education and greater freedom of movement than almost any other women, with the possible exception of a few in the royal family.

Among largely popular trends in Islam, Sufism should also be noted although, since its persecution by the Safavids, it is less important than in most Muslim countries. Sufism originally implied ascetic mysticism, although with the great growth of organized Sufi orders since about the twelfth century A.D., many persons joined Sufi orders and followed, to some degree, group mystic practices, without being themselves either ascetics or especially mystical. Sufi orders played and still play a partly social role, tying together people in one organized confraternity with a single leadership, its own doctrines and practices, and regular meeting dates. For those who are mystics Sufism, like Manicheanism before it, represents in part a rejection of things as they are and a search for a non-political way to escape the evils of the world. Sufi ideas have since 1500 been partly incorporated into the Shi'ism of some Iranian philosophers and theologians, a trend that continues among some current Iranian intellectuals. The popular Sufi orders, however, include many who are not adept in intellectualized forms of mysticism, and who chiefly use physical practices of various kinds to attain the trance or ecstatic state that is interpreted as unity with God. Although Sufi orders continue to exist, their importance, size, and elite following have greatly declined since the nineteenth century.

Another form of religious or semi-religious organization among the popular classes is the group or *hay'at* found especially among the bazaar classes, where it usually meets regularly in the home of one member. These small semi-religious societies provide an opportunity for socializing and discussion that has roots in the past but is also favored in the present partly because other forms of organization or discussion would be subject to stricter government surveillance and control. Bazaar festivals of a religious nature, which sometimes in their stress on the killing of past martyrs by past governments have an undertone of political opposition, may be planned by such groups. Hay'ats, mosque sermons, and religious processions formed one basis for organizing opposition to the government in 1978.

In stressing the informal and local organization and

manifestations of religion among the popular classes, it would be wrong to suggest that formally trained Shi'i mullas are unimportant. Although they have lost many of their educational and judicial functions, they continue to cater to religious, charitable, and other needs. Villages generally want a mosque and a mulla, and although village mullas may not be highly educated they remain on top of most village hierarchies in learning. Town and especially city mullas have more education. For most Muslims those educated in religious centers like the Iraq shrine cities or Qom, who tend to be independent of the government in their ideas as well as their training, have more prestige than those educated in relatively new government institutions like the University of Tehran's Faculty of Theology. Although, as recent studies have shown, students at Qom, which has no entrance or other examinations, tend often to be those who could not continue in regular high schools and universities, and the intellectual elite in general no longer heads for religious education or posts as it did through Qajar times, there are still men of considerable intellectual as well as moral power who come through the traditional system. With the trend to religion since the 1960s, it seems possible that the religious schools will soon have more intellectual graduates than was true in recent decades.

Higher in the scale of wealth and modernization than the rural classes and the urban masses and bazaar classes discussed above are the Western educated classes who have few very distinctive religious practices, since they tend, even if they are to some degree believers, to limit religion more and more to the private sphere and not to think too much about possible conflicts between their way of life and strict religious practice. It should be remembered that such things as wine drinking and graphic representation of humans continued to be widespread in Islamic Iran, despite religious discouragement or prohibition, so that current practices of the Western educated classes are often different in degree rather than in kind from what went on in the past. It is worth noting, however, that there has recently been a revival of such customs as *sufrehs* among 'modernized' classes. The reformist religious preachings and writings of men like Shariati, with their frequent references to Western thinkers, have also been popular with the educated classes, and the revival of religion among university students has been noted. Whether all this is a precursor of a new emphasis on reformed Islam by the educated class in general, which would be in part an emphasis on one more side of the national heritage as against the dominant West and Westernism, remains to be seen. Popular class pressures against the Westernism of the official and upper classes are strong. They have slowed reforms regarding women and the family, and they may become effective in other spheres, although not always in an anti-reformist direction.

Even before 1978 educated women privately voiced their fears of the religious opposition, which, if it gained in effective power, they saw as likely to brake or even reverse the movement for women's rights (such reversals have been seen in such countries as Algeria, Tunisia, and Egypt). Although secularist opponents of the government often tried to put the best face of the revivalist positions of the religious opposition, understandably believing that only this opposition could hope to have a mass base, the problem of social reform in the face of religious opposition in some spheres is a real one. On the other hand, those who promulgate reformist or radical interpretations of religion may mobilize new support for certain reforms.

The discussion of religious beliefs and practices of different social groups and classes has thus far been limited to those born within the fold or Shi'i Islam, who make up over 90 per cent of Iran's population, but the religious minority groups, whose strong inner identification makes them in part another kind of social group, should not go without mention. The position of several minorities, the Christians, Jews, and Zoroastrians, was strongly affected by the Western impact since the nineteenth century. Formerly disfavored and often impoverished, these groups were given educational and other support by their co-religionists abroad, so that they emerged, on the average, among the highly educated groups in society, with strong representation in varying kinds of businesses and professions.

The continuing high evaluation put by Iranians on pre-Islamic Iran favors the Zoroastrians, and Christians are very rarely persecuted. Although considerable popular anti-Semitism exists, now mixed with the widespread anti-Israel attitude of most Iranians, Jews generally did quite well under secularist modern rule. Bahais, despite their relatively good education and economic position, experience some discrimination, which for them (and in theory for the Azali Babis who exist in small numbers) is partly based on their apostasy from Islam, which is contrary to Muslim law. Bahais are also associated by many Shi'is with foreigners and with Pahlavi rule. Minority emigration was considerable in 1978–79. Smaller sects continue, such as the 'extremist' Ahl-Haqq or Ali Ilahis, found mainly among the Kurds – a sect whose radicalism has always included considerable egalitarianism regarding women; and the syncretic Mandeans, often called Sabeans, who live near the Iraqi border and do the gold- and silversmithing in the city of Ahwaz. Their religion antedates Islam, and has secret gnostic elements. In theory they are a protected 'People of the Book.'

Iran's Sunni Muslims are predominantly the Kurds of the West, the Turkomans of the north, and the Baluchis of the southeast, although there are pockets of Arabic and Persian-speaking Sunnis. The non-Persian Sunni groups have several points in common: all are tribal peoples who are or were largely nomadic; all live on Iran's borders and have strong ties to a related Sunni ethnic group speaking their language on the other side of the border. Although at various times Iran has, with some reason, feared secessionist or autonomist sentiment and/or movements among all these groups (as well as among their Shi'i Arabs and Azeri Turks) this fear was not based mostly on their Sunnism, but more on an autonomist identity that drew heavily on the presence of a related ethnic group outside Iran. On a world scale modern Iran's religious minorities have mostly been fairly well treated and little persecuted in this century; this record has been facilitated by the fact that the religious minorities are small. As of March 1979, it is too early to predict the conduct of the new government or of all Iranian Shi'is toward minorities.

CONCLUSION

From pre-Islamic times until now religious movements and ideas can in part be understood as representing the needs and aspirations of different social groups and classes, and these movements often take on a specifically political, and sometimes rebellious or revolutionary form. In Iran as in many other countries modernist ideologies long were distinguished by being more secular and less religious than past ideologies, and also by their emphasis on nationalist values above religious ones. Unlike many Arab countries, which are influenced by the fact that Mohammad, the Koran, and Islam form part of the Arab national heritage, Pahlavi Iran generally did not try to give its policies and reforms an especially religious guise, and in this the Pahlavis differed from nearly all earlier Iranian dynasties. As the government became the defender of a kind of secularism, and earlier of capitulation to Western Powers, so traditional Islam has since the late nineteenth century been frequently oppositional. In this situation heresy or sectarianism is no longer needed to express mass grievances, and so instead of the older dichotomy of the heretical masses versus the orthodox government, one gets in the 1960s and 1970s the orthodox masses versus the secularist government; in both cases hostility to the government was not limited to its religious views. How this situation will develop cannot be predicted, but it seems clear that political religious movements in Iran are not played out.

NOTES

1. For surveys of the complex and controversial religious history of pre-Islamic Iran, see especially Richard N. Frye, *The Heritage of Persia*, New York, New America Library, 1966 (original edition 1963); R. Ghirshman, *Iran: From the Earliest Times to the Islamic Conquest*, Harmondsworth, Penguin Books, tr. from the French, 1954; and Alessandro Bausani, *Persia Religiosa*, Milan, Saggiatore, 1959. On pre-Islamic religion and especially Mazdak, see N. Pigulevskaja, *Les Villes de l'état iranien aux époques parthe et sassanide*, The Hague, Mouton, 1963.

2. Marshall G. S. Hodgson, *The Order of the Assassins* ('s-Gravenhage, Mouton, 1955); Bernard Lewis, *The Assassins*, New York, Basic Books, 1968. On earlier Iranian Islam see the articles on religion in the *Cambridge History of Iran*, vols. IV, V, Cambridge, 1975, 1968; Bausani, *op. cit.*; G. H. Sadighi, *Les mouvements religieux iraniens*, Paris, Presses Modernes, 1938; R. N. Frye, *The Golden Age of Persia*, London, Weidenfeld and Nicolson, 1975; and the book on Iran's conversion to Islam by Richard Bulliet, in press, Harvard University Press.

3. This point is discussed, along with citation of Nasir-i Khusrau, Avicenna, and others, in Nikki R. Keddie, *The Middle East and Beyond*, Frank Cass, forthcoming, Chapter 2.

4. Nizam al-Mulk, *The Book of Government or Rules for Kings*. Translated by H. Darke, London, Routledge and Kegan Paul, 2nd ed., 1978.

5. On Safavid and pre-Safavid Shi'ism see Nikki R. Keddie, 'The Roots of the Ulama's Power in Modern Iran,' *Scholars, Saints, and Sufis,* Berkeley, University of California Press, 1972, and the sources cited therein; the articles by Hossein Nasr and Hamid Algar in *Studies on Isfahan,* special 2 volume issue of *Iranian Studies,* VII, 1–2 (winter–spring 1974); Michel Mazzaoui, *The Origins of the Safavids,* Wiesbaden, F. Steiner, 1972; and Jean Aubin, 'La politique religieuse des Safavides,' *Le Shi'isme imâmite,* Paris, Presses Universitaires de France, 1970.

6. See Hamid Algar, 'Shi'ism and Iran in the Eighteenth Century,' *Studies in Eighteenth Century Islamic History,* ed. T. Naff and R. Owen, Carbondale, Southern Illinois University Press, 1977. Mangol Bayat-Philipp has forthcoming papers that discuss the Shaikhis in the context of Iranian intellectual and religious history, one of them in M. Bonine and N. Keddie, eds., *Modern Iran: Continuity and Change* (Albany S.U.N.Y. Press, 1981).

7. Hamid Algar, *Religion and State in Iran,* Berkeley, University of California Press, 1969, and the sources cited therein. A. K. S. Lambton, 'The Persian Ulama and Constitutional Reform,' *Le Shi'isme imâmite;* in other articles she deals with the political role of the Qajar ulama.

8. See chapter 1 of this volume and the sources cited therein, which include the most important western language works on the Babis. They are also discussed in the Bayat-Philipp article cited above, which is a partial summary of a forthcoming book.

9. Nikki R. Keddie, *Religion and Rebellion in Iran: The Tobacco Protest of 1891–1892,* London, Frank Cass, 1966, and the sources cited therein; idem., *Sayyid Jamal ad-Din al-Afghani: A Political Biography,* Berkeley, University of California Press, 1972.

10. Algar, *Religion and State;* Keddie, 'Roots', and Chapters 1 and 2 of this volume.

11. On Reza Shah see Amin Banani, *The Modernization of Iran,* Stanford, Stanford University Press, 1961. Mangol Bayat-Philipp has an important forthcoming article on the two cultures in Iran, 'The Concept of Historical Continuity in Modern Iranian Thought,' *Asian and African Studies,* in press.

12. See Hamid Algar, 'The Oppositional Role of the Ulama in Twentieth Century Iran,' *Scholars, Saints, and Sufis, op. cit.* and A. K. S. Lambton, 'A Reconsideration of the Position of the Marja' al-Taqlid and the Religious Institution,' *Studia Islamica,* XX (1964), 115–35.

13. On Shariati see Mangol Bayat-Philipp, 'Shi'ism in Contemporary Iranian Politics: The Case of Ali Shariati,' in E. Kedourie and S. Haim, eds., *Towards a Modern Iran,* Frank Cass, London, 1980; Michael Fischer also discusses Shariati and criticisms of him by orthodox ulama in his *Iran: From Religious Dispute to Revolution,* Harvard Studies in Cultural Anthropology, 3, 1980. See also Ali Shariati, *On the Sociology of Islam,* tr. Hamid Algar, Berkeley, Mizan Press, 1979.

14. The position of women in Iran is discussed in the introduction and several articles in Lois Beck and Nikki Keddie, eds., *Women in the Muslim World,* Cambridge, Harvard University Press, 1978. Shahla Haeri is doing a UCLA

Ph.D. dissertation in Anthropology on temporary marriage.

15. See Algar, *Religion and State* and 'Oppositional Role,' and Gustav Thaiss, 'Religious Symbolism and Social Change: The Drama of Husain,' *Scholars, Saints, and Sufis, op. cit.*

16. Fischer, op. cit., discusses these women and the reason why they are not generally considered mujtahids despite their learning and functions. The role of Shi'i women mullas in Iraq was described in E. W. Fernea, *Guests of the Sheik*, Garden City, N.Y., Doubleday, 1969; their role in Iran has recently been studied, but not yet in published form.

SECTION II

Socio-Economic Change

5

The Economic History of Iran, 1800–1914, and its Political Impact

The economic history of Iran is a subject that has barely begun to receive the attention it deserves. Articles and parts of books on particular aspects of the subject appeared as early as the nineteenth century, but it is only since World War II that there have been extensive and serious studies in English, and these are still few and far between. Prof. Lambton's book *Landlord and Peasant in Persia* deserves to be singled out as a major pioneering study, and recently there has appeared Professor Charles Issawi's edited volume, *The Economic History of Iran 1800–1914* (Chicago: University of Chicago Press, 1971). This book brings together an outstanding collection of articles, excerpts, and sources, many of them translated from Persian, French, German, Russian, and Italian, that provide a basis for an understanding of the economic history of Iran in the nineteenth century. This essay will attempt a brief outline of the economic history of Iran from 1800 to 1914, using both Prof. Issawi's book and other sources, and adding some conclusions about political interaction with economic developments. Although for many countries such an essay would be superfluous, the economic history of Iran is so underdeveloped a subject that no such generalizing essay or book yet exists in the English language. (Figures not footnoted below are from Issawi's book.)

The first and perhaps most important impression that arises from an overview of the 1800–1914 period is the relative economic stagnation and very slow development of Iran in the period under discussion, particularly as contrasted with the Middle Eastern countries that border on the Mediterranean. The latter countries were in close contact with Europe by ship and

119

were opened up rapidly to a development that benefited primarily Western European nations, but also transformed the local society. The relatively rapid growth in the cultivation of cash crops, and of means of transport to handle them, and of large landownership to exploit them were Mediterranean features only palely reflected in Iran. By 1914 Egypt had some 250,000 European residents, while Iran had only some hundreds. At the same date Iran had less than 12 miles of railroads, no modern port, a few hundred miles of roads of any description, and a foreign investment below 30 million pounds including the national debt. Economic modernization, which in Egypt and Turkey got a serious start (however lopsided in favor of Europeans and religious minorities) in the nineteenth century, in Iran awaited the advent of Reza Shah in the 1920s.

Several reasons may be cited for this relative stagnation. Among those noted by Issawi are Iran's distance from Western Europe — over 11,000 miles until the Suez Canal was opened, and still great after that event; the lesser authority of the government than in Turkey and Egypt, especially over nomadic tribes; the weakness of the military, the archaic administrative and fiscal systems; the stultifying effect of the Anglo-Russian rivalry, with each country determined to thwart the schemes of the other; and the lack of large non-Muslim minorities with contact with Western ways. Here I will elaborate on a few factors which seem particularly crucial. One is the geography of Iran — not only its distance from Western Europe, but equally its rugged mountainous terrain and vast distances between population centers and its lack of navigable rivers except for the Karun in the South. This made Iran a less favorable territory for international trade than the countries of the Mediterranean, greatly increasing the price of transport and restricting the development of a national market. Second, there was the difficulty of setting up a strong central government of the type that encouraged economic change in Egypt and Turkey. In part this was a direct result of the geographic factors mentioned above, and in part an indirect result of these factors — the prevalence of nomadic tribes whom Issawi estimates at one-half of the total population of Iran in the early nineteenth century, removed large areas from direct government control. These tribes conducted their own economic affairs, getting whatever they lacked from nearby villages and towns, and they were politically almost independent. The shahs had a theoretical right to name their chiefs, but these were always named from the ruling tribal family. The shahs also relied on the nomadic tribes for their cavalry, and were prudent enough not to try to intefere with the internal workings of the tribes except in cases of open rebellion. Local governors were also virtually independent of the central government as long as they sent in their revenues, made the required annual presents, and did not rebel. The religious classes, or ulama, also retained considerable independence, based on their steady income from the Muslim community, their ownership of considerable land and property, their control of education and religious courts, and the respect in which they were held by the population. The Qajar dynasty, which ruled from 1796 to 1925, lacked any conspicuous centralizing ruler, and the few attempts at centralizing reforms met with opposition from the ulama and other vested interests and were generally soon abandoned or allowed to become dead letters. The old ruling classes – landlords, tribal khans, bureaucrats, and ulama – had a vested interest in keeping the central government from becoming too powerful and in maintaining the economic *status quo*, while the center had less foreign and internal impetus, and fewer talented individuals to push centralizing reforms than in Turkey or Egypt. Despite these unfavorable factors, there was some increase in the power of the bureaucracy and of the central government in the course of the nineteenth century, with the latter half of that century seeing fewer feudal and tribal revolts than had the first half. This increase in power was not accompanied by any real diminution in the power of the tribes or of the ulama, however, as was clearly to be shown when both groups demonstrated their strength in the course of the constitutional revolution of 1905–1911. Nor was the increase accompanied by any meaningful efforts by the center at economic development.

Issawi's mention of Anglo-Russian rivalry should be elaborated. In several instances each country did all it could to keep the other from getting economic concessions and from exploiting those it did get. The most obvious examples of this are Russian opposition to the notorious Reuter concession of 1872 which gave Baron Julius de Reuter, a British subject, exclusive rights to exploit nearly all the economic resources of Iran. The concession was cancelled due to Russian and Iranian opposition, but the British then used Reuter's unfulfilled claims to block Russian railway concessions. The Russian government then, having decided it did not want railways in Iran, signed a secret agreement with Iran which in effect blocked the construction of railways there for ten years, and this agreement was later renewed. Russia also helped foment Iranian mass opposition to a British tobacco concession granted in 1890.[1] In some of these instances the activities of the two powers coincided with Iranian anti-imperialism, but they also blocked some economic enterprises that could have led to a more rapid modernization of Iran, however exploitative they would probably have been. England and Russia both also often worked to block concessions by third powers. Finally, the enforced low tariffs and other privileges to foreigners combined with a social and economic system that stifled and penalized new forms of enterprise to help prevent rapid development from taking place.

Despite this relative stagnation there was, Issawi calculates, a twelvefold rise in the value of Iranian foreign trade in the period 1800–1914, an approximate doubling of Iran's population from about five million to ten million (both the trade and population rises are again much below Egypt and Turkey) and some important changes in the economic system. A study of the economic history of this period is therefore not devoid of interest both for its revelation of how one particular traditional economic system worked and how these workings were slowly changed under the Western impact.

Iran in the sixteenth and seventeenth centuries had reached relative heights of centralization and prosperity under the Safavid dynasty which ruled from 1501 to 1722. In this period agents from the chief Western Euopean mercantile countries opened trade relations with Iran, importing primarily silk and luxury items. The power of a central government has always been precarious in Iran, however, primarily for the geographic reasons mentioned above which encourage relative independence by tribal leaders and other local, vested interests. The Safavid central power rapidly declined in the late seventeenth and early eighteenth centuries, leaving the country easy prey to Afghan tribal invaders who devastated the capital of Isfahan in 1722. This invasion was followed by a period of struggles and civil wars, based primarily on tribal forces, which ruined the formerly flourishing economic life of the country and brought great suffering to the population. The externally glittering conquests of Nadir Shah, including his plunder of Mogul India, brought not riches but further exactions for the population, and his death left the country once more in anarchy, from which it was temporarily rescued by the short-lived but beloved Zand dynasty ruling from the southern city of Shiraz. The Zands were among the few rulers who tried to improve trade and the economic functioning of their territory. The Zands were overcome by another tribal dynasty, the Qajars, whose first ruler Agha Muhammad conquered Iran in battles between 1779 and his assassination in 1797. The Qajars were widely hated from the first and they had no ruler of outstanding ability. Nevertheless, their rescue of Iran from serious civil wars for over a century and the provision of relative internal peace and stability brought some recovery of the economy from the devastation of the eighteenth century and reduced the tribal raiding and brigandage that had added to that devastation.

The gradual change in world trade routes since the sixteenth century made Iran something of an international backwater by the eighteenth century. Nonetheless, with the Napoleonic wars Great Power interest in Iran revived quickly, and along with political interest there soon went concern with reviving trade.

Sir John Malcolm, sent by the East India Company on political missions to Iran in the early nineteenth century, has left the best account of the economic and social system of Iran in that period. Here his account of the tax system will be summarized. According to some sources Agha Muhammad Shah's successor, Fath Ali Shah (1791–1834), doubled the land tax from 10 per cent to 20 per cent of the produce, but Malcolm states that the actual tax varied from 5 per cent to 20 per cent depending on the water supply. He says that crown lands were rented by the peasantry for roughly half their produce. He notes a great increase in crown lands due both to the confiscation of *vaqfs* (inalienable religious lands) by Nadir Shah and to the disappearance of landowners in the civil wars preceding the rise of the Qajars. Malcolm states that the fixed revenues, mentioned above, were fair and moderate, but that people were continually exposed to irregular and oppressive taxes. Among these were usual and extraordinary presents which all high officials were forced to make on the Persian new year. In addition a present was always made on appointment to office, so that the office might be said to be bought. Most oppressive of all was the public requisition:

> If an addition is made to the army; if the king desires to construct an aqueduct, or build a palace; if troops are marching through the country, and require to be furnished with provisions; if a foreign mission arrives in Persia; if one of the royal family is married; or, in short, on any occurrence not ordinary, an impost is laid, sometimes upon the whole kingdom, and at other only on particular provinces.[2]

Malcolm estimated that the ordinary and extraordinary revenues amounted to about £3 million each, and that the extraordinary revenue in particular fell oppressively on the population. He noted that it was the custom to pay the principal officials, the royal household, and religious and other pensioners by assignments on the public revenue. He states that due to the public requisition peasants often had to sell their crops at a very low price while they were still in the ground. The shah hoarded a considerable portion of the national revenue.

The picture presented by Malcolm is supplemented by later sources, but it is striking how little conditions of taxation changed in the course of the nineteenth century. All sources agree that nearly all taxation fell directly or ultimately on the peasantry, with a smaller amount paid by the tribes and by the town artisans. Bureaucrats, landlords, the upper ulama, and merchants were largely exempt. The land tax was estimated by Curzon to amount to about 25 per cent of the produce on an average near the end of the century, a significant rise since Malcolm's time.[3] Villages, tribes, and city guilds were assessed as units, and it was the business of their officials to subdivide the assessment. In villages taxes, and especially the extraordinary taxes, often had to be collected by force, but they could almost never be avoided. Internal and foreign customs duties were further sources of revenues, and these were farmed out. The Treaty of Turkomanchai which ended a war with Russia in 1828 limited tariffs on Russian goods to 5 per cent *ad valorem*, and the same tariff was extended to other countries in later trade treaties. Foreigners were also exempted from the internal customs that Iranian merchants continued to have to pay. The government did not receive the full 5 per cent, as they farmed out the customs, and customs farmers often vied with one another to lower customs in their area even below this level so as to attract more trade to their own ports. Toward the late nineteenth century it was estimated that the government received no more than 2–3 per cent.[4]

Not only were irregular taxes standard and inequitably divided by officials, but even the regular revenue was based largely on increasingly obsolete assessments, so that it hit some districts much harder than others. There was no scientific reorganization of the revenue during the period under discussion, despite some abortive efforts by the reforming crown prince Abbas Mirza in Azerbaijan early in the century; by the equally reforming prime minister Amir Kabir in the mid-nineteenth century; and by Nasir al-Din Shah (1848–1896) later in the century.

As the century went on there appears to have been some change from the rather fixed presents from government officials noted by Malcolm to a situation which was almost an annual auction of office. The effect on the local peasant population can be imagined, as office was sought almost exclusively for the revenue it brought, and with the uncertain duration of office it was an almost universal practice to extort as much as possible as quickly as possible. Landlords often subfarmed their own lands – i.e., paid a fixed sum for taxes rather than subject their lands to the exactions of government agents. One source estimates that tax collectors took about three times as much as ultimately reached the government.[5]

As the shahs' and courtiers' tastes for foreign trips and luxuries increased in the late nineteenth and early twentieth centuries so did exactions on the peasants. Although Issawi believes it impossible to judge whether peasant conditions deteriorated in the course of the nineteenth century, travellers' and observers' reports suggest that they did – both Malcolm and James Fraser state that the peasants were rarely severely impoverished, whereas late nineteenth and early twentieth century reports often speak of them as such. This was partly due to landlord exactions, which increased with the rise of cash crops and of investment in land, but it was also due to extortionate taxes.

Despite the oppressiveness of the taxation system, the revenues that actually reached the central government were not large.

Nasir al-Din Shah at first appointed a reforming prime minister, Amir Kabir, who tried to eliminate the prevalent corruption and excesses in tax collection and introduce a regular system, which would have both benefited the peasantry and increased the revenues of the central government. This and other reform measures so antagonized the vested interests of the ruling classes at court, however, that they aroused the Shah's suspicions against his minister, whom he first dismissed and then had murdered.

Aside from the most elementary security measures taxation was not, throughout the period under discussion, used for public purposes and scarcely for self-strengthening. There were no roads at all in Iran until the very late nineteenth century, and those built then were almost entirely under concessions by the British and Russians for their own purposes. Bridges and caravanserais were rarely built, and then by private individuals. Individual charity was all the social security there was, while schools were built and run by the ulama. The Crown Prince Abbas Mirza made an attempt to modernize his army in Azerbaijan with European instructors early in the nineteenth century, but with his death in 1833 modernization of the army virtually died too, despite some abortive attempts late in the century. Only the Russian-officered Cossack Brigade founded in 1879 and centering in Tehran was an efficient force, and aside from that the shahs continued to rely mainly on tribal levies. The regular army was almost a farce, as officers bought their positions and appropriated their men's pay, while conscripted troops were generally neither drilled nor equipped but were permitted to make their living in ordinary trades in the towns and villages. Expenditures on education were miniscule, with one modern school, the Dar al-Funun at Tehran being the only one of Amir Kabir's reforms allowed to continue, to be joined by a very few other modern schools at the end of the nineteenth and beginning of the twentieth centuries. Revenues were spent mostly on the shah, the court, the bureaucracy, and pensions to princes, religious figures and others.

The public revenue and expenditure system thus presents a more retrograde picture under the Qajars than it did at the height of the Safavid dynasty, when efforts were made to promote trade and industry by the government.

Another aspect of the financial situation that was oppressive to the masses of the population was the rapid depreciation of the currency and the rise in prices throughout the century. Until the 1860s this was mainly due to the cutting of precious metals in the coinage, but after that it was even more owing to the world fall in the price of silver, the basis of Iran's coinage. This depreciation constituted a severe and indirect tax that hit the poor particularly, but it was also serious in its consequences for the Persian government itself, which kept raising its nominal revenues without its real revenues rising significantly. Issawi notes that the exchange value of Persian coinage fell to 1/5 or less of its 1800 exchange rate with the pound sterling by 1914. The rise in prices of basic foodstuffs in the late nineteenth century was even more dramatic, and was not equalled by the rise in wages. The depreciation of coinage continued in the late nineteenth century, as control of the mint was farmed out to the highest bidder, who naturally tried to recoup as much as possible through depreciation of the currency. Silver coinage increasingly disappeared from the market and debased copper coinage took its place. The export and hoarding of silver created serious shortages of currency for internal and international trade.[6]

Harmful to both the government and the peasantry was the fixed exchange rate by which the government agreed to convert taxes in kind to those in cash. As the value of Persian currency declined and agricultural prices rose, this brought increased income to landlords and meant that the government had to keep raising taxes just to maintain the same real income.

The period 1800–1914 saw increased private investment in land, the growth of large landownership, and of landlords' power over their peasants. Professor Lambton attributes these facts largely to the growing concentration of political, judicial, and economic power into the hands of landlords.[7] Other causes may, however, be cited – chief among them the economic impact of the West. This impact led to a new demand for cash crops, a new possibility of utilizing the largest possible agricultural surplus to buy Western luxuries, and to new income in the hands of some merchants, who were eager to join the profitable business of investment in land and to exploit it as efficiently as possible. At the same time the peasants, as Professor Lambton notes, were increasingly at the total mercy of their own landlord and hence frequently lost their ownership and other rights to the land. As the government's need for money grew, crown lands were more and more sold or sub-rented to new landlords who nearly always exploited them and their peasants more thoroughly and efficiently than had the government.

A study by Robert A. McDaniel notes that the fall in the value of silver and also in world prices of agricultural goods from 1873 to the mid-1890s were factors in the increased exploitation of peasants. The price of wheat on the world market fell from $1.50 a bushel in 1871 to $.23 in 1894, and though the amount of wheat exported from Bushire between 1869 and 1894 increased eight times, the value in terms of foreign exchange remained almost the same. According to the same study:

> In agriculture, the peasant was more tightly squeezed either by the tax collector or the landlord, or both. The long-range effect of this pressure was to cause a steady accumulation of the land in the hands of the powerful. Although there are no detailed studies of this phenomenon, the general trend of the period seems to indicate that the peasant proprietor could less and less stand on his own. He needed a friend at court. The 'friend' was usually a man who had political influence and used that influence to extend his landholdings. ...[8]

The rise in cash crops for export to Europe and the Far East, although less dramatic than in Mediterranean countries, was nonetheless significant, and is well covered by Issawi. Only increased production and exploitation could begin to pay for imports and make up for deteriorating terms of trade. There was a revival of silk cultivation in Gilan, in which capitalist relations increasingly entered, with speculators, chiefly Armenian, entering in to lend eggs and money to the landlords and peasants against the next crop. This profitable enterprise was devastated by the ruinous silkworm disease of the 1860s, from which it gradually recovered by the end of the century, only to face the competition of cheap Japanese silk, so that it never regained its former profits. Another major cash crop was opium, which had earlier been grown in small amounts, but from the mid-nineteenth century was encouraged especially by the British for export to the Far East. It was estimated to return three times as much revenue as wheat on the same land. The cultivation of opium on former wheat lands combined with a series of droughts to produce the terrible famine of 1871–72 in which estimates of deaths range as high as 10 per cent of the population or over. The opium habit also spread increasingly among the Persian population. Other important export crops were rice, cotton, tobacco, dried fruits and nuts. The export of wheat greatly raised its price in Iran. Cotton became Iran's chief export, responding primarily to the demands of the Russian market, and was encouraged by Russian cotton speculators who distributed improved cotton seeds in return for a lien on the crop.[9] In a few areas plantation methods were used for tea and other crops, but in general sharecropping continued to be the dominant method of exploitation.

Persian sharecropping was traditionally based on a consideration of who supplied each of five key factors of production – land, labor, water, seeds, and tools and oxen. The actual rents paid varied considerably despite these guidelines, however, and seem to have been based on providing the sharecropper with a minimum of subsistence. Nineteenth-century travellers' accounts tell of the reluctance of the peasant to adopt means that would increase his production because of his expectation that the entire surplus would go to the landlord or tax collector. The system thus discouraged initiative or modernization, and many of the gains that were made in cash crops appear to have been due to increased exploitation and the rise in population, although there were ways to induce peasants to grow more profitable cash crops. Despite the small percentage of Iranian land that was actually cultivated it was not simple to extend cultivation, as cultivation depended on irrigation, generally supplied by the expensive underwater aqueduct (*qanat*) system. Although Iran appeared underpopulated, there was in fact considerable emigration from Iran to areas of higher wages once opportunities opened up, and it is estimated that over 200,000 persons a year emigrated to Russia in the years before World War I (though many of these also returned).[10]

Peasant conditions differed in different parts of the country, with the peasants being most prosperous in the high rainfall areas of the Northwest, where some peasants paid a fixed cash rent and profited from any increase in production, and poorest in the dry and tribally populated Southeast. There was also the beginning of significant class differentiation of the peasantry, with a few peasants, especially village headmen, able to enter the class of small owners, while others fell to the status of casual day laborers. These trends were initiated by the introduction of capitalist relations on top of the former largely feudal ones.[11]

The government did very little to encourage agricultural production. Muhammad Shah's (1834–1848) prime minister Hajji Mirza Aqasi extended silk cultivation to Kerman, while the ubiquitous Amir Kabir helped bring dead lands into cultivation and repair irrigation works. After the mid-nineteenth century, however, the government hardly took any steps, except to lease out or sell crown lands.

As to the economic structure of the cities, it should be noted that these were the residences of the ruling classes – the chief government officials, the leading ulama, the landlords, the merchants, and even some of the tribal khans. These were the untaxed classes for whose consumption, as well as for the royal court, taxes were collected. The chief productive classes in the cities were the merchants and artisans, both of whom were organized into largely self-regulating guilds. The artisan guilds set up standards for production, established tests for becoming a master craftsman, regulated disputes among their members or between guilds, kept a treasury for their own social services, and apportioned taxes among their members. They also played a religious and social role. The merchants apparently paid no regular taxes, but only a rent on their bazaar offices, plus the road taxes involved in transporting goods from one city to another. Merchants were among the most respected classes in the community and, unlike their social superiors, were noted for their financial honesty, so that large sums and valuable goods would be entrusted to their care without any qualms. Merchants also played the role of bankers and moneylenders in the absence of a modern banking system, and often supplied money to the government and its representatives.

In the course of the nineteenth century most crafts and some merchants were severely hit by the progress of European trade. In the first half of the nineteenth century Great Britain rapidly entered the Persian market with cheap industrial goods, mostly textiles, which began to undermine Persian handicraft production. As early as 1836 the Shah tried fruitlessly to end the use of European cloth among his courtiers, and Issawi notes appeals from groups of craftsmen and merchants from 1837 on to the Shah to forbid European imports. Even had he wanted to do this, he was forbidden by the trade treaties he had signed with European powers. Late in the period there were renewed demands for boycotts on Western goods, some of which were successful.[12] The decline in handicrafts continued throughout the 1800–1914 period, and was only partially compensated for by the rise of European demand for Persian carpets which began to be an important export only in the last quarter of the nineteenth century. European firms systematized the production and export of carpets. The guilds suffered both from the decline of handicrafts and from the rise of the central government's judicial and administrative powers.

On the other hand some Persian merchants were able to take advantage of the new relations with Europe. Even though Persian merchants were at a severe disadvantage compared to European merchants because they had to pay internal customs duties which the Europeans did not, some managed through fair means or bribery to carry on both international and internal trade at a considerable profit. Some bought the protection of European consuls. Wealthy merchants and craftsmen were able to build up some relatively large manufactories to cater to domestic and international demand. Beginning in the 1880s there was also a development of Persian merchant companies combining several merchants, or representing a single wealthy merchant with manifold activities. The wealthiest merchant family was that of the Amin al-Zarb, or mint master, of Tehran who in addition to farming the mint controlled a network of internal and international merchant enterprises, with several offices abroad, which when he died in 1897 was inherited by his son, also known as the Amin al-Zarb.

Domestic and foreign efforts to set up modern industries were far less successful than were manufactories, primarily because of difficulties of transport and the impossibility of protective tariffs. Aside from some relatively successful gun and cannon foundries beginning with Abbas Mirza's work in the 1820s, almost no domestic industries were successful although numerous attempts were made. The Amir Kabir tried to set up several factories and sent Persians abroad to be trained for them, but his efforts were abortive as were almost all succeeding ones. At least one sugar factory failed because of Russian undercutting of prices.[13] Even European concessionaires did not do well with factories, although some gas and electric works did succeed. Iran had to await the 1930s before modern factories were seriously begun.

The situation in transport was scarcely better. The only railroad built in the period under discussion was a short line from Tehran to the nearby shrine of Shah Abdul Azim, built by a Belgian company which also brought horse-drawn trams to Tehran. The British succeeded in getting the Shah to open the Karun River to navigation as late as 1888, and a British and a Persian company made use of this. Late in the period the Russians got various road building concessions and built over 500 miles of roads, while the British also built some, but these were only a bare start towards an adequate road network. Animal pack remained by far the dominant mode of transport throughout the 1800–1914 period.

As for foreign trade, although it increased about twelvefold during the 1800–1914 period, the balance of trade became increasingly unfavorable to the Iranians. The period, like subsequent ones, brought a deterioration of the terms of trade as the price of Iranian raw materials fell relative to those of the manufactured goods that Iran chiefly imported. Added to the falling price of silver, this meant hardship for Iran, which must have been partially overcome by a rise in agricultural production. Real wages and salaries fell significantly in the last half of the nineteenth century.

Scarcely any source discusses the impact of the large-scale presence of nomadic tribes on the Iranian economy. Issawi estimates that the proportion of nomads in the 1800–1914 period fell from about one-half to about one-quarter of the total population. Given his estimate of a doubling of the population in this period, this would mean a static absolute number. In some important ways the nomads contributed to the economy, providing large numbers of sheep and goats with all their important by-products. On the other hand, the use for grazing of cultivable land and nomadic raiding of the peasantry, or exploitation of peasant villages, cut down on agricultural productivity, and it is difficult to judge which of these effects was the more significant.

The period 1800–1914 saw increased economic conflict between Iranians and Europeans, which eventually went from the economic into the political sphere. The rise in European trading companies in Iran, beginning with the Greek Ralli brothers in 1837, was looked on with jealousy by some Iranian traders, although others cooperated with or worked for

Europeans. European concessions beginning later in the century were similarly the occasion of mixed reactions. The first concession, for the Indo-European telegraph line, was generally regarded as helpful, and the spread of foreign and state controlled telegraphs increased the central government's control over the provinces. Later concessions were more a mixed story. The notorious Reuter concession, mentioned above, was negotiated with the help of two Iranian reforming ministers – Mirza Husayn Khan Sipahsalar-i A'zam and Malkum Khan. It met with Iranian hostility from the majority of informed opinion, however, which helped bring its cancellation. The British company navigating the Karun River also faced Iranian merchant opposition. So particularly did the British Imperial Bank of Persia, begun in 1889 as partial compensation for the cancelled Reuter concession, which was given exclusive rights of banknote issue. These rights annoyed Persian bankers, who had been accustomed to giving out their own bills of exchange and tried to continue to do so, but were forbidden to. The British (and the soon-founded Russian) banks' taking over of many loans also competed with Persian traditional bankers, and the latter organized runs on the British bank's specie, some of which came close to success.

The most dramatic economic conflict came with the concession of a monopoly over the purchase, production, and sale of all Iranian tobacco given to a British subject in 1890. Here the interests of Iranian tobacco growers and merchants were directly touched, and they played a prominent part in the nation-wide protest movement that brought about a cancellation of the concession early in 1892. There grew up a feeling among Iranians that their government was selling the resources of the country to foreign powers for petty personal profit, and this was a large factor in various protest movements that culminated in the constitutional revolution of 1905–1911. Interestingly at this time not much opposition was aroused by the later center of controversy – the oil concession to a British subject, D'Arcy, in 1901. This culminated in the only large-scale modern industry to be set up in Iran before World War I.

British and Russian merchants and their governments had a strong interest in promoting their own economic position in Iran, and this they did with considerable vigor. In the first half of the nineteenth century the British had the advantage, despite their distance from Iran, due to a relative lack of Russian industry or communications to Iran. With the growth of Russian industry and the building of the Transcaucasian and Transcaspian Railways in the 1870s and 1880s, however, the Russians gained the advantage, and Russian goods took over from British ones in northern and even parts of central Iran. It was in the late nineteenth and early twentieth centuries also that communications and transport concessions were given to the nationals of both powers, and the increased Russian and British economic and political power were felt to be galling by many Iranians. Russian rebates and bounties to manufacturers who exported to Iran meant that many Russian goods sold more cheaply there than in Russia itself, which made not only British but Iranian competition increasingly difficult. The Russian government vigorously promoted trade and concessions for political reasons, and the growth of Russian economic control was increasingly resented.[14]

Added to the feeling against foreign banks and concessions came that against foreign loans. Here again Iran entered the path of borrowing later than Turkey or Egypt, but Iran also used its loans less productively. The first foreign loan, for £500,000, was from England to pay the compensation demanded by the British tobacco company for its cancelled concession. Later much larger loans were made from Russia, primarily to pay for wasteful trips to Europe by Muzaffar al-Din Shah (1896–1907). Late in the nineteenth century also Belgians began to be hired to take over customs collection, which they did more efficiently than the Iranian customs farmers, but at greater expense to Iranian merchants, who were not slow to complain. Iran seemed to its merchants, artisans, and others to be falling more and more into the Russian and British economic and political grip, and the government appeared to be abetting this. It was, significantly, the beating of a merchant on the orders of the governor of Tehran in December, 1905, that set off the first demonstration of the constitutional revolution. Throughout that revolution merchants, including both the small and the wealthy, and artisans, played a leading role. Their interests were often voiced by the ulama, with whom the guilds and city dwellers had traditionally had close ties. Where traditionally a member of the ulama might intervene for an individual guildsman with the governmental authorities, now large numbers of the ulama helped express both their own and the merchants' anti-governmental and anti-foreign interests.

During the two parliaments that met in the course of the constitutional revolution there were significant reforms legislated in the economic sphere. Feudal land-holdings, or *tuyuls*, were abolished, taxes were regularized, an independent tax collecting gendarmerie was set up, a true national bank was voted for, pensions and sinecures were greatly cut, and a national budget was introduced for the first time. Unfortunately the parliaments had neither the military nor the financial means truly to enforce this legislation. The continued power of decentralizing forces was shown by the raiding of nomadic tribes and the reluctance of the provinces to send in taxes. When the American financial advisor, Morgan Shuster, tried to enforce the economic control of the central government over the whole country, the Russians accused him of ignoring the terms of their agreement with the British of 1907 dividing Iran into spheres of influence, and a Russian ultimatum, backed by the British, followed by a Russian invasion early in 1912 brought about the end of the revolution. The constitution it had provided remained, although henceforth it was more honored in the breach than the observance.

Merchant and artisan demands for a more independent national economy were partly met after the rise of Reza Shah to power beginning in 1921. During his twenty-year rule he built up a strong army and bureaucracy, reduced the power of tribal leaders, ulama, and independent landlords, gained tariff autonomy, and began significant work in communications and industry. This was all done at much cost to the common people, with a heavy burden of indirect taxation on items of mass consumption, but it laid the foundations for the current capitalist development of Iran.

However stagnant the period 1800–1914 may look in comparison to the half century that followed, there is no question but that the roots of later developments are to be found in the earlier period. The impact of the West on Iran's economy was already significant. The period brought Iran definitively into the international market, ending its former relative self-sufficiency and making it dependent on international trade. Some landlords began to produce for the world market and to feel the need for more efficient means of exploitation and transport. Some merchants were able to take advantage of new conditions to tie themselves to Western trade, while others were embittered against Western competition and sought to gain a greater measure of national independence. The power of the old ruling classes, with their heavy stake in decentralization and a weak central government was gradually undermined, as more and more Persians became aware that a new type of government was needed to keep Iran from being economically and politically swallowed up by the West. Economic changes during the 1800–1914 period followed by the disruption and famine brought by World War I form some of the basic causes of the Iranian political upheavals that characterized the period 1905–1925 and culminated in a dictatorial, centralizing, and modernizing government.

NOTES

1. See Nikki R. Keddie, *Religion and Rebellion in Iran: The Tobacco Protest of 1891–1892* (London: Frank Cass & Co., 1966); and Firuz Kazemzadeh, *Russia and Britain in Persia, 1864–1914: A Study in Imperialism* (New Haven: Yale University Press, 1968).
2. Sir John Malcolm, *The History of Persia, from the Most Early Period to the Present Time*, Vol. II (London, 1815), pp. 479–480.
3. George N. Curzon, *Persia and the Persian Question*, Vol. II (London, 1892, reprinted Frank Cass, London, 1966), p. 471.
4. Joseph Rabino, 'An Economist's Notes on Persia,' reprinted from the *Journal of the Royal Statistical Society*, LXIV, Pt. II (June 29, 1901), p. 4.
5. Muhammad Ali Jamalzadeh, *Ganj-e Shaygan* (Berlin, 1916–17), p. 122.
6. Rabino, *op. cit.*, p. 9.
7. A. K. S. Lambton, *Landlord and Peasant in Persia* (London: Oxford University Press, 1953), pp. 143–145.
8. Robert A. McDaniel, 'Economic Change and Economic Resiliency in 9th Century Persia,' *Iranian Studies*, Vol. IV, No. 1 (Winter, 1971), pp. 40–41.
9. *Ibid.*, p. 41.
10. Marvin L. Entner, *Russo-Persian Commercial Relations, 1828–1914* (Gainesville, Fla.: University of Florida Press, 1965), p. 60.
11. See Chapter 7.
12. Persian books and the British Foreign Office documents record some of these movements, particularly in Isfahan.
13. Jamalzadeh, *op. cit.*, pp. 99–100.
14. Entner, *op. cit.*; Kazemzadeh, *op. cit.*; and G. I. Ter-Gukasov, *Ekonomicheskie i politicheskie interesy Rossii v Persii* (St. Petersburg, 1916).

6

Iran, 1797–1941

Pre-modern Iranian society had what might be called an 'estates' type of class structure, with vertical ties within groups, such as tribes or *ulama*, having as much importance in many ways as horizontal class divisions. Society was also corporately organized, into guilds, urban wards and quarters, towns, villages, and tribes, with a rather diffused and decentralized total structure for the country as a whole. The story of modernization, on one level, has been the story of the creation of modern classes – the urban bourgeoisie, the proletariat, a class-stratified peasantry, a large bureaucracy, the army, and a professional and intellectual class. Some of these groups are still internally stratified to a significant degree, but there are more clearcut horizontal divisions and less vertical corporate life than there was in the traditional past. Two dates may be taken as crucial for the transformation from traditional to modern: the constitutional revolution of 1905–1911 which expressed overwhelming mass desire for the end of traditional forms of misrule and passed measures outlawing feudal property and taxation practices, and the coup d'état of 1921, which laid the groundwork for undermining tribal and *ulama* power and building a modern state, with an army, bureaucracy, and modernization programme. There had, of course, been quantitative changes in class relations before 1905, but it was only in 1921 that major qualitative changes really began.

In traditional Persian society one may speak either of an internally divided ruling class, or of several (chiefly four) ruling classes, with some overlap but other clearcut distinctions. First, there was the higher governmental administration, headed by the

137

shah, a variable number of ministers with somewhat varying functions, provincial governors and their ministers, and a rudimentary bureaucracy. Under the Qajars (1797–1925) many of the provincial governorships were in the hands of the royal family, and the governorship of the richest and most important province, Azerbaijan, was reserved for the crown prince. These governors, particularly the crown prince, were generally assisted by ministers, who were often the real rulers. Royal and non-royal governors had to give annual 'presents' for their offices, and by the late nineteenth century this was almost an annual auction of governorships, with the higher bidder generally receiving the post. The governors generally subfarmed the lower offices, and the net effect was to favour those who could fleece the most out of the common people in the shortest time. It has been estimated that many times as much in taxes may have been collected from the people as actually reached the central treasury. In mitigation of this is the fact that many governmental figures bought their offices rather than being paid for them; if they had been paid, more taxes would have been collected by the centre but more would also have been paid out in their salaries. Nonetheless, regularity in taxes and payment of civil servants is generally a less oppressive system for the masses than is sale of office and taxfarming.

Aside from the royal family, the governmental class was made up of local and tribal notables, who often bought office in their own area and, on the lower level, men of some education and polish who had enough pull or contact with the court to be brought into governmental service. Some of these men rose from within the royal household. Thus the reforming mid-century prime minister Amir Kabir had a father who was a royal steward; while the father of the powerful late century prime minister, Amin as-Sultan, was a royal water-carrier. Governmental bureaucrats below the highest level tended to be looked down upon by landlords and tribal leaders in the early nineteenth century, but as office made men wealthy by opening up all sorts of licit and illicit (or shady) avenues to wealth, governmental men tended to buy land and merge with the landlord class, and hence to become more accepted by them. On the other hand the government, particularly that of the Qajars, was generally regarded as oppressive and extortionate, and governmental men had relatively low prestige, especially considering their high *de facto* power. (When I was in Iran in 1959–60 I asked a large number of septuagenarians and octogenarians, 'When you were a little boy, what did you want to be when you grew up?' A large majority said, 'a great *mujtahid*,' or something similar. Not one said he wanted to be in the government, even though none of these men became *mujtahids* and many of them had held governmental positions.) Among the group questioned, at least, it was clearly *mujtahids*, and not governmental men, who were admired and formed role-models.

At the apex of the governmental class stood the shah. Theoretically absolute except for the limits placed on his power by the *shari'a*, the shah was surrounded by elaborate pomp and ceremonial, and supported by an absolutist ideology that declared him to be the shadow of God – *zill Allah* – on earth. He was essentially free to execute anyone he chose and to pardon anyone he chose – to choose anyone for government office, to set taxes, and fully to control foreign and domestic policy. There was no clear distinction between governmental and royal income, and the Qajar shahs who appropriated the crown jewels and expropriated properties at their accession were able to add greatly to their fortune in land and treasure in the nineteenth century. The *de facto* powers of the shahs were not as great as their *de jure* powers, however. They lacked a modern centralized standing army, despite abortive efforts to form one under crown prince Abbas Mirza early in the nineteenth century, prime minister Amir Kabir in mid-century, and prime minister Mirza Husain Khan in the 1870s. The army remained largely a paper organization whose pay was appropriated by its officers, while the men were esentially untrained and scarcely armed, and had to make their living at various trades in the towns. The shahs had to count mostly on unreliable and not totally loyal tribal levies, aside from the small Russian-officered Cossack Brigade begun in 1879. This situation, plus the lack of roads or any quick means of transport, meant that the shah was in no position to enforce his will on the tribes when they proved recalcitrant, nor to interfere in the details of people's lives. The despotism of the shah was felt by most people quite indirectly – chiefly through high and irregular taxes which were collected at several removes from any specific royal order.

Iranian despotism, like most traditional despotisms, should thus be distinguished from modern dictatorships. The latter tend to be more rational and less capricious, but they are also far more despotic, primarily because they have the tools to be so. The Qajar ruling group, from the shahs on down, seem to have been out primarily for money; at each level they thus did what was needed to maximize cash income. For the shah this was to sell offices as dearly as possible; to expropriate properties of the deceased or disloyal; to maximize tax income; and to rent or sell crown lands. Lower officials similarly got as much as they could from their subordinates, until the common people, who paid nearly all the taxes, were reached and fleeced. Outside the realms of taxes and law enforcement, however, the rulers might interfere relatively little with people's lives, although the rulers' and government men's own capricious lawlessness made them widely hated by the population.

Outside the directly governing class, although overlapping with it to some degree, were three ruling class groups – the leading tribal families, the leaders of the *ulama*, and large landlords. The first two were in a kind of corporate relationship with a lower group – the tribal chiefs with ordinary tribesmen and women, and the upper with the lower *mullas*. Ever since the Islamic conquest, and particularly since the Turkish tribal invasions that first became significant in the eleventh century, nomadic tribes have made up an extremely important element in Iranian society. Nearly all the dynasties that ruled Iran from the eleventh to the twentieth centuries have been tribal in origin, and even the Safavids (1501–1722), who originated in a Sufi order, not a tribe, came to power due to tribal military forces. The tribes have had a profound impact on the nature of Iranian social structure and development. With the growth in the tribal element of the Iranian population, beginning in the eleventh century, there was a rapid spread of military-feudal forms of landholding, in which large holdings were given over tax free by the government in return for military or other service. The Iranian shahs ruled to some degree like tribal *khans*, with a kind of segmentary divide-and-rule policy used to control subordinates in the absence of significant state power. It might be possible to dub the Iranian polity from the eleventh through the nineteenth century as one of 'tribal feudalism' – a system which had a feudal type of service fief, even if it lacked a feudal hierarchy – but was strongly coloured by powerful and essentially autonomous tribal enclaves within the polity.

Iran's tribal population has been estimated at half the total population at the beginning of the nineteenth century, and one quarter at its end – in a period when Iran's population approximately doubled from about five million to about ten million. The tribal leaders were generally both powerful and wealthy, but their relation to their tribesmen was rather different from that of the shah or a governor to his subjects. The necessities of the tribal economy involve a kind of rough democracy that is not at all a necessary feature of village life. The central feature of tribal life is the twice yearly migration, which must generally be undertaken in rather small camping groups. These groups must be self-sufficient, and must make their own decisions about when to start and when and where to stop each day. In addition to this type of self-sufficiency, tribal life necessitates a minimum level of capital, in the form of flocks, which must be maintained by each household if it is to continue to migrate. Once a family's flocks fall below this limit, they cannot feed themselves without selling or killing animals. Thus begins a vicious downward spiral that, barring outside help, ends when the tribesman is forced to leave his tribe and enter the bottom rungs of agriculture. This means that minimum subsistence for a tribesman, unlike a peasant, involves possession of considerable capital. A tribal leader, although he may take tribute from his tribesmen, is and was unlikely to push them to the wall. The tribe, or confederation of tribes, is a kind of corporate entity with considerable self-reliance at the lowest levels and a hierarchy of leadership, including often councils of elders, and members of the chiefly family, in which no individual wields despotic power. Some of the wealth of tribal chiefs goes for hospitality in which all tribesmen (and sometimes women) can participate.

Tribal leaders often had interests outside the tribe. They might be local governors or government officials, and might purchase land outside the tribal area. As time went on more and more of the tribal ruling families became city dwellers, who spent less and less time with their tribes. The ruling families were able to accumulate much or most of the economic surplus produced by the tribe, but they generally did this less capriciously and extortionately than non-tribal tax collectors. The tribes were usually able to keep government men out of their territory by paying a lump sum tax, after which the government was too prudent to try to push a claim for further interference. The military power of the tribes, with their mounted men who soon acquired rifles, made them hard for the government to interfere with, especially since the rulers had to conciliate them in order to utilize that military power.

Not only were men more equal in the tribe, but women were more equal to men in the tribes than outside them. Tribeswomen went unveiled (as did many village women), rode horses, shared in much of the work of the tribe, and often managed their husbands' affairs when the latter were away.

The tribe, then, was a virtually autonomous community, internally stratified, but generally lacking either extreme poverty or capricious despotism. All its members from chief to shepherd boy were engaged in essentially the same enterprise – the raising of flocks and sale or use of their products – and all tended to feel an identification with the tribe, and there is and was not the same alienation from tribal government that there was from the central government. Tribal chiefs wielded a large potential force because of the armed men at their command, but they were never able to unite together against the centre.

The next ruling class sector, and in many ways the most important one, were the leaders of the Shi'i *ulama* – chiefly the *mujtahids*, the *qadis*, and the government-appointed *shaikh al-islams* and *imam jum'ahs* of the main cities. In Twelver Shi'i Islam, unlike Sunnism, the door of *ijtihad* (endeavour in the interpretation of law and doctrine) was never closed, and Shi'i law can still be interpreted by those qualified to do so by education and popular esteem – the *mujtahids*. The Iranian *ulama* had far more independent power that the *ulama* of Sunni countries, for several reasons. (1) Since the eighteenth century the leading Iranian *ulama* lived in the Shi'i shrine cities in Ottoman Iraq, outside Iran's borders and beyond the influence of the shahs and their followers. Here the Shi'i *ulama* had endowments and income sufficient to support large numbers, and were quite independent of the Iranian government. Nearly all leading *ulama* who did reside in Iran were educated in Iraq and retained ideological and other ties there. (2) The Shi'i *ulama*, unlike the Sunni, were direct recipients of the *khums* tax, which was quite large. (3) According to Twelver Shi'i theory all temporal governments are illegitimate, and the theory grew up within Twelver Shi'ism that, pending the return of the Twelfth, Hidden Imam, his infallible will is best to be interpreted by well-qualified though fallible *mujtahids*. Since the Imam's authority extends to political as well as religious matters, the *mujtahids'* interpretations have superior force to the rulings of any temporal government, and it is the *mujtahids*, rather than the shahs, whose rulings should be followed. This theory was somewhat in abeyance under the Safavids, who had forged a descent from one of the Imams, and who retained a religious aura, but the theory came forth with full force under the Qajars, who had no such descent or aura. There were thus two competing ruling class ideologies – the strict Shi'i one which saw temporal rulers as illegitimate, and the governmental one which saw the shah as deriving absolute powers from God. (4) The *ulama* were not arranged into a government-appointed hierarchy, or even an *ulama*-appointed hierarchy. Rather, they often reached high positions of respect through a combination of education, ability, and popularity. A *mujtahid* could achieve his status only if he had a high level of popularity and following. This, together with the family ties of the *ulama* to the guilds, helped make the *mujtahids* representatives of public opinion and grievances. It was only the *ulama* who could voice popular grievances with impunity, and they did so with increasing frequency in the Qajar period.

There were, in a sense, two hierarchies of *ulama* in Iran. One was the one discussed above, and the other was the government-appointed one, including chiefly the *shaykh al-Islam* and *imam jum'ah*, or head of the Friday mosque, in each major city. Without question, however, the popularly recognized *mujtahids* enjoyed far more influence than the government-appointed functionaries, and it was widely believed that government appointment or connections tainted a religious leader.

As Twelver Shi'i theory developed, it emphasized that people must seek guidance from a living *mujtahid* and could not rely on the rulings of a dead one. This put an extraordinary power in the hands of living *mujtahids*, who became essentially legislators, or a kind of 'supreme court' interpreting Islamic legislation, for their own followers. In many cities, notably Isfahan in the late nineteenth century, the power of the *mujtahids* to arouse the population and bring pressure was such that the secular authorities often had to give way to their will. The *ulama* controlled religious law, virtually all education, and the administration of vast *waqf* properties. Many of the *ulama* and *sayyids* were paid pensions by the government, and in the course of the Qajar period their private and *waqf* wealth grew greatly. Many of them were large landowners, and this concentration of property in *ulama* hands increased through the Qajar period. The *ulama* formed a corporative sub-society whose leaders were increasingly in contact with each other, and whose followers included lower mullas, religious students, and much of the general population. Like some landlords and urban leaders the *ulama* leaders often had what amounted to private armies, made up particularly of religious students, who could cause disturbances and terrorize the government, particularly when they were joined by popular crowds.

Entry into the ranks of the *ulama* was one of the chief avenues of social mobility in Iran since, in theory at least, membership in the *ulama* class was not determined by birth but by learning. No studies have shown how much mobility actually occurred, but some broad generalizations may be essayed. First, straight nepotism through the inheritance of *ulama* office was much rarer in Iran than in the Ottoman Empire, and, in the popular hierarchy at least, a man had to display genuine learning before he was accepted as a leader. Second, the sons of the *ulama* had a headstart in the kind of family atmosphere and learning that would be conducive to success, and sons of respected fathers found it easier to attract respect than did newcomers. Third, a boy from a really poor family would find difficulty in supporting himself through the many years of education required for a thorough training for an *ulama* position. Nonetheless, some of them did make it. More frequent was success for the son of a bourgeois family.

Virtually unstudied in the West has been the informal hierarchy of women *mullas*, some of whom achieved enough education to command the knowledge necessary to be a *mujtahid*. These women were trained to meet the religious needs of Iranian women, for whom they conducted religious services, including recitations of the events of the martyrdom of the great Imam Husain. They formed an educated elite among women, made their own living, and moved about in many women's quarters with more freedom than most other women. There even developed full-scale women's passion plays, centering on the death of Husain, in which women took the men's parts, just as men took the women's parts in the male passion plays. Like tribal leaders and male *mullas*, women *mullas* continue to exist and play an important role.

The *ulama*, with their role as a widely-followed hierarchy largely independent of governmental control, became leaders of various minor and major protest movements in the Qajar period. The *ulama* and their followers were largely responsible for pushing the government into a disastrous second nineteenth-century war with Russia in 1826. As the century wore on the *ulama* became more and more concerned with the growth of foreign, infidel influence, and secondarily with governmental oppression. After a number of minor incidents expressing this concern, the *ulama* became the leaders of a major mass movement against a royal monopoly granted to a British subject, for the purchase, sale, and export of tobacco, given in 1890. This movement culminated in a ruling by the chief *mujtahid*, living in Iraq, that (pending cancellation of the concession) the smoking of tobacco was against the will of the Hidden Imam. The boycott was universally observed, even by non-Muslims and the shah's wives, and this, combined with the mass demonstrations that took place in the major cities, caused the cancellation of the concession early in 1892. Some *ulama* also played a leadership role in the constitutional revolution of 1905–1911, although they battled in the *majlis*, or assembly, against such proposals as equality of all religions before the law and the setting up of modern law courts. Others, seeing that constitutional parliamentarism was going to undercut their power, turned against the revolution, particularly in the city of Tabriz, where radicals and democrats had considerable power. Nevertheless, the role of the *ulama* as an anti-governmental class with popular ties appears in this unique participation by leaders of a traditional religion in a modernizing constitutional revolution.

With all that has been said above, it should not be imagined that the *ulama* were immune from corruption and venality, and were universally popular. They were popular as compared to the government, but many of them were after money and/or power more than anything else, and the *ulama* as a class were frequently regarded as oppressive, dishonest, and selfish. There were some honourable and ascetic *mullas*, such as the great Shaikh Hadi Najmabadi who lived in Tehran in the late nineteenth century and was ascetic, generous, enlightened, and uncorruptible; but his type was the exception and not the rule. There is no doubt that among the attractions of the *ulama* career line was the possible wealth and power it represented.

The fourth segment of the ruling class were the landlords. Unlike the tribal leaders and the *ulama*, they did not have a large band of devoted followers below them nor, unlike the *ulama* and the government, had they an ideology or any kind of national cohesion. Unless they were in the central government, then, their power tended to be local and individual. They almost lived in the cities, where they were often prominent in local affairs, and so their regional power could be both urban and rural. Within the villages as the nineteenth century wore on they gained more and more absolute judicial and other powers, rather than having these powers diminished by central government encroachments as in many other countries. This made the peasants more and more their subjects, and made them increasingly feudal patrimonial rulers.

Through the Qajar period large landownership grew, and new mercantile and governmental figures entered the landowning class. As the international market for Iranian products like cotton and opium grew the landlords, particularly the new men among them, exploited their land and peasants more thoroughly, and became richer. Landed wealth was sought as being secure, respectable, and profitable by most people who gained sufficient money. Landownership was a source of status as well as wealth and power. In turn those with landed wealth often sought government service, at least for one member of the family, partly in order to protect and increase their wealth. Various features of the taxation system, especially before the constitutional revolution, were very favourable to the landlords; and their role and power is suggested by the fact that the government did not try to change these features until they were partially reformed during the revolution. Government service, income from *ulama* positions and tribal leadership frequently led to landownership. Governmental confiscations and the division of property among the heirs in large families could cause landed fortunes to decline – as they might rise – relatively quickly.

Next to the above four ruling class groups in power, wealth, and prestige were the urban middle classes. Urban society had a partially autonomous structure, with the chief officials being named by the shah, who nearly always followed local public opinion. Towns were administered by *kalantars*, or mayors, assisted by a *muhtasib*, or market inspector with numerous public duties, and by heads of quarters, or *kadkhudas*. Most townsmen were organized into partially self-governing guilds, which were organized by occupation and trade, and which chose their own leadership. The guilds carried out functions demanded by the government, however, especially collecting tax from their members. The wealthiest and most respected townsmen, aside from those who belonged to the ruling class groups, were the long-distance merchants, who enjoyed a position of high status and trust. Stories are told of Iranians entrusting large amounts of specie or goods to merchants without even getting a receipt for them, and they appear to be the one class whose honesty at this level was believed in. The government frequently had to borrow from merchants, who often doubled as moneylenders and money changers in the absence of modern banking facilities before 1889. As elsewhere in the Muslim world, tricks and expedients were found to get around the Muslim prohibition on lending at interest.

The guilds were informally recognized as falling into a rough hierarchy in accordance with the lucrativeness and prestige of the occupation represented. The guilds had their own rules for becoming a master – only the two ranks of apprentice and master were generally recognized. The guilds regulated the crafts internally and kept down the number of master craftsmen. They had educational, religious, social, and tax collecting functions. The government also regulated prices, which sometimes made it unpopular, as in the incident in December, 1905, when the governor of Tehran bastinadoed several sugar merchants for raising the price of sugar and the resultant mass protest was the first event of the constitutional revolution. Urban crafts generally declined under the impact of Western competition.

The merchants were generally very lightly taxed by the government and the guildsmen were not too heavily taxed either.

Other urban classes of significance were the *lutis*, or armed popular toughs, and the servants and retainers of various magnates, including the shah. Conspicuous consumption encouraged very large retinues of retainers and servants – far beyond actual service needs – and these people formed a class loyal to their masters in times of difficulty. The shah's retainers formed a loyal royalist class during the constitutional revolution, and to a degree also the lower class tended to support the royalist cause as against the bourgeois and petty bourgeois guildsmen.

On the bottom of the economic scale were beggars – secular and religious – and paupers of various kinds.

Patronage and clientship were widespread relationships in traditional Iran, not only between employer and employee but between protector and client. The shah and high government employees were able to distribute jobs, money, and other forms of patronage, and even men of considerable independent wealth and power might seek the patronage and protection of the more powerful and wealthy. So there existed a number of overlapping formal and informal hierarchies which helped organize society in the absence of an all-pervasive central government.

In the countryside the overwhelming majority of villagers were cultivating peasants, who were the most heavily taxed and impoverished group in society. Some travellers' accounts suggest a possible decline in average peasant living standards during the Qajar period, and it can also be suggested that there was a strong beginning of class stratification within the peasantry as market agriculture grew. With the growth of commercialized agriculture merchants and moneylenders bought up or foreclosed land from peasants, and at the end of the Qajar period, a large proportion of the peasant class was landless. The peasants, like many other classes, were internally stratified; on top were peasants who owned adequate plots or rented them for fixed cash rents (the latter a very small group, found chiefly in the prosperous northwest). Below these were sharecroppers who had a fixed right to cultivate a subsistence plot of land – the plots might be changed by rotation, but the right usually remained. Below them were sharecroppers on plots too small for subsistence, or those who paid so high a share that they could not make ends meet, and also labourers, some of whom had fixed work, and others of whom were hired by the day in peak seasons. With many agriculturalists falling below the subsistence level rural migration to the towns was a growing phenomenon.

The peasant was under the virtually complete control of the landlord, who had judicial and administrative as well as economic powers over him. There were no written contracts between landlord and tenant, and a recalcitrant tenant could be evicted or deprived of his right to work a share of the land. The relative overpopulation of villages left the tenant without any bargaining strength, since men to work the land could easily be found. The village headman, or *kadkhuda*, was a landlord appointee, as were other village officials. There was very little autonomous organization within the village, and peasants tended to be politically apathetic, except for some parts of the more advanced and prosperous northern provinces of Gilan and Azerbaijan.

Merchants, money-lenders, and the top-level peasants could profit from Western demand, but the Western impact, as mediated through Iranian landlords and middlemen, did not help the majority of the peasantry. The situation was similar in the towns, where some merchants and the craftsmen in industries like carpets (Western demand for which grew rapidly from about 1875 onward) profited, but the majority of craftspeople found their livelihoods undermined by the competition of cheap Western goods. In those areas where there was demand, the Western impact encouraged the growth of larger manufactories than had existed before, as, for instance, carpet manufacture. It also promoted industries in several areas. Thus again in the carpet industry, looms, wool, and patterns would be provided for persons to work in their own homes, and they would be given a low wage for their work.

Qajar society thus presents a complex picture of social stratification. Outside of the class groups discussed above, mention should be made of two other groups that are not classes, but have a separate social identity – women and minorities.

Women ran the gamut from tribal women, who were unveiled and mixed relatively freely with men, to the members of an urban harem who went out only heavily veiled. Village women fell between the two. Women made up sub-societies whose members were in contact with each other, and who had their own religious and cultural life, including women *mullas*. Women could organize enough so that they had urban bread riots fairly frequently, and during the constitutional revolution there were several demonstrations by women, at least one women's *anjuman*, or revolutionary club, which started a school for girls, and there was a women's newspaper published by women in Tehran. For all these signs of independence and political interest, the position of women was clearly a second class one. As in other Muslim countries, the husband ruled in marriage, and he was able to divorce by simple declaration, whereas divorce was almost impossible for the wife. Girl children were made to feel their inferiority to boys, and urban women were kept strictly confined behind the veil. Remunerative labour was generally closed to women above the lowest levels. Polygamy existed, and there was also the Shi'i custom of temporary marriage whereby a woman could be married for a fixed term. When performed for short periods in return for money this was essentially legitimized prostitution.

Interestingly two break-off groups from Islam had a higher position for women. The Ahl-i Haqq, also known as the Ali Ilahis, did not believe in the veiling of women, and Ahl-i Haqq women went unveiled behind closed doors and participated with men in their ceremonies. The Babis and successor Baha'is also gave women a higher role and had them participate in joint religious ceremonies. But these groups were execrated by pious Muslims, over whom they had little influence.

The minorities had clearly second class status in Iran, and among the minorities only the Armenian Christians had been a prosperous community before the Western impact. Armenians were heavily represented in the crafts, in mercantile life, and in the diplomatic service. The Zoroastrians and the Jews were generally impoverished and poorly educated communities whose life began to improve dramatically in the nineteenth century. The Indian Parsis sent aid to Iran's Zoroastrians, helping them to build schools and otherwise advance themselves, while French and other European Jews similarly aided Iranian Jews. Several American and European missionary groups occupied themselves with the Nestorian Christians of Northwestern Iran and helped improve their economic and educational status. Apostasy from Islam was a crime, theoretically punishable by death, and this inhibited missionary efforts among Muslims and made them concentrate on Christians. Babis and Baha'is were considered to be guilty of apostasy and generally had to keep their beliefs a secret. These communities were increasingly well educated and often prosperous, and they formed a westernizing element in Iranian society. A relatively high proportion of Christians came also to be employed by Westerners, and this gave them an opportunity to advance themselves, though it might also have increased their unpopularity, and identification as Western agents.

As the nineteenth and early twentieth century progressed, the traditional class structure was gradually undermined by the effects of the Western impact. The commercialization of agriculture and the growth of foreign trade gave new opportunities to certain merchants, craftsmen, peasants and landlords, but on the other hand these helped impoverish other lower class peasants and craftsmen in threatened occupations as well as providing competition for many merchants and bankers. A small class of intellectuals with a modern education or modern ideas also grew up in the late Qajar period.

Both the tobacco protest of 1891–92, which resulted in the cancellation of a British monopoly tobacco concession, and the constitutional revolution of 1905–1911, which gave Iran its current constitution, were supported mainly by the merchants and artisans, a large section of the *ulama*, and the small but influential group of intellectuals with modern ideas. There was also considerable mass popular support in the cities from lower classes, although this was not universal. The two parliaments (*majlis*) of the revolutionary period passed measures, which, had they been fully carried out, would have initiated a significant modernization of the social structure. However, the *majlis* was dissolved, and succeeding governments, despite their constitutional form, had very little freedom of action and abandoned significant reform efforts. Feudal and Bakhtiari tribal leaders had made their way into the constitutional government, and they found it easy to work under conservative Russian tutelage.

World War I was disruptive. After the war there was serious and deadly famine in much of Iran. At the same time there was a great increase in middle class, intellectual, and mass nationalism, spear-headed by the war and, in its radical forms, by the Bolshevik revolution. The immediate post-war years also saw local uprisings with varying degrees of mass following and of radicalism – in Azerbaijan, in Khorasan, and especially in Gilan. In addition tribes in various areas were proving difficult to control, and there were many both in Iran and in the West who would have welcomed a strong government to put down these various movements.

Early in 1921 there occurred a coup d'état led by a colonel of the Cossack Brigade, Reza Khan, who became Minister of War, and a former influential journalist with ties to the British, Sayyid Zia al-Din Tabataba'i, who became prime minister. After his move for a republic on the Turkish model failed due to *ulama* opposition, Reza Khan had the last Qajar, Ahmad Shah, deposed and himself enthroned as the founder of a new dynasty, the Pahlavis, in 1925.

The policies of Reza Shah between 1921–1941 changed the social structure of Iran considerably, accomplishing much of what is often associated with bourgeois revolutions. In this case it was done from the top, although with support of bourgeois and intellectual groups. In the course of these years, two of the formerly powerful classes – tribal and *ulama* leaders – were greatly weakened, although they generally retained considerable wealth. Another major class, the landlords, was changed considerably in composition but generally retained their local power and wealth, and were often strong at the centre through ties to the government. A powerful bureaucracy was created, with greatly increased numbers and a degree of modernization, while the army, and secondarily the national gendarmerie and local police were modernized, enlarged, and given far more power and prestige than before. Businessmen and professionals developed in significant numbers for the first time. The first significant changes in women's status also occurred. Some more details are in order.

Regarding the nomadic tribes, who had been causing the central government trouble for several years, and whom many regarded as archaic and outmoded, Reza Shah's policy was first to put down tribal movements that refused to recognize the authority of the centre, then to disarm and settle some of the tribes, moving militarily against those who resisted. The rationale for disarmament is clear; but forced settlement of a group, when adequate agricultural land or year-round pasture in a single spot was lacking, often caused hardship. With the abdication of Reza Shah in 1941 many tribes went back to migrating, and many continue to do so today. They remain, however, disarmed, and the control of the government in taxation and other matters of concern to the centre is effectively enforced.

With the *ulama* the policy was not so clear-cut and simple, and the Shah did not launch the all-out attack on religious law and instruction undertaken by his admired Atatürk. He did attack the *ulama* violently when they preached against any of his measures, including the unveiling of women. He also undermined their positions in law and education. His measures in law and education were not undertaken primarily in order to weaken the *ulama*, but that was a desired secondary result. They were aimed at the modernization and self-strengthening of Iran, which they accomplished, whatever their weaknesses.

Since domestic capital was attracted mainly to well-known and profitable sources of income such as land, old style trade, and money-lending, and since industry tended to require much capital and be slow in returns, it was difficult to find private investors for the new industries the government desired, and hence most new plants were built primarily with government capital. The emphasis was at first on light to medium industry, such as food processing and textile plants, and Reza Shah's dream of a steel mill was interrupted by the war and his abdication.

By and large, the poor were not economic beneficiaries of Reza Shah's regime, although some benefited from the literacy training they got in the army or elsewhere. No serious steps were taken in the countryside, where the great majority of the poor lived, to reform tenure or tenancy or limit the share of the crop that went to landlords. The membership of the landlord class changed somewhat through favouritism but no basic changes occurred affecting either the landholders' class or the landholding pattern. It seems probable that the concentration of landlord power increased under Reza Shah. Legal and economic forces favoured the continued buying up of villages by landlords and the loss of land by indebted peasants. The growth in population, the settlement of nomads on the limited available arable land, and the increase in regressive taxes, have suggested to several observers that the condition of peasants and of settled nomads was worse at the end of the Reza Shah period than at its beginning. Little mechanization was begun, and there were only the bare beginnings of scientific agriculture – difficult to enforce in a primarily share-cropping culture where the peasant fears that a bigger crop will only result in bigger demands on him. The Qajar period had already shown that the old sharecropping structure, with some modification in the direction of increased social stratification in the village, could meet the elementary needs of commercial agriculture.

The new privileged groups in society were the army and the bureaucracy. Reza Shah saw in a powerful army the crucial instrument to ward off foreign control and suppress internal unrest. Several high army officers achieved a position of wealth, power, and influence. Even lower officers and enlisted men or gendarmes were generally privileged in comparison to their former class position, and everything possible was done to insure the loyalty of these men.

As for the bureaucracy, it both grew and became modernized with considerable rapidity. The former use of unspecialized officials who often bought their offices and brought along their retainers was increasingly abandoned in favour of somewhat educated and trained personnel, fulfilling definite bureaucratic functions. Although corruption, favouritism, passing the buck to the top, and wasting time continued to be problems, to which the problem of top-heavy over-centralization in Tehran was now added, there is no question but that the bureaucracy gradually grew in competency as it rapidly increased in size. Overcentralization has been one of the besetting evils of the Pahlavi period. As the power of local landlords, *ulama*, tribal leaders, and guilds was weakened, nearly all power came to be concentrated in Tehran, where all important political and economic decisions were (and generally still are) taken. At the same time other cities, provinces, and corporate groups lost much of their former importance.

Among the new classes below the ruling groups may be put the newly educated professional and intellectual classes, including teachers and professors, lawyers, doctors, and a small group of writers, journalists, and artists. Although behind their Western counterparts in many ways, they were a necessary force in modernizing their country. Although the business class continued to be numerically dominated by bazaar merchants, the growth of industry in the 'thirties brought forth some private entrepreneurs, particularly in light industries. The number of merchants involved in international trade increased significantly. In general the internal order and improved transport brought about under Reza Shah were favourable to trade and business and encouraged their growth.

Another result of the growth in business was the creation of an industrial working class of significant proportions for the first time. The largest single group of workers was found in the enclave controlled by the Anglo-Persian Oil Company, which had struck oil in 1908. Despite certain Company welfare efforts, workers' grievances were considerable, and broke out in strikes after world war II. Under Reza Shah strikes and independent trade unions were outlawed and minimum labour standards, although legislated, were not always met.

As for other social groups, women, partly due to the pressure of women's groups as well as government action, began to be emancipated in the Reza Shah period. Public education for girls on all levels was begun, women began to hold a limited range of lower-level professional jobs, chiefly as teachers and nurses, and in 1936 Reza Shah did what no other government has yet done (except some recent Communist ones) – he outlawed both the facial veil and the all-enveloping dark *chadur* that went with it. Gendarmes would tear these off woman in the streets, and some traditional women scarcely went outside. Although the law remained on the books, it was not enforced after Reza Shah's abdication in 1941.

There were only scant additions to women's legal rights under Reza Shah, since marriage and family law, including polygamy up to four regular wives and any number of temporary wives (a special provision of Shi'i law) continued to be religious law. A husband could veto his wife's working and could kill her and/or her lover with impunity if he caught them – a law which remains on the books. The wife had no reciprocal right. In practice polygamy, particularly of the multiwoman variety conjured up by the word 'harem', went out of fashion among the upper and educated classes with the end of the Qajar dynasty, and it had never been the predominant form of marriage among lower classes.

The life of lower class women probably changed little – until today they continue to work very hard in agriculture and among the tribes, a contribution masked by censuses that rarely record this work. In addition women worked and work in factories and workshops, and also in the home, where they are chiefly involved in difficult handicrafts and carpets. Both women's and children's work has tended to be very low paid, despite the high skill it involves, although in very recent years pay has improved somewhat and efforts have been made to enforce the law outlawing child labour under age twelve. These efforts seem largely successful in public workshops, but many children still work on carpets at home in villages, and this will be difficult to stop until universal education is achieved and cuts down the daytime hours available for work.*

* * * * * *

The rule of Reza Shah thus saw considerable economic and social achievements, accomplished partly at the expense of the lower classes. Traditional 'decentralizing' classes and groups were weakened and the army, bureaucracy, and monarchy strengthened. There was considerable modernization from above. These trends continued from 1953 to 1977.

Without discussing in detail the social aspects of the reign of Mohammad Reza Shah, 1941–1979, one may say that it saw continued efforts at centralization of the economy and of control over nearly all social groups based on rising oil income and ties to Western powers, especially the United States whose government helped bring the Shah back to power after the Mosaddeq period 1951–53. A continued growth in the bureaucracy, in the army,

* The paragraphs that follow have been added in order to provide a conclusion.

and in the production and import of goods and services catering to the Westernized middle and upper classes strengthened classes that generally supported the Shah, but also increased the growing gap between the 'two cultures' – the Westernized middle and upper classes on the one hand and the 'traditional' bazaar and religious classes and subproletarian urban migrants from the countryside on the other. The various stages of land reform and encouragement of large mechanized agriculture left most peasants poor and subject to a huge migration to overcrowded cities – a process which, like other processes increasing the income gap between rich and poor, sped up after the great oil income increase that began in 1974. As inflation, shortages, urban overcrowding, and other economic and social problems grew, so too did organized opposition to the regime in several forms: student strikes and protests; urban guerilla action by Marxist and religious radical groups; petitions and open letters of protest by intellectuals and professionals beginning in 1977; and the mass religious-led movements of 1978–79. Although not all the opposition followed the ideology of the ulama leaders, the latters' relative impunity and the respect in which they were held by the masses made them ideal leaders for a victorious opposition, and intellectuals and other Westernized classes were willing for a time to subordinate their doubts and differences to a common revolutionary effort.

7

Stratification, Social Control, and
Capitalism in Iranian Villages:
Before and After Land Reform

INTRODUCTION

The 'City Feudalism' of the Middle East and much of Asia (so designated because the major landlords lived in cities) is sometimes cited as one of the reasons modern capitalism did not develop indigenously in these areas. In many studies, stress has been put on the lack of independent municipal communes in Asia and on the stifling economic effects of landlord domination of the cities. However, recent research indicates that the agricultural sector was perhaps more important than the urban one in causing strikingly different rates of economic change in different parts of the world.

The manorial system of Western Europe and Japan, and the high productivity of agriculture in these areas of heavy soils and rainfall, seem to have produced an increasing agricultural surplus. In both Europe and Japan, men with rural origins played a key role in the development of modern capitalism. In the arid Middle East, however, agricultural production seems to have shown a general decline over many centuries, due in part to deforestation, soil erosion, changes in the water table, and the salinization of irrigated lands. There appear to have been no major agricultural improvements in the area for centuries preceding recent imports from the West. Perhaps improvement was more difficult in the Middle East than in the West — such an important European innovation as the heavy wheeled plow is useless on most of the soils of the Middle East. One may also suspect that the residence of landlords in the cities and the vulnerability of the villages to pillaging by nomads, conquerors, and brigands were obstacles to

158

the accumulation of a surplus or to heavy investment in the countryside. Investment was confined to such things as the traditional irrigation networks, which were essential to maintaining a minimum productive level; the countryside continued to provide a surplus for the cities, receiving almost nothing in return.[1] With neither the capital nor the incentive to raise production, the peasantry remained conservative in its ways, not generating an innovating gentry or bourgeoisie.

The most serious natural limitation on agricultural production is lack of water, which can be met by sinking deep wells and by large-scale irrigation efforts. Due to the lack of such efforts, not only is there much more potentially cultivable land than is in use in any one year, but in most areas yields on cropped land have been among the lowest in the world. However important they may have been, natural limitations have been less responsible than structural ones for the continuation of poor peasant conditions and low productivity in modern Iran. With a different agrarian structure, comparatively simple improvements might turn Iran into a land of agricultural surplus.

PRE-TWENTIETH CENTURY CONDITIONS

Until the mid-nineteenth century, Iran had a social system which might be termed 'tribal feudalism,' although a phrase encompassing both tribal and upper-class urban dominance of the countryside would be better. Beginning in the eleventh century A.D., a large proportion of landholdings were under essentially feudal land grants, based on governmental, religious, or military service. The conduct of war was largely in the hands of tribal leaders, who held some of these grants, and feudal dues and services were demanded of the peasantry, the main productive class. Iranian feudalism differed from Western feudalism in the following respects: the lack of feudal contracts and of serfdom; the residence of Iranian ruling classes in the cities rather than on manors; the prevalence of nomadic tribes, leading to frequent wars and destructive raids; and the importance of water control and irrigation. For various reasons, related to differences in climate and social structure between the Middle East and the West, there was no indigenous evolution of capitalism in Iran, no agricultural or industrial revolution. When Western powers showed their first strong concern with Iran in the early nineteenth century, Iran had barely recovered from a period of breakdown during which tribal rivalries and wars had reduced the country to a state of anarchy.

Although the periods of anarchy and war were hard on the peasants, in periods of peace before the mid-nineteenth century the peasants were apparently better off than they were subsequently (although they probably never attained anything like a level of comfort). That the period of Western impact has seen a worsening of peasant conditions, and not simply a maintenance of traditional standards, is suggested by comparing Western travelers' reports before the mid-nineteenth century with later conditions. Jean Chardin, an observant and thorough reporter on seventeenth-century Iran, spoke of the comfortable standards of Iranian peasants, which he compared favorably with those of the West (Chardin 1811, p. 391). As late as 1833 another perceptive observer, the Englishman James Fraser, similarly noted high peasant standards.[2]

> The cultivators of the soil ... are those on whom the tyranny of their rulers falls the most heavily. Yet their houses are comfortable and neat, and are seldom found without a supply of good wheaten cakes, some mast or sour milk, and cheese – often fruit makes its appearance, and sometimes a preparation of meat, in soup or pilau. Their wives and children, as well as themselves, are sufficiently though coarsely clad; and if a guest arrives, there are few who cannot display a numed or felt carpet in a room for his reception. In fact, the high rate of wages proves that the profits of agriculture are high, while food is cheap; and we may be satisfied that in spite of rapacity, enforced by torture, no small share of the gain is hoarded by the farmer. (Fraser 1833, p. 204)

Even allowing for possible exaggeration, it is difficult to imagine such a description of peasant conditions being made in the mid-twentieth century. Since the late nineteenth century, eyewitness descriptions show most peasants living on the bare edge of subsistence, with the poorest kind of food and lodging. The best recent study of Iranian agrarian history, Lambton's *Landlord and Peasant in Persia*, also points out that the condition of the peasantry was better in the early nineteenth century than it was later (Lambton 1953, pp. 143–45).[3]

Why the Western impact encouraged large landholdings and a

decline in peasant standards is a question that has not been studied thoroughly, but an attempt can be made here to summarize the outlines of an answer. In general, landlords and leaders of nomadic or seminomadic tribes took advantage of economic changes brought by Western contacts to enhance their position, and new groups were encouraged to invest in large estates run for profit.

Already in the second half of the nineteenth century a reinforcement of landlord power may be noted beneath the apparently static facade. In this period the central government was in constant and acute need of money, partly in order to buy Western goods, including arms to defend itself. This need encouraged the systematization of the sale of offices.[4] Local governorships were sold to the highest bidder every year, so that governors were most concerned with raising enough taxes to keep up their bids and make a good income. The governors also recruited lower officials on the basis of promised monetary returns. Since officials at all levels retained a profit from collected taxes, the peasants were forced to support an increasingly oppressive official hierarchy, whose main duty, in turn, was to fleece them.

Nineteenth-century wars with European powers put a strain on the central government, which weakened its control over tribal areas and over some of the areas given out as feudal land grants. This meant a loss of tax revenue from these areas, as some landlords and tribal khans pocketed all the local revenue, and the government had to raise taxes or insist on higher bids for governorships elsewhere. Peasants in the area freed from central control did not profit, since landlords raised their rents and dues to equal the increased government taxes. When the central government in the 1920s reestablished firm control over tribal leaders and independent landlords and set up an efficient paid bureaucracy and army, the pattern of high rents and taxes was continued.

The late nineteenth and early twentieth centuries saw the inauguration of a number of economic trends that have continued until today. The government began to ask for cash taxes; to pay these the peasant had to sell his crops at artificially low exchange rates, often giving profits to middlemen who could resell the grain on the open market elsewhere (Mochaver 1937, p. 161). Then as now, the peasant had to sell grain immediately after the harvest, or even pledge his crop before the harvest, and often had to repurchase grain in the season of high prices to keep himself and his family fed.

Western influence brought a gradual development of modern private property in place of the various forms of feudal tenure that had previously existed. Traditionally, both peasants and landlords might have had certain rights to a given area without either being considered absolute owner. Now, rights of peasants and nomadic commoners to certain areas or flocks began to be abrogated, as the wealthy used their superior power to assert absolute property rights on the Western model. Feudal dues on the peasants were not removed, and although individual peasants could not be sold as serfs, whole villages were freely sold, with implied rights to the labor of their inhabitants.

Loss of land by the peasants took place not only through such expropriation, but also through the new use of land to secure loans. The government's preference for cash taxes and the landlords' increasing demands led to the growth of moneylending to peasants. The peasant often had to borrow for food or implements, and inability to repay sometimes meant loss of land. Unpaid debts could also tie the peasant to a landlord's property, since landlord and moneylender were often one and the same.

The Western impact favored investment in land and a more thorough exploitation of it than had been traditional in Iran. Foreign demand for certain crops turned parts of Iran into areas of specialized raw material production, dependent on the foreign market. Opium, for example, began to be cultivated widely after the decline in silk production in the 1860s. The English encouraged the growth of opium, which they transported and sold in the Far East. Much opium was also consumed in Iran once its cultivation became widespread. In the North, cotton became a specialty because of Russian demand. As had happened in Eastern Europe in previous centuries, landlord income and power increased with the growth of a profitable Western market for agricultural goods. The sale of crown lands in the late nineteenth century resulted in more intensive exploitation of the peasants than had been traditional.

Another continuing trend which began in the late nineteenth century was the replacement of some Iranian handicrafts by

Western manufactured goods. In certain areas, peasants, nomads, and city artisans gradually lost the employment and income that home industries had provided. Unlike the West, Iran did not compensate for the decline in handicrafts by developing manufacturing industries which could provide both employment and capital growth. Although some handicrafts, notably carpets, were actually in greater demand than before, due to Western interest, the general trend was in the opposite direction, particularly in articles of mass consumption, such as textiles. The former almost self-sufficient village economy was undermined, without any satisfactory modern replacement being created.

The drain on Iran's economy caused by its dependent economic relation to the West is indicated, in the best available figures, by the fact that in the late nineteenth century Iran exported a volume of raw materials five times larger than the volume of finished goods it imported, and paid three times more for its imports than it received for its exports (Kia 1937, pp. 87–8). The increasingly adverse trade balance was ultimately paid for primarily by exploitation of the agriculturalists.

Certain groups benefited directly or indirectly from the Western impact. Among these were many landlords, who strengthened their hold on the land and peasants and who profited if they owned land producing goods for export. Various middlemen, moneylenders, traders, and lower officials also found new opportunities of enrichment, sometimes leading to landownership, and a small proportion of the peasants profited by lending tools and goods to others. Social stratification among peasants seems to have increased in market-oriented areas, where some peasants profited from the new demand for agricultural raw materials and opportunities for entrepreneurial efforts.

The traditional ruling classes generally increased their local political power as well as their economic position in the nineteenth century. There was an end to an earlier relative division of functions between landownership and the administration of law and taxes. Local administration and judicial processes increasingly became the monopoly of the same men who owned villages and received feudal dues. Village headmen and other local officials were appointed by the landlords, and the peasants rarely had recourse to any outside authority (Lambton 1953, p. 143).

The Western impact not only indirectly increased the power of old landlords but also added new families to their ranks. The growth of trade with the West brought an increase in the merchant class, and merchants invested in land. Land became freely alienable as buyers increased, the shahs sold state land to meet fiscal needs, and some money-lenders, village headmen, and prosperous peasants also succeeded in becoming landlords after their wealth increased. In the relatively prosperous Northwest, even tenants who owned oxen or rented sizable tracts could profit from the growth of a market economy.

The Western impact at the same time that it helped the wealthier groups, and by the very fact of doing so, also helped to create a largely destitute peasantry. During the late nineteenth and early twentieth centuries traditional land rights were abrogated, and the growth of a market economy enabled landlords, moneylenders, and a few peasants to enrich themselves at the expense of the peasant majority. This result seems to have been particularly pronounced in villages accessible to the influence of the government or its feudatories or tax-farmers:

> Everything in Persia depends on whether a village is brought into direct intercourse with the Government or not. In the more retired valleys, where grasping khans do not penetrate, fertility and contentment reign, but if the Shah or the Governor of a province cannot pay inferior officers they give them a village or villages to do their worst with, and woe to the village thus given – nobody therein can call anything his own. (Bent 1891, p. 366)

In addition to worsening the conditions of the peasant in Iran, the impact of the West also undermined a number of traditional Iranian institutions – the monarchy, feudal armies, self-sufficient local economies – and encouraged the formation of more modern ideas, groups, institutions, and economic changes. The struggle between modernizing groups and the traditional ruling classes makes up much of the history of twentieth-century Iran. This history is not easy to summarize, since in every major situation there have been Iranian leaders with one foot in each world – men who have a limited interest in reform for purposes of efficiency, modernization, or lessening popular discontent, but who also have economic ties to the old system of landownership. Such men include some leaders of the Persian Revolution of 1905–1911, Reza Shah (1925–1941), and some moderate reformers who back Muhammad Reza Shah (1941–   ). Western powers have shown a similar ambivalence toward agrarian and other reforms, and have usually desired increases in productivity and economic efficiency without the development of a government or economy strong enough to limit Western prerogatives in Iran. Without an attempt to unwind all the threads in the story of Iranian efforts for social reform, its main outlines and relevance to the current agrarian situation will be summarized below.[5]

THE REVOLUTION OF 1905–1911

The growth of modernizing groups and ideas was demonstrated in the constitutional Revolution of 1905–1911. This was the first attempt to break with the immediate past and to reconstruct Iran partly on the basis of concepts derived from the West, although a religious revivalist element was also important. The Revolution provided Iran with a constitution, still in force, and an elected legislature. Although landed tribal and religious leaders with grievances against the Shah helped lead the Revolution, it was notable for the participation of the new city intellectuals and the urban middle and lower classes. There was also a peasant movement in a few areas in the North, expressed in refusals to pay rent and taxes and in raids on the landlords' storehouses.[6]

Under popular pressure, the revolutionary legislature passed a number of reforms, the most important of which from the agrarian point of view were in the revenue system. These were mostly directed at the power and privileges of the top feudal group, which paid no taxes and often profited from government favor but was virtually independent of government control. The *majlis* (parliament) declared taxes universal and outlawed the following outstanding abuses: (1) large pensions and sinecures to relatives of the Shah and hangers-on of the court; (2) the retention by local governors of the surplus of what they collected above what they were asked to collect, i.e., tax-farming; and (3) feudal land grants. The court budget was limited and separated from the national budget (Mochaver 1937, p. 215). On paper this was an impressive group of reforms, and might have gone far to weaken abuses had the new government been able to put it into effect. However, efforts to implement a sound financial program failed.

AGRARIAN CONDITIONS 1914–1941

The First World War had a devastating effect on Iran. The country was used as a battlefield by the Turks, Germans, British, and Russians; many Iranians were killed, and invading armies ruined agricultural areas. Peasants were taken from the fields and forced to work on military roads and other war projects. Irrigation works, which required careful upkeep, were destroyed in many areas, and the number of livestock and total cultivated area decreased. Other countries were similarly hurt, but in some Asian cases, such as India and China, the War also stimulated industrial and urban development; however in Iran it caused a fall in urban enterprise and population. The central government became weaker in the war period, and local landowners and tribal khans rebuilt local armed forces and reasserted powers of feudal control (Razi 1957, p. 286).[7]

The Russian revolution removed Russian forces from Iran. The British tried to create a virtual protectorate, but were stopped by Iranian nationalist and American hostility. The War and post-war crisis gave rise to nationalist, reform, and radical movements, but these differed in goals and lacked nationwide organization.

A *coup d'état* in 1921 put down radical movements which had taken power in the North. The strong man of the new government had himself declared monarch, under the name of Reza Shah, in 1925. The new regime was supported by those who wanted to build a strong and efficient nation without undermining the economic position of the landlords or the middle classes. As summarized by one scholar, the rule of Reza Shah meant a change in power from a tribal-feudal group to a middle class-intellectual-(new) landlord coalition. The regime 'initiated a policy of disfavor to tribal leaders, peasants, urban lower classes, and the clergy; and of favor to intellectuals, the urban and semi-urban middle class, and landowners' (Razi 1957, p. 297).

The necessity for some economic and social reform merely to retain national independence and unity was clear to Reza Shah and his followers. Economic life was stagnant, social structure was essentially the same as before the War, and in relation to the West, Iran was more backward than ever. In 1926 an observer noted:

In its social and economic structure, there can be no doubt that

Persia is one of the most backward countries in the world. Except Tibet, Afghanistan, and Abyssinia, no other organized nation presents quite the same spectacle of medievalism ... Practical serfdom still exists, education is extremely restricted, and does not extend even to all of the upper class; there has been no beginning of industrial development ... (Sheean 1927, pp. 231–32)

The suppression of the post-war popular movements and the institution of a centralized government with strong police power to put down lower-class discontent discouraged agrarian reform in the 1920s. Without reform, agriculture recovered very slowly from the wartime decrease in production, which was not overcome until after 1925.

In the 1920s, however, the growth of westernized groups and of demands for fundamental change encouraged Reza Shah to launch an impressive program of reform and modernization outside the agricultural sphere. Modernized law codes, improvements in transportation and communication, and the end of tariff limits and other treaty privileges for foreigners laid the basis for industrial development in Iran.

In the agricultural sphere, on the other hand, Reza Shah relied on the support of old and new landlords and made himself the largest landlord in Iran. Many of his measures strengthened the position of the landed group. For example, the government passed a law declaring any village which had been in the continuous possession of one man for thirty years to be his private property. This, in effect, legalized expropriations accomplished since the mid-nineteenth century. In some areas there was still a feudal division of ownership. This law, plus laws of 1928 and 1929 requiring registration of property, supported claims to land by the rich and powerful over those peasants and tribesmen previously considered as having some rights of possession on the land they worked. The wealthy were able to register land to which peasants had old titles, since the upper classes had influence in the courts and bureaucracy and could make their viewpoint prevail (Lambton 1953, p. 297). The land registration laws were a step to modernization accomplished at the expense of the peasants.

The Civil Code of 1928, still not altered despite its incompatibility with recent land reforms, also strengthened the position of the landlords. Like the registration Laws, the Civil

Code recognized *de facto* possession as proof of ownership rights, and helped confirm acts of usurpation. The Code had no provisions protecting the peasants or insuring them of any minimum share of the crops, and the section of the Code dealing with crop-sharing agreements was weighted in favor of the landlords. Tenants were legally liable for keeping harvests at a certain level and for carrying out the terms of sharcropping agreements, regardless of obstacles. The Code assumed a written contract between landlord and tenant, but did not require such a contract. Generally, there were no contracts, and the tenant had to comply with the landlord's interpretation of an informal oral agreement. According to Lambton:

> It will ... be clear that very little attention is paid by the Civil Code (or any other body of legislation) to the regulation of the relation of landlord and tenant. In general the scales are weighted in favor of the former and little or no protection is afforded to the latter. (1953, p. 209)

The only agricultural laws of the 1920s which encouraged modernization were the exemption of agricultural machinery imports from customs duties and of industrial crops from taxes. These laws favored the development of large-scale capitalist farming, but, in fact, few mechanized or unified farms were begun. The old system continued to be highly profitable, since labor was extremely cheap. The exemption of certain areas from land taxes did not help the peasants who, not being owners, were no longer directly responsible for these taxes.

From 1930 on, Reza Shah launched a program of industrialization which gave the country its first modern factories and railroad. His programs of army modernization and educational and social reform continued in the 1930s. Yet, despite some impressive economic achievements, the position of the great majority of the population that lived off the land did not improve, and the social structure of the countryside remained much as before. The industrialization program itself was limited by the lack of an expanding national market, and it provided only a bare beginning toward overcoming Iranian backwardness.

The key to Iranian backwardness remained agrarian conditions, which encouraged low productivity, medieval methods, and investment in land and usury. A study of Iranian agriculture made in 1934 shows an increase of traditional evils, with the government supporting, rather than reforming, the old system. According to this detailed work, based on observation and primary sources, large landlords having several villages owned about one-half the land (estimates for the 1950s are usually higher, suggesting the continuation until recently of forces leading to concentration of landownership) (Sandjabi 1934, p. 138).

There were several methods of exploitation of the land, all of which have continued to the present. Direct peasant proprietorship was rare, and found mainly on marginal lands. Even peasant owners were under the thumb of the local landlord, and their economic position and agricultural methods were quite similar to those of tenants. Middle proprietors owning 'only' one village were usually descendants of headmen and other rich peasants and nomads. Even when they lived in the village, these proprietors put only 5 to 10 per cent of their land under direct cultivation with hired help and improved tools. The majority of the land of middle and large proprietors was sharecropped by tenants. Sharecropping contracts were nearly always verbal, unclear, and designed to keep the tenant from accumulating any surplus (ibid., pp. 143–62).

In a few relatively prosperous areas in the North there was another system of exploitation, according to which the peasant paid a fixed rent. This allowed the peasant to accumulate some surplus and was opposed by landlords. Much more prevalent, and continually growing, was renting by an intermediary. This consists of a short-term contract by a renter, often of the middle class, from a landlord. The renter then subcontracts to the peasants. This system is a logical result of the increased holdings for which the landlord could not be directly responsible. Over half the total land was estimated to be rented this way, including most of the state and *vaqf* land (ibid., pp. 169–73).[8] Renting hurt cultivation, since it encouraged high profits on a short-term basis and discouraged any investment or improvements. Renters generally treated peasants worse than did landlords, who had some interest in their remaining alive and active over a long period.

By the 1930s the peasant village in Iran was a purely agricultural unit. The peasants usually worked for one landlord, and the land was periodically redistributed in most areas, so that peasants had no permanent stake in any plot. The work of the tenants was under the constant supervision of landlord-appointed agents. The village headman, who had once represented the villagers to some degree, was now a landlord appointee, as was the official in charge of water distribution (*ibid.*, pp. 183–88).

Iranian tradition based the crop division on five factors – land, labor, water, seed, and animals – with the provider of each to get one-fifth of the crop. In practice, the weight allowed to each factor varied. The peasant's share varied from one-fifth to seven-eighths of the crop, depending on where he lived and what he supplied. The peasant was also subject to feudal dues, to state taxes, and to a share in the pay of local officials, so that his final portion was meager.

Peasant conditions were bad throughout the Iranian plateau, but they were much worse in the South and East than in the North and West. Housing and health conditions were primitive and unsanitary, bread and rice were the only staple foods, and peasants were usually hungry. Landlords had *de facto* control over the peasants' lives. Settlement of the nomads, carried out by Reza Shah, often reduced them to the economic level of the peasants.

No agrarian reforms were attempted in the 1930s, although a few technical improvements were made. When the government realized that the state lands were bringing in little income, they were put on the market in 1934, but on terms which only large proprietors could afford. A relatively painless way to inaugurate land reform through the sale of state land to peasants on easy terms was thus avoided (*ibid.*, p. 110; and Esfandiary 1945, p. 45).

A law in 1935 stated that the village headmen were the landlords' representatives and were responsible for law and order in the villages. No provision was made for peasant participation in village administration. A gesture toward increasing low agricultural productivity was made by a 1937 law making landlords responsible for proper cultivation of their estates, by Iranian standards, on pain of confiscation for neglect. Landlord opposition prevented this law from being put into effect and the rules for enforcing it were never drawn up (Lambton 1953, pp. 190, 193).

In 1937, in the province of Sistan an attempt at land reform was made through the sale of state lands to peasants. So many complaints came from the peasants about landlords flouting the law that Reza Shah set up investigating commissions, but these took no action to ensure that peasants got the land. Instead, landlords and government officials were able to use their power to take over the state lands. Through various forms of pressure, such as withholding needed water from the land, many peasants were expropriated, and productivity and living standards fell. Peasants in Sistan who retained their land, however, said in the mid-1950s that, bad as their lot was, it was still better than it had been before they became owners (*ibid.*, p. 252).

The only agricultural reforms carried out were aimed at increasing productivity. A 1937 law encouraged the improvement of badly cultivated land and wasteland through agricultural loans. A few agricultural schools and experimental stations were founded. These measures had minimal results, and in 1940 an ambitious Five Year Plan for agriculture, whose aim was to raise productivity substantially, was launched. The plan was interrupted by the War, but the record of the 1930s makes it seem doubtful that it could otherwise have reached its aims.

The lack of agrarian reform under Reza Shah made thorough modernization and economic improvement impossible. Landlords and merchants had little incentive to invest in modern enterprises when moneylending and exploitation of land and peasants continued to be so profitable. Improvement in agricultural methods and productivity were unlikely to occur as long as the peasant lived on the edge of subsistence and labor was so cheap that the landlord had no desire to replace it by machinery. Some measures by Reza Shah actually lowered the living standards of the peasants. Among these were high taxes and import duties on articles of mass consumption, the forcible settlement of nomads, and the encouragement of large landed estates, particularly in the hands of the Shah himself. In the depression years the peasants were especially hard hit, as prices of the agricultural goods they sold fell more than the prices of the manufactured goods they bought (Bank Melli Iran 1934, pp. 2–4). The peasants gained no protection against dispossession or arbitrary raises in rent and remained without economic rights. The extension of police and army control, which enabled rapid suppression of any movement for better conditions, helped keep down the economic and political status of the peasants. The growth of landlordism and declining agricultural standards were the clay feet of the whole modernization program of Reza Shah.

Modernization in both city and countryside was held back by the persistence of the old social and economic structure in agriculture. Although the Reza Shah program registered some impressive achievements and increased the number of prosperous people by adding to the army, bureaucracy, middle classes, and intellectuals, it also increased the gap between these groups and the agricultural mass of the population. According to one examination of Reza Shah's program, its costs meant that 'by the time of the outbreak of World War II, the economic position of the average Iranian was considerably and chronically worse than it had been in 1925' (Cooke 1952, p. 238).

AGRARIAN CONDITIONS 1941–1962

The anomalous and economically harmful state of agrarian relations became more acute after 1941, when Reza Shah abdicated and the Anglo-Russian occupation began. World War II put another severe strain on the Iranian economy and brought a new rise in nationalist and reform movements, with revolutionary attempts, including agrarian reforms in some areas. As after World War I, the situation led to a politically conservative, Western-supported government which repressed its enemies on the left while promising, and to some extent producing, economic reforms.

Many of the trends discussed above continued in the post-war period. Wartime inflation and scarcities meant further loss of land and growing debt. Discussing the typical peasant in post-war Iran, Lyle J. Hayden wrote:

> Hosayn does not, of course, own any land himself, and since he has no money to buy land, irrigation water, seeds, food, or even his house, he must borrow from the village owner and return a percentage of what he raises. (1949, p. 143)

The main economic burdens on the peasant are debts, rents, and taxes, and these burdens have tended to increase until recently. The processes leading to peasant indebtedness are well described by Lambton:

The peasant performs all the operations concerned with the production and disposal of his crops himself. ... His need almost always forces him to take the price offered however disadvantageous it may be.

Inadequate communications and costly means of transport greatly add to his costs of production and make it difficult for him to do anything but sell his goods at the nearest market at whatever price is offered. The almost permanent state of need and the series of temporary crises which are the normal concomitant of peasant life force him to dispose of his produce immediately after harvest, if it is not already pledged before. This means that he has no alternative but to sell or barter his surplus crops at the period when prices are lowest ... he then has to buy when prices are at their peak.

It is thus not surprising that debt should be one of the curses of Persian rural life. (1953, pp. 379–80)

A peasant proprietor was almost always forced to borrow money for seeds, tools, livestock, and other current expenses. The tenant, paying exorbitant rents, was also forced to borrow in order to feed himself and his family. High interest rates and low peasant income made it difficult for the peasant ever to repay the principal on such loans. These high rates not only impoverished the peasants, but lured capital from productive ventures and directed it toward the economically parasitical field of moneylending. The fact that investors, including landlords, often turned to unproductive uses of their funds does not necessarily mean that they were following traditional cultural values irrationally. On the contrary, any rational calculation of returns within a private enterprise framework would normally lead *any* investor to do the same.

In many cases the peasant borrowed from his own landlord. This led to further loss of peasant land due to inability to repay, and to perpetual indebtedness which tied the peasant to a single area. Thus tenants were often in a state of peonage. As the American advisory group, Overseas Consultants, Inc., pointed out, 'The villages and, for all practical purposes, the peasants are the property of the landlords, most of whom live in the larger cities or even abroad' (1949, vol. 2, p. 8).

The post-war growth of large landholdings increased the kind of middleman renter operations described for the 1930s. Renters and subcontractors, forming a nonproductive hierarchy over the peasants, took over more of the agricultural surplus, without doing anything to increase productivity. Renting and usury remained most profitable occupations for those in the middle class who did not have enough capital to become landlords. Even landless sharecroppers with oxen increasingly subfarmed their shares to laborers or sharecroppers who supplied only labor, while the original sharecropper generally supplied animals and tools, and the landlord land and water.

Until the mid-1950s the lack of capital investment in agriculture resulted in a decline in irrigation and hence of cultivable land in many areas, increasing population pressure and peasant dependence on the good will of the landlord or his agent. Not only was there insufficient annually cropped land for the agricultural population, but low yields compounded the problem. Despite high migration to the cities, a growing number of villagers were reduced to the ranks of landless laborers.

With the growth of mechanization of dry-farmed areas in the 1950s and 60s, population pressure on the land has increased in some areas. In Iran machinery has chiefly benefited landlords, and hurt peasants who have often been evicted, although large tracts of marginal land brought under machine cultivation have provided some new employment for laborers (*ibid.*, vol. 3, p. 13; Vreeland 1957, p. 154; and especially Okazaki 1968). Recent studies have shown that rich and powerful men close to the court have used their positions to purchase the state lands that have been sold, supposedly to benefit the peasants. The continuation of a regressive system of primarily indirect taxation has further increased the burdens on the peasantry.

Profiting from this agrarian situation has been a whole galaxy of middlemen, overseers, village headmen, rich peasants, tax officials, and moneylenders. The most direct beneficiaries of the exploitation of the peasants and tribal peoples have been large landlords and tribal khans. (The composition of the large landlord group changed significantly after World War I, since Reza Shah confiscated the lands of those old families who refused cooperation.) New groups of merchants, contractors, bureaucrats, army officers, and village officials bought up land from the 1920s through the 1950s, and became a new landlord class. The new landlords were reputed to treat their peasants worse than the old families, and to seek short-term profit at the expense of land and peasant.

Most landlords continued to be absentees, concerned with receiving the maximum profit without any investment after the original land purchase. Coercion and dishonesty in elections in the past insured landlord control of the *majlis*, and the purchase of land by government leaders and army officers reinforced the ties between landownership and political power.

Since the War there have been various attempts at reform, including notably the Shah's sale of (disputed) crown lands to some of the peasants working them,[9] and the law under Mosaddeq raising the peasant's share of the crop. The most important reforms were those begun in January 1962, which required landlords to sell land above 'one village,' excluding several categories such as mechanized farms, to the government, which in turn would sell them to certain of the cultivators. These reforms will be discussed later.

SOCIAL STRATIFICATION AND AGRARIAN REFORM

Several informative studies made in recent years have underlined the magnitude of problems faced by any land reform program in Iran. They have especially emphasized problems linked to the stratified structure of agrarian society. One such study, whose results have not been published, was done in 1954 by a three-man team (two Americans and one Iranian) under the auspices of the Iranian Ministry of Agriculture and the Ford Foundation. Since the reasons for its non-publication no longer exist, it seems useful to publish results of this study, tabulated from its data sheets.[10]

The sample survey's purpose is indicated by its title: 'A Reconnaissance Survey to Determine the Possibilities of a More Equitable Distribution of Farming Population on the Arable Lands of Iran.' It was hoped that some parts of Iran would turn out to be relatively under-populated, and would hence provide room for resettlement from over-populated areas. However, it turned out that none of the villages surveyed, which were scattered throughout Iran, was underpopulated in terms of resources that were then in use or that could be brought into use without considerable capital outlay. On the contrary, nearly every village was relatively overpopulated. There was general disguised unemployment, and many redundant laborers eked out the barest existence on land where their labor was needed only in the peak agricultural seasons.

This survey, like other studies, documented the extremely low living levels, poor resource use, lack of landlord investment, and low yields of Iranian agriculture. More important were its conclusions regarding regional variations of income, class stratification within each village, and the conservative function of the village hierarchical structure below the landlord level. To speak of regional variations first, there were villages in the southeast of Iran where the poorest stratum of peasants had an income of eight, ten, or fourteen dollars a year, and even the richer cultivators made only five or six times that much per family; at the other extreme in one atypical village in Mazanderan, a prosperous province below the Caspian Sea, the peasant families averaged $1037 per year. Average family income, computed from all cases in those thirty-seven villages where the number of families receiving a given income was noted, was $516 (38,610 *rials*) in the prosperous northern provinces of Gilan, Mazanderan, and Azerbaijan (a bit under half as much if the atypical village were eliminated), but only $47 (3500 *rials*) for the rest of the country.[11] The difference between regional averages, even disregarding the differences within a village, was thus of the order of *one to eleven*, or, if the untypically prosperous village is eliminated, *one to five*. Even assuming that these figures might be skewed because there was no practical way of assuring a random sample, the differences are large enough to be significant.

The median income for all peasant families in this survey was $112 (8425 *rials*), excluding casual agricultural laborers whose incomes were not given but were included in the incomes of the peasants who paid them, thus making the median *too high*.

This survey was taken following a period of political instability and financial crisis resulting from the international oil companies' boycott of Iran's nationalized oil industry; thus these figures may have been lower than usual. Instability plus the vague threat of land reform may have influenced the disinvestment by landlords noted in the survey in village after village. Underground irrigation channels and other water supplies had been allowed to fall into disrepair, and nothing was being done to keep up, let alone improve, the investment level. It would thus be unfair to take these figures as firm averages, or especially to use them as a base from which the progress of land reform a decade later would be judged.[12] It seems likely, however, that the regional and class variations revealed by the survey are a more persistent phenomenon.

The most significant finding of this sample survey, and one which retains its full relevance in the era of land reform, was the existence and social importance of a pattern of class division or stratification among the peasants in virtually every village surveyed. *This pattern existed even in that majority of villages surveyed where the peasants were all landless*, meaning that any analysis of peasant stratification based purely on amounts of land owned is inadequate.

The stratification pattern among landless sharecroppers usually worked as follows: Peasants worked a certain area of land (which might be periodically redistributed) in organized work-teams, headed by an oxen-owner. Theoretically, every owner of two oxen might head such a work-team, but in many villages there was not enough land to make this possible, while in other villages there were not enough owners of two oxen, so that a team might be headed by a man with only one ox. In any case, the crucial 'top-class' sharecropping position went to a man with one or two oxen, who received extra income both because of his supplying one of the factors of production and because of his position at the head of the work-team. Anyone owning oxen was assured of a position on the work-team and of a higher income than was received by the peasants without oxen.

The non-oxen-owning peasants, who often made up the majority within a village, had the lowest incomes and were in the most precarious position. Due to the relative overpopulation of all villages, they had to vie for favor with the work-team heads and with the landlord-appointed headman, who usually assigned the positions on the work-team. If they got a position on a work-team they were assured of a regular, although very small, share of the crop (or, in some cases, a fixed cash income). If they did not get such a position they were often forced to migrate or become casual laborers, getting a daily wage only in peak agricultural seasons. Some owners of oxen or other factors of production (i.e., tools, water) chose to rent these out without working.

From this survey, plus other recent studies of rural Iran, one may construct a table showing the main socioeconomic strata found among agriculturalists. In Table 1, Persian terms are excluded, since it was found that such common terms as *gavband*, *khoshneshin*, and *khordeh malik* are used in different senses by different authorities, reflecting regional variations and possibly misunderstandings. This table also excludes mechanized areas and strata not in direct relationship to the land, even though these make up part of the rural stratification picture (e.g., moneylenders, peddlers, shopkeepers, artisans, teachers, mullas, and shepherds). For a complete picture of village stratification one would have to include especially moneylending classes. Recent surveys have demonstrated that the majority of peasants are in debt and that the vast majority of their debt is owed to sources other than the government or landlords. Interest rates of 50 per cent and more help make the shopkeepers, townsmen, peddlers, and others who indulge in rural moneylending one of the most powerful rural classes.[13]

The strata are listed in the table in generally declining economic and prestige order. Almost every village has several (usually between four and seven) of these strata. Some peasants are found in more than one stratum.

Extreme regional variations, especially in the need for irrigation and in the degree of orientation of agriculture toward distant markets, make it impossible for the table to be totally comprehensive, either for all existing strata, or for their relative prosperity.[14] However, this relatively simplified list gives some idea of the complexity and importance of stratification in the villages. (One could further simplify the classification by speaking of landlords and of three major peasant groups: upper 'entrepreneurial' farmers, middle subsistence sharecroppers, and lower laborers.)

The 1954 survey found indescribable conditions among the poorest peasants: locusts and clover as the main food supply in a few areas; a majority seriously diseased; interest rates of 240 to 800 per cent per annum, etc. Later surveys show that, apart from landlord advances, annual rural interest rates rarely fall below 50 per cent, and it is common for a peasant to mortgage his future crop for half the amount he will later have to pay to buy the same amount of grain.[15] With the end of advances from large landlords, the need for credit to fill the gap and to increase investment is

TABLE 1
Strata of Adult Male Agriculturalists Widely Found
in Iranian Villages*

Non-Cultivators

1. Absentee landlord, including the state, crown, and *vaqf* trustees.
2. Large-scale renter, often absentee.
3. Village officials: headman, landlord's agent, water official, field-watcher, etc.
4. Non-cultivating small owner.
5. Non-cultivating small renters from strata 1 or 2 (one village or less).
6. Non-cultivating leaser of productive instruments, usually cattle, sometimes water.
7. Non-cultivating head of work-team, providing at least one instrument of production.

Cultivators

8. Cultivating small owners.
9. Cultivator paying a fixed cash rental.
10. Cultivating head of work-team.
11. Sharecropper with some productive instruments, usually oxen, not head of a work-team.
12. Sharecropper with only his labor to sell, but with a regular position on a work-team or on land.
13. Laborer with regular wage, in cash or kind.
14. Casual laborer, without a place on work-team or land, often hired by the day only in peak seasons.

---

* To anticipate, one may note here that *only* (part of) strata 1 and 2 were eliminated in the villages distributed in the recent reforms. Below that, stratification remained, and in some cases became more acute. The 1962 land reform law gives priority in receiving land to those who hold a recognized right to cultivate a share of village land, and who own some instruments of production; it calls them cultivators, but does not ensure that they actually work the land themselves either before or after reform. In practice this has generally meant that non-cultivating classes 5, 6, and 7 got land, while cultivating classes 12, 13, and 14, who probably comprise 40 to 50 per cent of the villagers, did not.

immense. Unless it is met the poorer will lose out to the richer, whatever the legal provisions discouraging sale of distributed lands.

Almost nowhere did the survey find minimally decent conditions, and it found only one village where the landlord was making the investments necessary to improve production and village life.

Most significant are the survey team's conclusions on the role of hierarchical stratification and overpopulation in maintaining conservative social control in the villages. The team notes several times that overpopulation forced the poorest to vie for positions on the work-team. This is told of in a quotation from one *kadkhoda* (headman):

> Every year we must go to the landlord at harvest time and give him gifts for the opportunity of cultivating his land for the next year. Those outside of the *govband* [work-team] compete by saving what they can from their earnings during the year to buy presents for the landlord in hopes they can replace some govband member. For example, a man works the harvest in Gorgan. His family stays alive by gleaning the fields of the govbands here. Then this family spends most of their earnings for presents for the landlord to get a place in a govband ... owners throw out govband members at their slightest whim. If one of us would forget to say 'Goodmorning' to the landlord he would throw us off the land.[16]

Discussing a village where a few families headed two work-teams each and could gross about $435 a year, while a laboring family might average only $27, the survey goes on:

> This fact indicates an insight into the part played by the govband in the land tenure pattern of Iran. It may be observed here and in all other villages visited in Iran by this team that the govband system, which provides a vested interest group in a village, provides stability for the landlord or his representative to maintain control. This system is also partly responsible for overloading the land with underemployed people because there is a tendency for the govband owner to withdraw from actual work and to perform merely a management function while hiring cheap labor for only part of the agricultural season.[17]

In villages where the top landlord stratum has been removed, the continuation of the rest of the stratification pattern, including competition for scarce work, has perpetuated a pattern of social control by the top classes, to whom some of the power formerly held by the landlord has been transferred.

The survey team also had some general remarks about settled tribesmen which may be relevant to the continuing governmental efforts to settle the tribes:

> No groups of people in Iran are more poverty stricken, more miserable, more exploited, than the sedentary tribal peoples – the Baluch, the Arab tribes, the peoples of Sistan, and the Kurds, to name only a few. They are ground down by their own khans or Sardars or Sheiks under the guise that the government is the culprit while the government answers any signs of unrest by stationing large bodies of troops in the areas with no apparent attempt to solve one of the basic difficulties of an archaic and vicious land tenure system.[18]

The team also commented significantly on a village in Sistan, where land had been distributed with none of the accompanying investment and services that could have made the distribution program a real success. Although the farmers were earning only $32.50 per family and were all in debt, the team noted:

> Despite the contention that the Sistan land distribution is a failure, the individual farmer on the Zabul plains cultivating land only one-third as productive as that in Jiroft is making a net cash return three times that of the Jiroft *Khoshneshin* (farmer in a govband without oxen) [who nets $10.25]. Despite their abject poverty, when the freeholders of these villagers were asked if they were better off under their former landlords, than now, they defended to a man their present independence on their own tracts of land.[19]

The general conclusions of the survey team, several of which are relevant to land reform, were as follows:

1. More people are trying to make a living on the land than it can presently support.

2. There is considerable evidence to suggest to us that the governmental institutions in the rural areas of Iran are derived from, and give support to, the present land tenure system; that the social and economic institutions are conditioned by the same pattern of land ownership.

3. It follows (from 2 above) that the political and economic structures in the provinces are maintained to a large extent by the land tenure system. Under the present government, the power is divided

between the land-holding power groups in the provinces and the army.

4. There is conclusive evidence that benefits from public works in the provinces – dams, factories, etc. – are enjoyed in the main by special interests, i.e., those power groups also benefited by the present land tenure system.

5. Our data would suggest that lands operated by government agencies (the Irrigation Bongah, the Ministry of Agriculture, Amlak, etc.) are merely an adaptation of the local land tenure, crop-division system, that the farmers on these lands are not materially better off than the private landlord's tenants.

6. In certain areas where it is possible to supplement the normal one cereal crop per year by supplementary summer crops or dates, it was noted that if the increased level of a few persons in the villages rose above that of the average, such farmers tended to stop work and hire labor which actually reduced their cash incomes. We believe this phenomenon to be due to:

a. The cultivation pattern in which the landlord design is the preferred living pattern.

b. The pressure of unemployed population in every village which puts social pressure and moral obligation on the better-than-average-to-do villager to provide employment for unemployed persons.

c. On the observational level it would appear that the lack of *alternative investment opportunities supports* the relative preference for leisure attitude.

7. It was observed and our data support the conclusion that there is a tendency for landlords to maintain a vested interest group within each village as evidenced by the *govband* system in which a preferred economic group helps maintain stability and preserves the land tenure *status quo*.

8. There has been a retrogression of agriculture in Iran during the last three years due to lack of capital investment on the land (principally ganat repair and maintenance) due perhaps to a period of general political instability.

9. There is not evidence in our sample (which covered every province of Iran, even to the remotest agricultural areas) that there is any cessation whatsoever on the part of the farmers to pay the landlord's share. By virtue of the *govband* vested interest system and the forces of social control such as the gendarmerie, the Minister of Interior officials down through the *kadkhoda*, and the legal processes, the farmer cannot escape payment.[20]

Many of the conclusions of the 1954 survey are reinforced by an excellent study by R. C. Alberts. This detailed examination of a farming district not far from Tehran, and particularly of a single village within it where equal sharecropping rights to public domain land were distributed in the 1930s, shows the rapid development on such land of new stratification, with the poor and unlucky losing their effective rights through population growth, debt, or misfortune, while right-holders with key positions like the *kadkhoda* and his family, or even shopkeepers who double as moneylenders, were able to gain control of theoretically inalienable sharecropping rights and buy land in other villages. Although the original distribution of rights to cultivate equal territories had made the sale or transfer of these rights illegal, their *de facto* transfer has moved so rapidly that within twenty-five years the control of about 50 per cent of the village land passed into the hands of the *kadkhoda* and his family, while many former right-holders were frozen out. The continued growth of population without an equal growth in employment opportunities put growing numbers of agriculturalists in a highly dependent position, often as laborers without rights, which the younger generation was no longer inclined to accept as simply the will of God or fate. Even the newer landlords quickly adopted the status prerogatives of the old families. After recounting instances of mistreatment of the poor by the rich, including the unprosecuted rape of a tenant's wife by a *kadkhoda's* son which was treated as a joke by high-status persons, Alberts says:

> As status inferiors, *amaleh* (laborers) are treated by kadkhodas and *arbabs* (landlords) as little more than units of labor. They are seldom greeted, addressed, praised or thanked – which anywhere in Iranian society, urban or rural, signifies extreme social indifference indeed. In conversation between *arbabs* they are often referred to by impersonal pronouns normally appropriate for livestock. ...
>
> In sum, Garmsar (district) landownership is the essential ingredient of an economy which supports a system of social organization characterized by marked stratification and status difference. Social distance between the bulk of society and the landed aristocracy is in fact such as to make it difficult to imagine that the situation could soon evolve into free and equal opportunity for all. Prerogatives for wealth are in turn prerequisites for increasing wealth; and wealth, in the last analysis, commands the good things of life. Despite the many

programs of reform – private, national and international – of which
Garmsar has had more than its share, the overwhelming
preponderance of villagers have no belief that sharecroppers will one
day have equality with *arbabs*. ... To *arbab* and tenant alike, the *first*
step and every step toward both economic security and social
ascendancy hinge on the acquisition of land. (1963, pp. 752–55 and
passim)

The difficulty of effective land reform under such conditions, in
the absence of social revolution, may be imagined.

An even more rapid stratification has taken place on state and
crown lands sold for mechanized farming since the mid-1950s.
Mechanization has developed rapidly in the past two decades, and
mechanized farms were excluded from the land reform of
1962–63. A recent study of Gorgan province, much of which had
been expropriated for the crown by Reza Shah, shows that large-
scale and relatively heavily capitalized mechanized farming has
developed rapidly, with the purchase of crown lands by tribal
khans and influential Tehran-based entrepreneurs. Peasants
entered the process where they came under the Crown Lands
distribution program. Mechanization has resulted in the
reclamation of former wasteland and a rise in production, but also
in a growing class differentiation among the peasants; the rich
peasants have grown richer and have employed laborers, while
many peasants with lesser resources have failed in their efforts to
adapt to the new technology by such means as purchasing
machinery and hiring themselves out as tractor or combine
drivers. The spread of cotton cultivation in Gorgan has had
similar results, since the crop is lucrative, but also requires greater
capital resources. In summary:

Some machinery owners raised money through the pre-harvest sale of
cotton on disadvantageous terms, bringing exploitation by the
merchants and creating a vicious circle. Others sold their lands to
cover the deficit; the rest were obliged to part with their machinery, or
to have their machinery confiscated ... a drastic change in land tenure
has been taking place as a result of the above-mentioned changes. In
Tilan, for example, where three hectares of Crown land were
distributed to each of the forty-four peasants in 1955, only nineteen
peasants still held three hectares in 1962; ten peasants reduced the
scale of their holding and fifteen peasants expanded in scale through
the purchase of land from ruined peasants or the reclamation of virgin

land. ... [Throughout Gorgan province] The lands lost by the poor peasants were accumulated by the rich peasants. On the one hand, a group of poor peasants and a rural proletariat was created; on the other hand, a circle of rich peasants who showed increasingly progressive management capacities was initiated. (Okazaki 1968, pp. 44–5)[21]

The tendency of market-oriented farming to increase class divisions among the peasantry is shown both in Alberts' study and in this study of Gorgan. In both cases, due to market pressures and entrepreneurial possibilities, peasants who originally held equal lots of sharecropping rights have been differentiated into upper (entrepreneurial), middle (cultivator), and lower (laborer) groups. Although comparable data does not exist for earlier years, and there was probably never a period without some village stratification, we may surmise that the growth of market-oriented agriculture and of mortgaging land to moneylenders (from the mid-nineteenth century on) similarly increased the stratification of the peasantry. The two studies just cited also indicate the difficulty of maintaining relative peasant equality in areas of land reform, given a basically free enterprise framework.

Similar conclusions arise from a more extensive Agricultural Sample Survey done in 1960 by the Iranian authorities and the FAO, whose results have been published (in Persian) in fifteen volumes. This survey took place in a period of greater prosperity than the 1954 survey, but the general features it reveals are the same. According to this survey the rural population of Iran was about 15.4 million, and the cultivated area was 11.4 million hectares, of which 39.9 per cent was annually left fallow. Almost 2 million rural families had regular positions on holdings averaging about 6 hectares (14.83 acres, including fallow), enough to earn a subsistence in Iranian conditions, but another 1.3 million rural families had no such regular positions and most of these lived off the same holdings. Half the total farm units were under 2.9 hectares (7.2 acres, including fallow). In addition to the widely varying sizes of holdings, even within the same area, the survey found overall that 14.4 per cent of the employed rural population were wage laborers and 33.1 per cent were 'family workers' (corresponding to the non-oxen-owning members of the work-team in the 1954 survey).

Thus, an estimated 47.5 per cent of the employed rural population with nothing to offer but their labor generally received no land in either phase of the land reform. They have remained dependent on capitalistic farmers or on the new land-owning peasants for most of their employment, or else they have continued their growing migration to the cities, where unemployment and underemployment are still prevalent.

Hossein Mahdavy, an Iranian economist who participated in on-the-scene studies of the earlier effects of land reform, has noted:

> About 10 million out of the 15.4 million rural population of Iran belongs to the poorer classes who have either no land at their disposal or have less than 4 hectares to cultivate. [A.S. Table 301.] This is at the root of Iran's 'Agrarian Problem,' irrespective of the ownership of land which undoubtedly aggravates the situation. The land reform program, as will be explained below, left the existing land allotments untouched. In the villages affected by the land reform, only the title deeds of the lands previously farmed by the peasants were passed on to them. No redistribution or leveling of the existing disparities between different classes of peasants took place.

> The distinction between different classes within the village community is seldom appreciated by those who have not had loose ties with rural Iran. The peasants have their own *bourgeoisie*. These richer men of the village usually control the better lands, operate the village mills, own the village shops and act as general money-lenders and traders and can afford to acquire more land and livestock and even aspire to become some sort of a government appointed or landlord appointed functionary in the village.

Mahdavy goes on to note the communal pattern of agriculture in Iran, with open fields for grazing, and frequent redistribution of farms by landlords. A modernization pattern based on individual farms could result in enclosing the common lands to the detriment of the poorer peasants, as happened in much of modern Europe. Writing early in 1965, Mahdavy gives his view as follows:

> The communal open-field system of agriculture, prevalent in Iran, is by nature more amenable to a cooperative form of production than to a system of production based on individual enterprise. In a cooperative system, the overfragmentation of lands and the grazing problems can be overcome by introducing production plans for the

entire village. The need for enclosures on tiny plots of land will thus not arise.

The incompatibility of the communal form of production organization with a land system based on individual initiative and enterprise is not yet fully appreciated or perceived in Iran for an obvious reason: there has been little time for any intended change to encounter difficulties. But this difficulty will increase proportionally with the attempts on the part of the village *bourgeoisie* to break away from the communal and traditional patterns and to undertake more profitable farming in cash crops, fruits and vegetables. (1965, pp. 15–17)[22]

The government hoped that the extension of cultivated land through new irrigation schemes and the increase of crop yields on cultivated lands through improvements in productive techniques might meet the problem of agricultural unemployment and underemployment. It seems doubtful that agricultural improvement will mean significantly more agricultural employment, since some improvements actually reduce the number of men who can be employed, as is the case in mechanization of cultivated areas, a process which has been expanding for years especially in dry-farming areas near some cities. Within the existing limitations the government might have opted either for a cooperative farming solution that would have given all villagers a similar stake in agricultural improvement and modernization or for a bourgeois-individualist solution that counted essentially on the initiative of farmers and of capitalist landholders. Unsurprisingly, in view of Iran's general political and economic orientation, the government chose the second option. A bourgeois land reform that lessens the control of parasitic and nonproductive absentee landlords is a significant reform whose positive effects on production and modernization are already being felt; it is, however, a reform that contains within it contradictory features that promise continuing problems.

LAND REFORMS OF 1962–1963

The crucial land reform measures in Iran were adopted in 1962–1963, at a time when the landlord-dominated parliament had been dismissed and a reformist government dominated by

Premier Ali Amini and Minister of Agriculture Hasan Arsanjani was in power. The Shah had already indicated his interest in land reform, and a rather mild reform bill had been introduced in parliament late in 1959. There were political reasons for land reform, including foreign and internal pressures and some change in peasant attitudes (from fatalism to disaffection).[23] Moreover, land reform was imperative if the country were to become stronger and more modernized.

The traditional pattern of draining the entire agricultural surplus to the cities and leaving only the barest minimum for agricultural investment was a result of absentee-landlord dominance that could not be overcome by the various foreign-sponsored technical aid programs that were so abundant in the post-war years. Middle-class and technically educated strata of the Iranian population were growing and were entering government agencies in ever larger numbers. Like the Shah, many of them saw that the large absentee landlords were hurting Iran's chances for further economic development. The early 1960s was a period of sharp economic recession and stagnation after a boom in the late 1950s. If Iranian growth were to be started again, on a less speculative and more productive basis than before, the growth of agricultural production and of a peasant market would be essential ingredients.

Although Muhammad Reza Shah's rule did rest in large part on landlord support, there were some fundamental differences in interest between the Shah and the absentee landlords. The Shah was interested in modernizing and strengthening Iran, and hence in increasing production, as quickly as was compatible with the safety of his own rule, while the landlords as a class were not. The Shah seems to have been willing to take the risk of alienating the absentee landlords in order to do what was necessary to put Iran's economic growth on a sounder basis, particularly since he could hope to replace landlord support with that of some of the middle-class and peasant elements.

In January 1962, the Shah and Arsanjani announced a new decree-law, the work of the latter, among whose main features were the following: (1) No one was allowed to own more than one village (or selected fractions totaling one village). Excluded were orchards, tea plantations, groves, homesteads, and mechanized areas worked by wage laborers. (2) The government was to indemnify landlords in ten years (later changed to fifteen) on the basis of the taxes they had been paying ; this sum plus 10 per cent administrative costs was to be paid over fifteen years by the purchasing peasants. (3) Only persons who were members of a village cooperative were eligible for land, and the deeds would remain with the Agricultural Bank as security until all instalments had been paid. Another major feature of the reform was that peasants should be allotted the land they were actually farming and those providing more than labor received first priority.[24] In practice this seems generally to have meant that the heads of work-teams got land, while laborers, who constituted approximately 47.5 per cent of the rural population according to the 1960 survey, did not.

Landlords, having had fair warning (at least since the 1959–60 bill) that a division of their land based on maximum holdings might be enacted, had had two years to transfer ownership of their villages to their wives, children, and relatives, and this land was allowed to remain where it was.[25]

The actual area distributed under this 'First Phase' of reform is a matter of some dispute. The official government figures are between twelve thousand and thirteen thousand villages (out of a total of forty-eight to fifty-four thousand villages in Iran). According to Mahdavy, however, who helped survey the effects of reform:

> The information released by the government in Tehran is invariably found to be inconsistent with data provided by the authorities in the field. ... Even if $1/100$ of a village were to be sold to the government, in most statistics issued by the government, that village would be classified as 'reformed.' More accurate statistics can be obtained from provincial offices of the Land Reform Agency. ...
>
> From time to time the government issues information concerning the number of households affected by land reform. The figures are not reliable as they include manyfold counting. ... If only a fraction of a village is sold by one landlord, the entire households of the village are claimed to have benefited from the reform. If a second landlord sells another fraction, the entire village household is counted again as having benefited from land reform. (1965, pp. 22, 23, and notes)[26]

Mahdavy, extrapolating for the areas he studied, judges that the equivalent of about five thousand complete villages, or about 10 per cent of all Iranian villages, had been distributed by mid-1964, at which time the First Phase had been declared completed. However, further distributions have occurred since that period.

A detailed published study of one reformed village in a relatively prosperous region south of Zanjan reveals trends that are so in accord with what might be expected from a previous knowledge of peasant stratification that they may be of general validity. Also, this study provides another cautionary note about official statistics. The land reform law specified that only peasants who joined cooperatives would get land; therefore many cooperatives were formed in theory that were never brought into effective use. In the village studied and in other villages in the area, cooperatives existed only in official statistics (Miller 1964).[27]

The following represent the most relevant portions of this study:

Under the old landlord system, lots were drawn every three or four years by the farmers for the lands to be farmed. In this way, a poor farmer might draw the best land, and with hard work and good harvests could improve his position. The land distribution law has done away with this possibility. Under present circumstances, except for a few fortunate small holders who are on exceptionally fertile land, the larger peasant landowners have already begun to grow richer in comparison with their fellow villagers who own less land. In Hosseinabad, several families out of fifty-two peasant landowners own half the village. A tendency has already begun to emerge: the larger farmers, two and a half *joft* or more, lend their surplus capital at a high rate of interest to their less prosperous fellow villagers and as a result are gradually replacing the land capitalism of the former landlord with the oxen and cash capitalism of the new system.

... The removal of the landlord from the power structure has put control of village government firmly in the hands of the wealthier landholders. It was in the landlord's interest to balance power between the wealthier farmers, the small farmers and the *khoshneshin* [laborers]. The removal of the landlord has broken the balance and the *rish sefid* [council of elders] as a consequence primarily press for the interests of the larger and wealthier landholders with little regard for less privileged groups.

... a feeling of discontent is growing among the *khoshneshin* [who comprise 40 per cent of this village] even though they still harbor some hopes that the government will give them some land as well. The development of new lands through large-scale irrigation projects could absorb some of the *khoshneshin*, but the limited land available for new farmers and the introduction of labor saving techniques will make the problem of providing work for the *khoshneshin* a major national problem. (Miller 1964, pp. 487, 489, 594)

The writer later expresses the hope that the introduction of effective cooperatives and election of the village council by secret ballot will overcome the problems of exacerbated class division that he observed. Judging from the example of India, with a longer experience of cooperatives and of village self-government, one may be skeptical of this suggestion. Although it is true that effective cooperatives can meet the immediate problem of low-interest loans, it seems probable that the cooperatives and the village council, even if secretly elected, will continue to be dominated by, and to favor, the wealthiest elements in the village.[28]

This criticism of the land distribution program does not imply that it is a meaningless fraud, as some of the Shah's more strident critics have alleged. The reduction in the amount of income going into the hands of absentee owners and the consequent increase in local funds available for both investment and consumption has evidently given an impetus to both production and living standards in the villages, to judge by recent reports. Similarly, one class of peasants (the more prosperous villagers) can know for the first time that the benefits of capital investment and time spent on their land will accrue to them. This has resulted in some enclosure of farms, a rise in the use of chemical fertilizers, and new receptivity to the suggestions of the government's growing extension services.

However, the poorest stratum, variously estimated as including 40 to 50 per cent of the population, have not had their needs met even in the areas affected by land reform. Their situation may even be worsening, regardless of whatever temporary relief they receive in a good harvest year. Even if the cooperatives spread more effectively than they have until now, land reform remains an essentially bourgeois reform, favoring both the large capitalists, who farm reform-exempt plantations and fields with hired labor, and the more prosperous villagers, who can now profit from more rational investment and agricultural techniques. The large laboring class, however, is given no protection – no minimum wage, no unemployment compensation, no gleaning rights on the now-private fields, and no land.

The second phase of land reform was proclaimed in decrees and regulations in 1963–64, and its implementation began in 1965. It covers most of the large majority of villages untouched by the first phase and is of a much more conservative nature than that put through by Arsanjani. Landlords are allowed to retain a maximum of 30 to 150 hectares of nonmechanized lands, depending on the region, and must dispose of the rest in one of several ways, chosen by the landlord, who may: (1) rent the land to the peasants on the basis of the average net income of the past three years, the lease to be for thirty years and subject to five-year revisions; (2) sell the land to the peasants at a mutually agreed price; (3) divide the land with the peasant, retaining a section equal to the share of the crop he formerly received; (4) by mutual agreement set up a joint stock company with the peasants, with the landlord share in the company to be equal to his former share of the crop; or (5) sell his share to the government to be resold to the peasants on terms equal to those of the first phase.

These stipulations may involve more of a *regularization* than a reform of the existing situation. Where leases revisable every five years are chosen, the landlord loses nothing and gains a government-enforced lease, while in the other alternatives (except for number 5) the peasant may lose as much as he gains. The percentage of self-sufficient farmers, even among those who buy or receive land, is smaller among those affected by the second phase of reform than among those affected by the first, since most of the new owners in the second phase either have to meet a price set by the landlord or else be given a plot of land based on the crop division, which in most cases is too small to provide subsistence and rarely provides a surplus for improvements.

Some well-informed observers regard the first phase of reform as a well-thought-out and rather radical initial program that Arsanjani hoped to promote throughout Iran, while the second phase represented the recrudescence of conservative forces. According to Doreen Warriner, a successful National Congress of Peasants held in Tehran in January 1963

> was Arsanjani's triumph, and therefore the cause of his downfall. He was reforming too vigorously and becoming too popular. Shortly after the congress the government began to try to control the reform, allegedly for financial reasons, in reality because it could not face the implications of the principle that the land should belong to the tiller.

This principle was never stated explicitly in the law, but it was announced; Arsanjani had posters with this slogan put up in the land reform offices in the capital and the provinces.

... [The second stage] was much less radical than Arsanjani's first version, and represented some concession to the interests of the landowners, which ran contrary to the land-to-the-tiller principle ... in March he resigned, provoked to do so by a government-prompted television attack on his policy. ...

During the spring and summer of 1963, violent anti-government demonstrations broke out in Tehran, and a large number of people were shot down in the streets. In order to preserve the image of the Shah as a progressive ruler, the blame was laid on the mullahs, as the enemies of the reform. To a certain extent it is true that the mullahs were used by the landowners and their supporters to attack the reform, but the demonstration also represented a popular and genuine opposition to arbitrary rule and the suspension of the constitution by the Shah. ...

Unrest in the country nevertheless continued, and with the object of allaying it the government announced that the second stage of the reform would be put into effect. ... In fact, they [the regulations for the second stage] represented a step backward. (1969, pp. 120–22)[29]

The second phase was declared completed in January 1967. According to official figures – which are incomplete and may be biased, as has been noted – of the over one million tenants affected, only 46,000 were able to purchase land from their landlords, while 17,000 landlords chose to distribute their land on the basis of the former crop division to their 153,000 tenants. Landlords who bought out their tenants numbered 6,392. Only *3,238* landlords sold any land in this phase, as contrasted with 203,049 who chose to lease their land. Official figures show 199,000 ex-tenants getting *some* land in the second phase, although over three-quarters of these got significantly less than they formerly farmed, while the rest of the over two million peasants (with families totaling 11.4 million), who are said to have benefited from this phase, got no land. The procedures and figures of the second phase must be kept in mind when grandiose claims about the Iranian reforms are made (Economist Intelligence Unit 1967, p. 11; Bank Markazi Iran 1967, p. 194).[30]

A generous estimation can be made that, of the approximately 14 to 16 per cent of Iran's villagers affected by the first phase of reform, about one-half (or 7 to 8 per cent) received land. Relying on official figures we can say that of the 60 to 70 per cent of villagers affected by the second phase, under one-tenth of these (6 to 7 per cent) received any land. Therefore, 14 to 15 per cent seems a reasonable estimate for new landholders created by the reform. (Let me emphasize that *this is not an insignificant figure* in spite of its divergence from more extravagant propaganda claims.) However, probably no more than 10 per cent of Iran's peasants received enough land to support them and enable them to make necessary improvements.

POST-REFORM CONDITIONS

The success of land reform is difficult to measure but it is clear that many problems remain unsolved. A United Nations study, *Progress in Land Reform* summarized the situation in 1966 as follows:

> These land reform measures have, however, by no means solved the problems of Iranian agriculture. In the first place, it is not clear that they have solved the social and political problem of landlord dominance. There was nothing to prevent landlords from reordering the cultivation pattern in their villages before the land reform reached them in such a way as to ensure that the best land – or indeed any land at all – went only to their friends, relatives, and loyal dependents. Again landlords who exercised their option to retain a collection of parts of villages might contrive to retain the best of each and even, perhaps, those parts which dominate the water supply for the rest of the village. It also remains to be seen whether the second-stage reforms will, in fact, end traditional forms of tenancy.
>
> ... Again, in those districts where there was a tenancy hierarchy, the land has sometimes gone to the entrepreneurial *gavband* who did not cultivate directly, rather than to the crop-sharing labourers who have derived no benefits from the reform. Thus a new class of landlords may have been created. It is, indeed, the explicit intention of the reform not to establish equality, but to create an extended tenure ladder. As the Shah said in one of his speeches, 'our aims are not to destroy small landlords. What we are doing is a means of making it possible to become small landlords. Those who become owners of land today, we hope, will become small landlords in the future.'[31] The shift in power from the feudal magnates to the new larger class of small landlords could still represent a significant political change, however, and it may be that these new landlords, being closer to the productive process, are in fact more concerned with raising

productivity than were the original absentee landlords, though there may be compensating disadvantages in an increase of social tension.

... A second problem concerns the cost of the land to the beneficiaries. ... Many will find this too large a sum to pay off over fifteen years.

... The third immense problem is to find some rapid substitute for the organizational and physical services formerly provided by the landlords and their agents.

... The potentialities of these [village] councils are great. At the same time, in those villages where the land reform has left a stratified population with a few of the large landholders being the only obvious candidates for office, there are equally clear dangers – the possibility of an oligarchic system of exploitation of the poor by the rich, for instance, or, alternatively, of debilitating factional struggles between rival leaders and their dependent followers of the kind which has plagued the Indian *panchayat*. (United Nations 1966, pp. 24–25)

Professor Lambton's book *The Persian Land Reform* (1969b) gives a generally more positive assessment. In view of the partial and contradictory nature of the reforms, however, it seems too early to predict the degree to which they will succeed even in introducing more productive capitalist relations into the countryside outside of the more prosperous areas. In the majority of villages not covered by the first phase old patterns may continue under new forms. It seems clear that the *trend* is toward capitalism and increased investment and productivity in agriculture, due to favoring cash rents and large farmers and exempting mechanized farms with hired labor from redistribution; but it is unclear when and whether this trend will come to dominate the traditional patterns of Iranian agriculture. The experience with similar reforms by other countries with impoverished land-hungry peasants does not inspire easy confidence.[32]

One of the numerous remaining problems is that the success of cooperatives and of extension and educational services depends on having numerous dedicated government representatives in the villages, whereas the government and its agents have in the past acted more as additional exploiters than as productive aides. This pattern is changing, but it is too soon to say how much.

Recent figures and impressions indicate that agricultural production and village consumption are rising, and although it will take several years to show that this is a steady trend rather than one based on a few good harvests, there seems no reason to doubt that the reform will continue to have a favorable effect on the average production and consumption of villagers (Issawi 1967, p. 455).[33] There is still a great need for increased government services and more effective cooperatives if the reforms are to result in more than momentary improvements.

An on-the-spot survey of the results of land reform has recently been published by Doreen Warriner (1969), and A. K. S. Lambton has published both an article (1969a) and a complete book (1969b) on the Iranian reforms (see also McLachlan 1968). Both authors stress the positive effects of reform in the minority of villages covered by the first phase, while noting that the second phase shows a much more mixed picture, although its results appear to have been generally positive. Professor Lambton's article also discusses the so-called third stage of land reform, embodied in measures passed from late 1967 to January 1969. The first of these measures encouraged the establishment of agricultural corporations comprising two or more villages, with the aim of increasing output through mechanization and an economic use of manpower.

> It is too early to appraise the economic or social effects of these corporations, but in some respects they would appear to be a reversal of the original reform, which, because it gave the peasant security of tenure, stimulated agricultural development. In an area run by a corporation the land is taken away from the peasant, who no longer has any responsibility for its cultivation. In return, he is given a share in the corporation, which employs him, if at all, as an agricultural laborer. The declared aim is eventually to hand the corporations over to their members, but whether it will meanwhile be possible to maintain the interest and confidence of the peasants seems doubtful. ... Some fifteen or sixteen corporations have been set up, in districts where good land with adequate water is available. A better case could perhaps have been made for the corporations had they been established in districts where consolidation is a pressing problem or where poverty prevents the peasants exploiting the land. (Lambton 1969a, pp. 144–45)

Professor Lambton's book also notes a disturbing trend toward increased governmental control of cooperatives (1969b, Chaps. 16, 17, and Postscript).

Another bill that became law in January 1969 provides for the abolition of remaining tenancies except in the *vaqf* land administered by religious authorities. If carried out, this law should convert all members of non-*vaqf* village communities either into small owners who theoretically cultivate their own land (although they do not always do so in practice) or into paid laborers who work for the first group, for the new corporations, or for larger capitalistic farmers, most of whose lands have been exempted from the various stages of reform. It is too early to say how and to what degree the third phase of reform (as of 1969) is being carried out.

An important element in the above discussion is the socio-political effects of the reforms. As already indicated, land reform in Iran has had a bourgeois-capitalist bias. In this sense land reform policies fit in well with other changes now occurring in Iran, such as the boom in productive investment. It is something of an irony that Iranian capitalism, because of oil and strategic location, has been able to profit from the rivalries of two groups not always friendly to the successful independent capitalists of new nations – the old capitalist powers and the new socialist bloc. Partly benefiting from the rivalry of these two groups, Iran may be on the way to setting up a largely self-sufficient capitalist economy. Although it may prove to be as planless, wasteful, and frequently indifferent to human suffering as that of the United States, it is bringing an upward swing to the magic GNP curves and a rise in average living standards.

Those who rightly note the inadequate and contradictory nature of land reform sometimes conclude that the majority of the peasants excluded from significant benefits in the reform will become for the first time a revolutionary class (Mahdavy 1965).[34] I have usually found historical trends too complex and contradictory to make any such prediction. Specifically, at least two factors that will operate against rural revolt should be noted. First, if increases in agricultural production should continue, most laborers may improve their lot even though they are getting relatively no more of the crops, or even less, than they used to. Second, and more important, if it is true that a dissatisfied class with new aspirations has been created, it is also true that a relatively satisfied class with a greater stake than ever before in existing relations has also been created. For the moment it seems clear that the power and resources of this new landed class enable them to keep effective control over the landless. No matter what the institutional formalities, it is almost certain that this class will continue to dominate village government and institutions, and will continue to hire workers from a pool that exceeds the demand. How long the stabilizing effect of the new owners and the old hierarchies will continue to outweigh the dissatisfactions of the excluded laborers is not a matter for confident prediction. Since one general effect of the reforms (as of 1969) has been to improve peasant income and agricultural productivity, one might argue that they have, for the present, foreclosed rather than encouraged revolutionary potential.

In the past, neither Iranian peasants nor those of most other Middle Eastern countries have entered into political struggles over their own destiny to an extent similar to that of the peasants in several Far Eastern countries. Scholars have scarcely explored the reasons for this difference, but one may guess that the widely scattered and sparsely populated settlements characteristic of the arid regions of most of the Middle East have made organization of peasants far more difficult than in the densely organized territories of the Far East.

The rapid economic and social changes being introduced by land reform and new technology as well as the new information available to agriculturalists through the mass media and increased literacy may help to politicize Iranian agriculturalists. There seems no reason, however, to expect any rapid end to the governmental controls, rewards, and punishments and the hierarchical deference patterns that have kept political opposition from being effective even in the highly politicized cities in recent years. Even if a significant section of Iranian agriculturalists were to develop a revolutionary perspective (which is not the case at present), the open terrain, strong army, and good transportation network of most of Iran would discourage, if not preclude, a revolutionary movement from finding a widespread base in the countryside.[35] The most that would seem politically possible at present and in the immediate future is that both the landed and the landless peasants might be moved from old patterns of fatalism and deference to new attempts to influence or control their own destinies.

The most important political question now facing the peasants affected by reform as a group is whether they can achieve the independence foreseen by Arsanjani's original reforms and expand their control over their lands and cooperatives, or whether a trend, already evident in 1968–69, toward increased governmental control of cooperatives and retraction of individual plots in favor of agricultural corporations will continue. If peasant objection to the imposition of new outside controls over their lives can be made politically effective it will be an unprecedented political success for Iranian peasants; but whether peasants can make their will prevail over those who have been reimposing bureaucratic controls on them is still unclear.

NOTES

1. Three books touching on the consequences of the urban drain of agricultural surplus in the Middle East are of special interest: Adams 1965; English 1966; and Weulersse 1946. For a firsthand account of the workings of a 'feudal' area of irrigated agriculture see Forbes-Leith 1927.
2. Xavier de Planhol informs me that Fraser's optimistic picture may, however, be colored by the centering of his travels on the prosperous Caspian area.
3. Professor Lambton believes that the control of landlords and fief holders over local land jurisdiction was the main cause of the decline, and does not stress the Western impact in this regard.
4. On nineteenth-century economic trends see Mochaver 1937, pp. 147–83.
5. For a more detailed discussion of the interaction of political history and social change see my work 'The Impact of the West on Iranian Social History' (1955).
6. See *Correspondence Respecting the Affairs of Persia*, in *Accounts and Papers*, CV, 4, 26, No. 25. In an important analytic article, Abrahamian points out that there were *only* three recorded incidents of peasant ferment during the revolution; he sees this as part of peasant passivity lasting into the 1950s, a passivity which he thinks will probably be analyzed by social psychologists (historians and political scientists having failed to explain it). (See Abrahamian 1968, p. 209.) I would agree that Iranian peasants have been more passive than those in many areas of Europe and the Far East, but I think that peasant political activity has been somewhat more significant than Abrahamian implies. The concentration of this political activity even since 1906 in the prosperous and relatively densely populated and well-watered regions of Azerbaijan and Gilan (which resemble Europe and the Far East far more than do the arid parts of Iran) suggests that patterns of peasant settlement and economic organization are more important influences on peasant political activity than is social psychology.

7. The devastating impact of World War I and the subsequent famines are discussed in Forbes-Leith 1927.

8. *Vaqf* land is inalienable land donated for religious or charitable purposes. Often descendants of the donor and other private persons profit from it.

9. As of 1969, the only scientific evaluation of the results of part of the Shah's program is Gharatchehdaghi 1967. The author, who surveyed the first twelve villages to be distributed before their sale to peasants in 1952, returned to evaluate results in 1964. He found that although there was a dramatic original rise in average incomes, due to the difference between the 50 per cent share formerly taken by the crown and the twenty-five-year redemption instalments, real income stagnated or declined between 1955–64, due partly to drought, but also to rising debt, poor government planning, and other factors. He also found some alienation and subdivision of plots (despite rules designed to prohibit this), a trend toward restratification, the bankruptcy of the local cooperative after a few years, and a return to traditional high-interest credit sources. In addition to such problems in Varamin, an area which received an unusual amount of governmental and American aid, C. Webster Johnson discovered (without publishing) the fact that approximately one-third of the crown lands distributed throughout Iran were reserved for wealthy landlords, including members of the royal family and other favorites.

10. Two of the participants, Howard Bertsch and H. L. Naylor, wrote up the survey results. Additional tabulation from the survey's data was done by myself and W. H. Keddie in 1960, and by Professor Gene Garthwaite of Dartmouth College, a former research assistant, in 1968.

11. In the survey Dr. Garthwaite found a conversion ratio of 80 rials to the dollar. Our tabulations here are at the official 75-to-1 rate.

12. This is shown by a resurvey of the same areas conducted by Iranian specialists in 1964 and gradually being published, along with the 1954 survey, in *Tahqiqat é eqtesadi*, 'Rural Economic Problems of Khuzistan,' 3 (August 1965): 153–222; and 'A Study of Rural Economic Problems of Gilan and Mazandaran,' 4 (January 1967): 135–204. From these it is clear that except for day laborers, who often get the same wage as in 1954 despite the rise in living costs, peasant prosperity increased in the decade 1954–64 quite apart from land reform. This contrasts with the apparent *fall* in real peasant income from the late 1920s to the 1960s noted by M. Atai in reports published over several issues of *Tahqiqat é eqtesadi*. What is suggested by these incomplete figures is thus a notable fall in peasant income between the 1920s and 1954, and a partial recovery since then. Unfortunately, the published data on the 1954–64 study do not cover the same areas as the 1920s to 1960s study, and one wishes that both studies would now be published *in toto* instead of piecemeal.

13. The articles listed in note 12 give details on peasant debt and its sources.

14. Thus, cultivators paying cash rentals are concentrated in prosperous and market-oriented areas like Gilan, and are often much wealthier than small owner-cultivators, who before reform were found mainly in areas with little surplus to tempt a landlord. In areas where irrigation water is crucial, ownership or even leasing and subletting of water may give more income

and power than landownership. This has created problems for a reform based on landownership, and it is too soon to say how the recently announced nationalization of water resources will affect the situation.

15. In addition to the sources in note 12, see especially the excellent and comprehensive paper delivered at Harvard in 1965 by Hossein Mahdavy, who participated in the 1964 survey, 'Iran's Agrarian Problems,' only part of which has been published.

16. This is a description of Khorasan, Kashmar area, Fark village (survey village no. 20). It is to be noted that the 1954 survey uses the word 'govband' (*gavband*) to mean work-team, though its more usual and correct use refers to an ox-owning peasant who rents out his oxen to others, or, in a few areas, it may refer to an ox-owning cultivator. A widespread although not universal Persian word for the work-teams that characterize Iranian agriculture is *boneh*.

R. C. Alberts states on the basis of his careful study of an area not covered by the 1954 survey:

> What principally keeps the tenant in line is rigidity of the system which for him means lack of alternatives. The recalcitrant peasant may be penalized by economic sanction, since the local merchant or money-lender, to whom he is surely indebted, is typically the landlord in another guise. He may be transferred to another area – and many landlords rotate tenants periodically as a purely prophylactic means of frustrating clique alignment. He may also be assigned inferior land. Or he may be flogged ... the peasant who proves overly troublesome may be permanently ejected. It is the threat of this – a fate worse than usury, penury, abject status or hard labor – which seems to account most for resigned servility. The outcast tenant is an illiterate, unskilled, indigent soul with a family to support and nowhere to turn. It is no accident that a high percentage of beggars, petty criminals and social misfits in the cities have rural background and histories as village troublemakers.

On the other hand, Alberts continues, the peasants do have some underhand ways to gain small concessions (Alberts 1963, p. 241). Even in relatively prosperous Gilan, Paul Vieille similarly found landlords using their control over land and water allotments to keep their peasants insecure, vying for favor, docile and isolated from each other. The individualism and competitiveness of Iranians have been encouraged by the ruling classes to prevent united opposition to their rule or control on the village level as well as higher up. (Vieille 1965).

17. Azerbaijan, Miandoah area, Mamahdel village (no. 26).

18. Kermanshah, Kurdistan area, Salehabad village (no. 33).

19. Sistan, Zabol area (no. 7).

20. 'Some Tentative General Conclusions,' at the end of the 1954 survey.

21. Another recent careful study emphasizing stratification and significant inter-generational upward and downward mobility of peasant families is Ajami 1969.

22. With writers using the 1960 survey there is a confusing usage of 'peasant holdings' and 'peasant holders,' which in this survey refer not to peasant ownership but only to peasants having a regular position on plots of varying sizes. I have seen no indication of ownership statistics in this 1960 survey. The statistics above are cited in Mahdavy 1965, pp. 13–19.

23. On the politics of land reform, aside from Mahdavy, see Land 1966, pp. 80–122, and Scarcia 1962, which appends an Italian translation of the January 1962 decree-law. Growing peasant disaffection before the reform is noted in Alberts 1963, pp. 48–9.

24. The most detailed and complete study of the land reform, based on extensive first-hand observation, is Lambton 1969b. It covers many aspects of reform not dealt with, or dealt with only very briefly, in this article.

25. That such transfers were widespread is indicated by the great discrepancy between scholarly and official estimates that the majority of Iran's villages were owned by large landlords, and the official decision that 13,904 villages out of Iran's 49,000 were eligible for distribution. As noted below, this figure includes villages of which only a part was to be distributed, so that the number of eligible villages probably equalled fewer than 9,000 complete villages. By contrast, as noted in the excellent section on agriculture in the U.S. Army *Area Handbook for Iran* (1963), in 1962 the Minister of Agriculture estimated that about 15,000 villages belonged to landlords with *over five villages*, and the government stated that 400 to 450 large landlords owned 57 per cent of all Iranian villages (p. 443). Lambton 1969b (*passim*) also notes post-reform transfers.

26. Another analysis of official figures casts similar doubt on them: 'A Review of the Statistics of the First Stage of Land Reform' *Tahqiqat é eqtesadi* 2 (March 1964), 139–150. The authors state that of the 13,904 villages stated to be eligible for distribution, 3,788 were fully eligible and 10,116 only partly eligible. In the absence of data as to what proportion of the latter was eligible, the authors guess that it averaged half of each village, thus reducing the eligible figure to 8,836 whole villages, or 18 per cent of the Iranian total (p. 140). According to the *Iran Almanac* (Tehran: 1966) 12,875 villages of the 13,904 had been bought and distributed by February 1965. With so many gaps and inaccuracies in official figures, it seems impossible to estimate the proportion of full villages distributed beyond saying that it should lie between 10 and 18 per cent, and one may guess at 14 to 15 per cent.

27. 'In the Khamseh only land distribution has taken place. Cooperatives have been formed in theory; they have not yet been brought into effective use in any of the villages observed. Money has been collected from the peasants for the cooperatives, but after a year the government has done nothing about contributing its share of funds or allowing these funds to be used in the village' (Miller 1964, p. 496). Similar conclusions are found in other recent studies.

28. 'A Survey of Rural Co-operatives up to Mehr 1342 (September 1963),' *Tahqiqat é eqtesadi* 2 (March 1964), 151–60, notes on page 160, for example, that cooperative regulations allow much larger loans to those who contribute larger shares to the cooperative, thus increasing that land reform's favoritism to the more prosperous peasants.

29. Similar views are expressed in Lambton 1969b, Chapter 9, ff.

30. Aside from statistical inflation, noted above, confusion is sown by the practice of referring to land leased to peasants on terms revisable every five years (including the ninety-nine-year leases for *vaqf* property stipulated by

the reform) as having been *distributed* or *given* to them. Under such semantic rules the vast majority of Iran's peasants may be claimed as beneficiaries or even as new 'owners.'

31. The citation is to *Facts About Iran*, no. 156, November 20, 1962 (Iran Government, General Department of Publications and Broadcasting). A related view is expressed by the Shah in Pahlavi 1961, p. 200. 'Much of the worst-managed land in Iran is in the hands of the biggest landlords ... as a class the big private landlords are parasites. ... Quite different are many of the smaller landlords, who may own one or a few villages and not infrequently live in close association with their tenants. While some of them are selfish and self-centered, many take a lively interest in the families who live on their land. Often they freely give land for schools, clinics, or mosques, and many of the best-managed villages in Iran are run by them.' It is unclear to what degree this distinction is supported by scholarly studies.

32. See especially reports on the failure of reforms favoring the wealthier peasants even to spread capitalism significantly, such as Thorner and Thorner 1962, Chapter 1; and Mosse 1965.

33. Issawi notes the primacy of weather conditions as a factor in three successive good harvests. On some other points this author seems too ready to utilize inflated official statistics.

34. Several other sources note the early active discontent of excluded peasants and villagers, including Lambton 1963, pp. 111–116. I have seen no reports indicating whether this discontent has become more or less active in the past few years, although according to Ajami 1969, p. 65, the omission of laborers from land reform

> has stimulated bitter class consciousness in these villages. There is a sense of isolation and lack of belonging to the village community among the Khooshneshin families. They rarely participate in community development projects. They are not represented on the village council and cannot join the village co-operative.

35. Many Iranian students abroad have talked for years as if Iran were on the verge of social revolution. In fact, the 1960s have seen not only economic development but also related improvement in the government's political position and stability, despite the continued opposition of many intellectuals and some additional urban groups to the lack of democracy and to other ills.

BIBLIOGRAPHY

Abrahamian, E.
    1968. The crowd in Iranian politics. *Past and Present* 41 (December): 184–210.
Adams, Robert M.
    1965. *Land behind Baghdad*. Chicago: University of Chicago Press.

Ajami, Ismail.
1969. Social classes, family demographic characteristics and mobility in three Iranian villages. *Sociologia Ruralis* 9 (no. I): 62–72.
Alberts, R. C.
1963. Social structure and culture change in an Iranian village. Ph.D. dissertation, University of Wisconsin.
Bank Markazi Iran.
1967. *Bulletin.* July–August.
Bank Melli Iran.
1934. *Bulletin.* March.
Bent, J. T.
1891. Village Life in Persia. *The New Review* 5.
Chardin, Jean.
1811. *Voyages du chevalier Chardin en Perse.* Paris: Le Normant.
Cooke, Hedley V.
1952. *Challenge and response in the Middle East.* New York: Harper and Row.
Economist Intelligence Unit..
1967. *Quarterly Economic Review:* Iran. March.
English, Paul W.
1966. *City and village in Iran: settlement and economy in the Kirman basin.* Madison: University of Wisconsin Press.
Esfandiary, Amir.
1945. *Les Propriétés et entreprises de l'état iranien.* Geneva: Imprimerie genevoise.
Forbes-Leith, F. A. C.
1927. *Checkmate: fighting tradition in Central Persia.* London: Harrap.
Fraser, James B.
1833. *Historical and descriptive account of Persia.* New York: Harper & Bros.
Gharatchehdaghi, Cyrus.
1967. *Distribution of land in Varamin: an opening phase of the agrarian reform in Iran.* Opladen: Leske.
Hayden, Lyle J.
1949. Living standards in rural Iran: a case study. *Middle East Journal* 3 (April): 140–150.
Issawi, Charles.
1967. Iran's economic upsurge. *Middle East Journal* 21 (Autumn): 447–461.
Keddie, Nikki.
1955. The impact of the West on Iranian social history. Ph.D. dissertation, University of California at Berkeley.
Kia, A. C.
1937. *Essai sur l'histoire industrielle de l'Iran.* Paris: M. Lavergne.
Lambton, Ann K. S.
1953. *Landlord and peasant in Persia: a study of land tenure and land revenue administration.* London: Oxford University Press.
1963. Rural development and land reform in Iran. In *Symposium on rural development.* September 25–30 1963. Tehran. Ankara: CENTO.

1969a. Land reform and rural cooperative societies in Persia. Part I. *Royal Central Asian Journal* 56 (June): 142–155.

1969b. *The Persian Land Reform, 1962–1966*. London: Oxford University Press.

Land, C.Opt'.

1966. Land reform in Iran. *Persica*, vol. 2. The Hague.

Mahdavy, Hossein.

1965. The coming crisis in Iran. *Foreign Affairs* 44 (October): 134–146.

McLachan, K. S.

1968–. Chapter 21. *Cambridge history of Iran*. Vol. I. Cambridge: Cambridge University Press.

Miller, William G.

1964. Hosseinabad: a Persian village. *Middle East Journal* 18 (Autumn): 483–498.

Mochaver, F.

1937. *L'évolution des finances iraniennes*. Paris: Librairie technique et économique.

Mosse, W. E.

1965. Stolypin's villages. *The Slavonic and East European Review* 43 (June): 257–274.

Okazaki, Shoko.

1968. *The development of large-scale farming in Iran: the case of the province of Gorgan*. Tokyo: Institute of Asian Economic Affairs.

Overseas Consultants, Inc.

1949. *Report on the seven-year plan*. Vol. 2. New York.

Pahlavi, Mohammed Reza.

1961. *Mission for my country*. New York: McGraw-Hill.

Razi, G. H.

1957. Religion and politics in Iran: a study of social dynamics. Ph.D. dissertation, University of California at Berkeley.

Sandjabi, Karim.

1934. *Essai sur l'économie rural et le régime agraire de la Perse*. Paris: Domant-Montchrestien.

Scarcia, G.

1962. Governo, riforma agraria e opposizione in Persia. *Oriente Moderno* 42 (October–November): 731–801.

Sheean, Vincent.

1927. *The new Persia*. London: The Century Company.

Thorner, Alice, and Thorner, Daniel.

1962. *Land and labour in India*. New York: Asia Publishing House.

United Nations.

1966. *Progress in land reform*. 4th report. Department of Economic and Social Affairs. New York.

United States Army.

1963. *Area handbook for Iran*. Washington, D.C.

Vieille, Paul.

1965. Un groupement féodal en Iran. *Revue française de sociologie* 6: 175–189.

Vreeland, H. H., editor.
　　1957. *Iran*. New Haven: Yale University Press.
Warriner, Doreen.
　　1969. *Land reform in principle and practice*. London: Oxford University Press.
Weulersse, Jacques.
　　1946. *Paysans de Syrie et du Proche-Orient*. Paris: Gallimard.

8

Oil, Economic Policy, and Social Change in Iran*

Iran was the first non-Western country in which oil was discovered and exploited on a commercial scale, and hence the 'oil era' for Iran is significantly longer than for any of the other oil-exporting countries. Discovered in 1908 by a British company that had held a concession since 1901, Iranian oil became of central strategic concern to the British after the British navy switched from coal to oil and the British government purchased a majority of shares in the Anglo-Persian Oil Company in 1914, making it in essence a British government enterprise. The British retained monopoly control on Iranian oil, disturbed only by a short interruption and re-negotiation of terms by Reza Shah in 1932–33, until the nationalization of the then Anglo-Iranian Oil Company in 1951 under Mossadeq. Although the theory of nationalization was retained after Mossadeq's overthrow in 1953, real control passed in a 1954 agreement to a consortium consisting of AIOC (today British Petroleum), several American

* This is a revised version of a paper presented to the conference 'Stratégies de Développement et Changements Sociaux dans les Pays Producteurs de Pétrole d'Afrique et d'Asie,' held in October, 1977, under the auspices of the Association Française de Science Politique, Centre de Hautes Etudes sur l'Afrique et l'Asie Modernes, and organized by Yves Schemeil. Thanks are due to E. Abrahamian, L. Beck, and E. Hooglund for comments on the 1977 paper. Some material from these papers was used in shorter articles in *Iranian Studies*, 1979, 'The Midas Touch' (where there are more details on Ayatollah Khomeini and the religious opposition) and in *Race and Class*, 'Oil, Economic Policy, and Social Conflict in Iran,' where there are more statistics and more details on land reform than in this essay. Editorial help on those essays from Ali Banuazizi and Eqbal Ahmad contributed to this one. Unless otherwise specified in the essay, the policies referred to in the essay were those followed before the 1978–79 events.

majors (later joined by small shares for the so-called 'independents'), Royal-Dutch Shell and the Compagnie Française des Pétroles. The National Iranian Oil Company took charge of drilling and exploration in the poorer areas not covered by the Consortium agreement, and later entered into more favorable agreements with Italian and Japanese companies. The 1954 agreement raised Iran's oil income (thus showing Iran had profited from the 1951 nationalization) and after two decades virtually full Iranian government control was established over Iran's oil policies, with the consortium participating lavishly as a marketing organization in the high profits of Iranian oil, but no longer directly setting prices or production levels.

Even the above bare summary of Iran's oil history is sufficient to suggest that the impact of oil on Iranian society is both longer and more varied than on societies where the discovery of oil was more recent. To discuss 'pre-oil' Iran one must go back before 1908 since, even though the impact of oil on Iranian society in the first years after oil's discovery was relatively small, this impact did have some importance.

The socio-economic structure of pre-oil Iran can be discussed in terms of the Qajar period (1796–1925), excluding the years after 1908. Iran was one of many states in the Middle East in which aridity, difficult terrain, great distances in comparison to population size, and a large nomadic or semi-nomadic population made control by the central government difficult, and necessitated a devolution of power on to local governors, landlords, and nomadic chiefs who often held and administered territory in return for an (often theoretical) duty of military service. Provisional land grants in return for military or other service, which partly reflected the government's inability to pay salaries, bear some resemblance to Western feudalism, although Western features like manorialism and hereditary aristocracy were lacking. In addition to the relative independence of many tribal chiefs, landlords, and governors (all of whom tended to be left alone as long as they turned in revenue due and did not rebel), Iran had another feature which was not found in other Middle Eastern states that might resemble Iran in other respects. This was a considerable political, ideological and financial independence on the part of the Iranian ulama: an independence which grew, rather than decreasing, in the century before 1908.

The growing political, ideological, and economic power of the Iranian ulama in Qajar times was based on several factors: (1) 'Twelver' Shi'ism was the state religion, followed by the vast majority of the population. This branch of Islam held that religious and political leadership passed hereditarily from Mohammad's cousin and son-in-law Ali through a line of *Imams* ending with the Twelfth Imam who went into occultation but will return at the end of time as the *Mahdi* (messiah). Pending his return there is no truly legitimate rule, but Shi'i doctrine came to hold that the best interpreters of the will of the Twelfth Imam were the leading ulama, or *mujtahids*, whose education, knowledge, and popular following gained them recognition. Already in the seventeenth century Jean Chardin quotes mujtahids who attacked the legitimacy of the Safavid shahs, and ulama attacks on the Qajar dynasty increased through the Qajar period. (2) In the eighteenth century the religious center of Shi'ism moved outside Iran to the Shi'i shrine cities in Ottoman Iraq. There the Shi'is had ample revenue based on the donations of the faithful, and from there Shi'i leaders could direct attacks on the government with impunity – a situation very different from that of the capital-based ulama of Cairo, Istanbul, and most Islamic states. (3) The Shi'i ulama, unlike their Sunni counterparts, were the direct recipients of major religious taxes, which elsewhere were usually collected for religious or charitable ends by the government. (4) Since the Shi'i ulama had no formal appointed hierarchy their status was largely based on popularity, and they therefore tended to voice popular grievances (which they could do with relative impunity), particularly those of the urban guildspeople and merchants, to whom they were often allied by family and other ties.[1]

In addition to tribal leaders, holders of land and/or office, and the ulama, who were frequently wealthy, there were other groups with some power. One was the large royal household, in which those relatives of the Shah who were not refractory may be included. The three most important nineteenth century prime ministers sprang from humble origins within the royal household, and the Queen mother or favorite wife often played crucial political roles.

Other important groups with semi-autonomous organization were merchants and craftspeople. Long-distance merchants were often wealthy, respected, and powerful, while guildspeople through their organizations and their ties to the ulama several times played important political roles. The economic and political strength of *Muslim* merchants were greater in Qajar Iran than elsewhere in the Middle East.[2]

A striking feature of the Qajar period, particularly when Iran is contrasted with more 'central' Islamic lands on the Mediterranean, is the almost total lack of effective reform or centralization initiated by rulers. Whereas Egypt, the Ottoman Empire, and Tunisia saw a series of reforms in the nineteenth century that laid the basis for more modern armies, bureaucracies, educational systems, and economic structures – reforms directed for the most part from the top – Iran experienced the barest minimum of such reforms from above. In large measure this was due to Iran's location and ecology, and to the decentralization these encouraged. The power of tribes, ulama, and other groups who balked at modernizing and centralizing reforms, the great difficulty of communication (no roads, only one short navigable river), the distance from Mediterranean trade, and the widely scattered nature of Iran's small population all made centralization, which is a prerequisite to reform from above, extremely difficult. In this Iran partly resembled such areas of the Middle East as Central Asia, Afghanistan, Arabia, and Morocco.[3]

Also hindering reform were relations with Great Britain and Russia, whose balanced rivalry in Iran was the main factor in Iran's continuing formal independence. Once Britain and Russia had, following two victories by Russia in the early nineteenth century, extracted favorable commercial and extraterritorial rights from the Qajars, they both supported the widely disliked Qajar dynasty, which otherwise might have fallen prey to revolt or have been forced to reform. While encouraging certain, chiefly raw material, exports – cotton, dried fruits and nuts, opium, and carpets, in particular – British and Russian policy in Iran as elsewhere was to promote Iranian imports of their own manufactured goods, which undermined Iranian handicrafts and competed with Iranian merchants. Largely because of British and Russian fears of each other, nothing was done to build an infrastructure (which might be used for military purposes). Despite innumerable railroad projects, both countries finally decided railroads would endanger their interests, and hence none were built. Often the British and Russians also entered into independent relations with leaders of tribes and of the ulama and with landlords and governors – relations that were scarcely compatible with the supposed sovereignty of Iran. The Imperial Bank of Persia with exclusive rights to issue paper money was a British institution; the Russian Bank was largely less powerful; and British and Russian nationals controlled other important economic institutions.[4]

A final factor in the lack of reform was the weakness of the Qajar shahs. The only energetic Qajar was crown prince Abbas Mirza, who introduced military and other reforms as governor of the province of Azerbaijan, but died in 1833 before he could take the throne. The most culpable was perhaps Naser ad-Din Shah, whose long reign, 1848–1896, encompassed the period in which reform might have been expected. He briefly appointed two reforming prime ministers, but bowed to the pressures of vested interests against them. These pressures, which included ulama and courtier influence, suggest the difficulties of reform. Nonetheless, it is surprising that such an elementary measure as basic army reform, which would have been in the self-interest of the center, was never seriously attempted, and only a small modernized unit, the Russian-officered and -influenced Cossack Brigade, was formed in 1879.

Qajar oppression and complaisance to foreigners, and the sufferings caused by Western incursions in the Iranian economy, gave rise to various movements of revolt and discontent, which grew in strength from the late nineteenth century. The two most important such protests were the successful movement against a private British monopoly concession on the growth, sale, and export of tobacco in 1891–92, and the constitutional revolution of 1905–1911. Both these movements saw an alliance of the leading oppositional ulama living in Iran and Iraq and the merchants and guildsmen of Iran. Also important were a small but influential group of intellectual reformers, who generally spoke in Islamic terms, which some of them adopted only because they knew they were needed to sway the religious majority. The tobacco movement, culminating in a decree by the leading Shi'i mujtahid forbidding tobacco which was followed by a universal boycott, resulted in the cancellation of the concession. The constitutional revolution gave Iran the constitution that it retained until 1979, but the revolution was suppressed by a Russo-British ultimatum and invasions based on the Anglo-Russian division of Iran into spheres of influence in their entente of 1907. Both of the above Iranian movements had features of classic Western European revolutions, such as prolonged popular fighting rather than military coups. In Iran's case these long popular struggles were possible partly because Iran lacked a standing regular army that might either suppress popular movements or join them to bring about a coup.[5] The 1978–79 events, however, show that a broad-based movement with religious leaders can even stand up to a modern army.

OIL AND SOCIETY, THE EARLY PHASES

The British Legation in Tehran helped the British subject William Knox d'Arcy obtain his 1901 concession for oil rights in all Iran outside the five northern provinces, partly by the ruse of casually communicating the concession in Persian to the Russian legation when the Russians' translator was out of Tehran, and then taking a brief silence to indicate consent. The British government, however, apparently did not take Iranian oil very seriously before its discovery in 1908. Hence, the area in which explorations were proceeding was not included in the British zone of influence in the Anglo-Russian entente of 1907, but rather in the neutral zone where either country was free to act and get concessions. Shortly after the discovery of oil in 1908, however, the British government began to be actively concerned, a concern that culminated in the government's purchase of a majority of shares in the company in 1914. In addition, both the company and the British government were concerned to have cooperative relations with the tribes that dominated much of the Southwestern area where the company operated. This resulted in separate treaties with Shaikh Khaz'al, head of the Arab tribes that dominated Khuzistan, the locus of the oil port and of the huge new Abadan refinery, and also with the Bakhtiari tribes located in oil areas and along the pipelines. These treaties involved payments to tribal leaders and also implied British protection for these tribes, both of which had pretensions to autonomy (although during the constitutional revolution the Bakhtiaris tried to control the government rather than simply be independent). During the early years of oil production the combination of payment and protection to these tribal groups, although smaller in absolute terms, was more significant than the relatively small royalties and payments that went to the center, and hence it can be said that the earliest social effect of oil revenue was to strengthen tendencies toward decentralization and tribal power, and to weaken the already weak center. (By the 1901 concession royalty payments equalled 16 per cent of net profits, but profits were reduced by discount prices to the British navy.)

Iranian nationalism, based on discontent with the government and with foreign control, and a desire for self-strengthening and democracy, grew during World War I, when Iran was disrupted by fighting by the troops and agents of several powers, despite her declared neutrality. During the war the Russians agreed to let Britain add the neutral zone to her sphere. After the war, a desire to protect the Iranian oil supply was one reason why the British, spearheaded by their Foreign Secretary, Lord Curzon, tried to impose on Iran the Anglo-Persian treaty of 1919, which would have made Iran a virtual British protectorate. Opposition to the treaty by Iranians, by the Soviets, who had renounced their concessions in Iran, and by the U.S. and France, who wanted an open door to the Iranian economy, including oil outside the concession area, meant that the treaty was never ratified by the Iranian *majlis* (parliament). Acting on his own, but with no opposition from his government, the head of British military forces in Iran encouraged first the advancement as head of the Persian Cossack Brigade and then the coup d'etat in February 1921 of Reza Khan.[6] The latter first became Minister of War, building up modern military forces; then prime minister; and in 1925 had the *majlis* depose the Qajars and make him Shah. Both the British and Iranian conservative nationalists hoped he would strengthen Iran against radical threats.

Reza Shah was the first ruler to increase oil income and he made use of it especially for military modernization. However, oil income during his reign remained a small to moderate percentage of the budget (never comprising over 25 per cent of the state's revenues), and cannot be said to have been a crucial determinant either of his policies or of social change. As was true earlier, it rather strengthened trends already in existence – in the prewar period it strengthened the autonomy of certain tribes, while in the centralizing phase of Reza Shah it strengthened the trend toward government-controlled modernization. In the 1920s Reza Shah successfully suppressed the autonomy of the large tribes and tribal confederations, using military force when necessary. Shaikh Khaz'al in Khuzistan resisted and expected British backing, but did not get it and was brought to heel. Bakhtiari autonomy was similarly crushed and British payments to the tribes were ended, with all payment going to the center. The Anglo-Persian Oil Company's royalty payments were low and fell further with the world depression, with a dramatic decline in 1931, and when the British would not agree to new terms in 1932 Reza Shah cancelled the concession. It was renegotiated the following year on terms somewhat, but not dramatically, more favorable to Iran, but the new agreement also greatly extended the life of the concession and post-World War II nationalists took a negative view of the renegotiated concession.

Oil income from the time of Reza Shah's suppression of the tribes went exclusively to the Iranian government, giving the government a monopoly on the internal revenue from Iran's major resource, and on the internal component of decisions on how it should be used. These facts made of oil income, even when it was relatively small, an important factor in the strengthening of the central government that has been a feature of all periods of royal rule from 1921 to 1978. After the rise of Reza Shah the trend of Iranian government and society was the opposite of that of the Qajar period; toward greater government control, based on an ever stronger army, police, and secret police and an expanding and increasingly specialized bureaucracy; toward the suppression of the independent power of the ulama, the landlords, the tribal leaders, the urban classes, and indeed all social groups and organizations. Increasingly rapid economic and social modernization have largely replaced pre-industrial and traditional modes of organization and operation. Already under Reza Shah roads, telephones, automobiles, a railroad, and various state-owned factories were introduced, as well as modern schools, a university, some education for girls, the unveiling of women, and new legal codes. Foreigners' power was reduced through the ending of capitulations, the regaining of tariff autonomy, and the beginning of protective tariffs. Parliamentary rule during the constitutional revolution and after World War I had proved too divided and too susceptible to landed and foreign influences to carry out effective modernization, especially in view of Russian and British efforts to dominate Iran; while radical movements in the northern provinces after World War I never gained the scope necessary to fight both the British and Iranian conservatives. Reza Shah thus could appeal both to non-radical middle class and modernizing landlord elements in Iran and to the British and later to the Germans as a non-threatening nationalist to whom some economic and legal concessions would have to be made (as they were to Chiang K'ai-shek and Ataturk), but who could be relied upon to put down communists and radicals. Under Reza Shah leftist movements were outlawed, as were trade unions, and there were numerous jailings, although death was mostly reserved for those formerly close to the seat of power (as it was in Qajar times) and for far fewer radicals than since 1953. Under Reza Shah, as since, it was realized by both sides that Iran's oil income depended on sales to the West, and hence any fundamental break with the West, whether based on oil or other issues, would sharply cut into Iranian government income. Concomitants of centralization were the weakening of ulama and tribal power and a strengthening of the new army and bureaucracy, which were facilitated by oil revenue.

WORLD WAR II AND MOSSADEQ

In the late 1930s Germany became increasingly influential in Iran, and when war began between Germany and Russia in June 1941, Russia and Britain, now allies, needed Iran as a supply route to Russia, and made demands on Reza Shah, including the expulsion of Germans from Iran. Reza Shah felt he could not meet the Russo-British terms and after a brief attempt at military resistance he abdicated in favor of his son, Mohammad Reza. An active parliamentary regime was reinstalled, with considerable influence exercized by Britain, Russia, and later the U.S. The Russians requested a northern oil concession but a majlis deputy, Muhammad Mossadeq, who had years before opposed the accession of Reza Shah, got the majlis to vote a law forbidding any negotiations for concessions without prior majlis approval. This blocked both the Russian concession and Western projects.

Iran became an early terrain for the Cold War, and the U.S.

increasingly supplemented the weakened British as backers of an anti-Soviet policy by Iran. For Iranian nationalists, however, once more strengthened by the dislocations and changes in power and ideology brought by a World War, the crucial issue was not so much the Russo-American cold war as the regaining of Iranian control over her resources, and particularly her major resource, oil. Nationalist concentration on oil was favored by the Anglo-Iranian Oil Company's payment of more in British taxes than in Iranian royalties; by Iran's lack of control over the Company's accounting procedures; by royalty terms adversely affected by inflation; and by the far more favorable terms offered by U.S. companies in Saudi Arabia and Venezuela. In the early phases of postwar Iranian oil negotiations with the British, Iran had some support from the U.S. Ambassador, which may have created illusory hopes of later U.S. support. Gradually, as negotiations resulted in no satisfactory agreement, the demand for the nationalization of the oil industry took the fore. The demand was put forth especially by two political groupings: the National Front, a coalition of dissimilar groups ranging from socialists to religious elements and headed by the liberal nationalist Mossadeq; with varying support from the Tudeh party, which started with elements of a left united front but became increasingly a community party – the party with the largest mass base in Iran. In social class terms the movement culminating in oil nationalization represented, in part, the same classes found in the revolutionary movement of late Qajar times – the bazaar classes of merchants and guildspeople, along with an anti-imperalist ulama and a liberal section of the traditional landed classes, like Mossadeq. They were joined by large numbers of the new middle and working classes, and by the majority of Iranian intellectuals (all groups involved in the 1977–79 movement).

The exacerbation of the oil issue brought about a high level of mass participation in politics and culminated in the choice of Mossadeq as prime minister in 1951 and the nationalization of AIOC. An atmosphere of crisis and panic was created in the West by this act – approached perhaps only by Egypt's nationalization of the Suez Canal. The impression given in the U.S. was that Mossadeq was either unstable, or next thing to a Bolshevik, or both; that Iran was about to 'fall' to the Russians; that Iran could not possibly produce oil without British help, etc. When Iran was unable to sell the oil produced after nationalization, the vast majority of Westerners were given the impression by the media that this was due to Iran's inability to produce oil without Western help. In fact, Iran was producing some oil despite the British departure, but an effective boycott by the major international oil companies, backed by their governments, prevented this oil from being sold. The attempts of Italians, Japanese, and others to buy Iranian oil were blocked by the U.S. Ambassador to Italy and by others who threatened that these countries could not expect U.S. direct and indirect aid and at the same time oppose U.S. policy, which was that Iran must settle the dispute.[7] The British also blocked purchase attempts.

The Iranians, having perhaps overstressed signs of competition between the governments and oil companies of the U.S. and Great Britain, somewhat unexpectedly had to face the prospect of a 'no-oil' economy. An objective economic and social history of the Mossadeq years has still to be written, but it can be noted that, for all the tremendous difficulties caused by cutting off a major source of government revenue and an important source of employment, Iranian industry developed in the years 1951–1953, although limited by difficulties in paying for capital goods imports. This was in part a simple case of necessity: Iran could no longer afford the imports supported by oil exports and hence had in part to substitute for them with her own manufactures. This development under difficulties generally took place without undue favors to large governmental or private industry, and did not result, as has later development, in the building up of a small class of wealthy business men, with middle and small scale entrepreneurs disfavored.

In the agrarian field the record of the Mossadeq government is more doubtful. Although some writers claim that he had a comprehensive program for agrarian reform, the evidence of this is not yet incontrovertible, and the only real measure taken was a palliative. This involved rent reduction for Iranian farmers (mostly sharecroppers) of 20 per cent, of which half was to go to village councils. It is not clear how universally even this measure was carried out. Some important elements in the Mossadeq coalition favored land reform, which might have been carried out in time.

The hostility of the U.S. and the world boycott of Iranian oil were unexpected blows to Mossadeq's governing coalition, and these setbacks, plus the disparate nature of the coalition, help explain the defection of some of Mossadeq's early followers, although he retained his general popularity to the end. The Eisenhower government took a more activist role in Iran than had the Truman government, helping to overthrow Mossadeq and to re-establish the Shah's power in 1953. Before nationalization Iranians had had the illusion that the Western world would be vitally hurt by the loss of Iranian oil, but in fact this loss had been made up very quickly by the expansion of new and old sources, particularly in Kuwait. The main lesson of the Mossadeq era for other oil-producing countries and for Iran, as far as oil was concerned, was probably that nationalization was a highly risky and unprofitable business, since one's own product would be boycotted and the West could recoup its oil losses elsewhere; at this early date the possibilities of concerted action by the oil exporters for nationalization were slight. For many years after 1951 no oil country tried nationalization (Mexico's 1930s experience was not that of a major exporter, and appeared in any case unpromising). The path taken in Iran and elsewhere was rather that of gradual accretions of income and control, in which favorable deals with 'outsiders' like Italy's E.N.I., the Japanese, and the U.S. Independents helped set the pace. Only recently has national control and income become so great and widespread that the step of nationalization could again be tried, with the Western majors retaining such a preponderant share in the huge profits of marketing that they no longer seem to care much whether an oil industry is nationalized.

The above does not mean that Iran's nationalization was, even in the most apolitical economic terms, a 'mistake' that had predominantly negative results for Iran. On the contrary, it is probable that nationalization and the scare it gave the majors were key factors in the increasingly favorable oil terms that Iran obtained from the majors and other companies from 1954 to the present. From the time of the 1954 agreement between Iran and the newly formed Western consortium the theory of nationalization was retained, but until recently this was mainly a myth. In the 1954 agreement, royalties ('payments') to Iran were raised considerably (50–50) but control over production and marketing decisions was handed back to a consortium of AIOC,

U.S. majors (later also 'Independents'), Royal-Dutch Shell, and the Compagnie Française des Pétroles. Over the years the Shah, ever eager for higher production and prices, both entered into more favorable agreements with companies outside the consortium area and renegotiated consortium terms so that since the early 70's both production and pricing have been in Iran's hands (limited by OPEC). The foreign companies provide technical aid and do most of the foreign marketing, and there has been a kind of coalition still between these companies and the Iranian government and its NIOC. The foreign companies have not suffered, as the rise in oil prices and the very low production costs of Middle Eastern oil mean that both Middle Eastern governments and foreign companies can draw huge profits from the production and sale of oil.

OIL, PLANNING, AND DEVELOPMENT STRATEGIES

From the first of the post World War II Plans to 1978 there was an intimate link between oil income and planning, with ca. 55–90 per cent of Plan Organization funds (the low figure is for the 2nd Plan and high figure is for the 5th Plan, 1973–77) coming from oil. The vast majority of the government's receipts come from oil, 88 per cent in 1974, and the percentage for plan funds is even higher.

Outside the Communist world the vogue for planning, or for talking about planning, is essentially a post World War II phenomenon. Reza Shah did not talk of planning, and yet a huge long-term project involving heavy expenditures and complex engineering like the Trans-Iranian Railroad would today be considered a phenomenon of planning. On the opposite side, it has been doubted that the first two or three Iranian plans can meaningfully be called plans, since they mostly grouped together disparate government projects with no provision for enforcing an effective government strategy towards the economy and society as a whole.[8] Despite these caveats, we will here deal briefly with the whole period since 1949 partly under the heading of planning, since it evinces some of the elements of planning and shows certain consistent trends in governmental economic and social strategies.

Iran's first plan was a seven-year plan that was to run from

1949 to 1956 and to be financed chiefly out of oil revenues. It was heavily influenced by preliminary studies made by the American engineering consultant firm, Morrison-Knudson Company, and by Max Thornburg, an influential American private oil man. Its strategy emphasized agriculture, private enterprise, and infrastructure, and like later plans it foresaw no major socio-economic transformations. It was largely vitiated by bureaucratic and private interests even before the cut-off of its main source of income, oil revenues, effectively killed it in 1951.

Later plans have become increasingly sophisticated in technique and personnel and increasingly comprehensive in coverage, although a running battle between the 'independent' Plan and Budget Organization and the ministries that are supposed to carry out its projects but would often prefer to develop their own, was a continual cause of delays and immobilization. In the late 1950s an Economic Bureau was set up for the Plan Organization assisted by a group of Western advisers under the auspices of Harvard University. The only general evaluative published work by a member of this bureau is almost totally negative regarding planning in Iran, and notes that the main economic advances experienced by Iran in the past half century have occurred not through planning but because of nationalism – such as the increasing control over oil, tariffs, and relations with foreigners.[9] It is thus perhaps best to be wary when talking of 'planning' in Iran. The government has, indeed, followed a general economic strategy and this strategy has been highly influenced by the presence and increase of large oil revenues. It seems likely, however, that much of this strategy might have been followed without the mechanism of a Plan Organization, although the latter has had at a minimum the ideological role of making it appear that the government was thinking ahead for the benefit of the whole country, and using the most up to date mechanisms to insure rapid economic and social progress. Often the dictates of Mohammad Reza Shah in fact determined economic policies.

Governmental strategy toward the economy, especially since the 1960s, was rapidly to develop large enterprises, using as much modern and labor-saving technology as possible. Despite a few showy 'crack-downs' extremely large profits were encouraged for both domestic and foreign companies, while little was done for those on the bottom rungs of the economic scale. The above policy was justified by some according to the partly fashionable theory that in early stages of development income distribution must worsen, and that those at the top of the scale should be favored since they save and invest more than those at the bottom. The rival theory that, at least at the stage Iran has reached, much greater equality of incomes is needed for self-sustaining development if a mass consumer market where people can buy back what they produce is to be achieved, is rarely stressed. The vogue for bigness and modernity, with its concomitants of underemployment, unemployment, and poverty, affected agriculture as well as industry, and deserves as much study as the more publicized land reform. In both industry and agriculture heavy inputs of foreign capital, personnel, and many imports were favored by official policies.

The essential mechanisms of the above economic strategy are fairly simple, although not well known to non-specialists. Oil income was one factor in a generally regressive tax structure, encouraging the government not to enforce its mild income tax and not to institute other progressive taxes. The government can essentially do without tax income, and did not try seriously to use taxation either as one means for more just income distribution or to prepare Iranian tax-collectors and citizens for the day not long hence when oil will start to run out.

More seriously, the impetus given by oil to the dramatic economic boom experienced by Iran from 1963 until the late 1970s, with her per capita g.n.p. rising from ca. $200 to $1000 in real terms, and with one of the highest growth rates in recent history for a sizable country, did not lead to a narrowing of the already wide income gap between the rich and the poor, but quite the contrary. Gains were concentrated at the upper levels, and this was largely the result of government policies.

In industry, government policies, at least since the 1960s, favored the private production of relatively expensive consumer durables with a large foreign component and a concentrated market in Tehran, and also encouraged the concentration of economic enterprises in or near Tehran. This helped both Iranian and foreign investors, who by law were free to repatriate their profits. The role of oil income in these policies could be direct; as when the government forgoes industrial taxes to favor certain industries, and can do so because of its oil income, or itself builds industries or infrastructure that favor other large industries; or it could be indirect, as when the government is able on the basis of oil income to pay higher salaries to the higher administrative echelons, thus enabling them to purchase consumer durables.

The relevant government policies included preferential high tariffs to lower foreign competition; prohibition of certain imports for the same reason; very low rates for bank loans to large industries; tax holidays; licensing of only a few industries in each field; and preferential treatment for foreign capital. Critical economists do not deny that high tariffs and prohibitions may have been needed in some cases at an initial stage in order to launch an industry, but they note that tariffs are seldom lowered, so that there is little incentive to operate efficiently, or to direct capital toward those branches of production using local inputs (tariffs on capital goods are low and do not discourage inappropriate production). A bewildering variety of unneeded automobiles were assembled and partially produced, while many goods that could be made for popular use in small plants were either imported or handmade in insufficient quantities. Lowered tariffs could rationalize production by reducing the production of complex goods requiring many imported elements and encouraging production of simpler, more popular goods, which should need less tariff production as their manufacture is relatively less expensive. Capital goods production, which often requires small plants, could be encouraged by new tariff policies.

Credit policies in industry, as in agriculture, were similarly designed to favor large factories and the rich Iranians and foreigners who own and run them. In general, rates of 6–9 per cent, which are considerably below the market price of money, were available only to large enterprises, while small shopowners and craftsmen were starved for bank credit, since their plant did not provide sufficient collateral for a loan. They were generally not even eligible for normal bank rates of ca. 12 per cent, but had to borrow in the bazaar for 25–50 per cent. Economists concerned with the provision of employment, better done by small than large concerns, and with reversing the trend toward greater income inequality, suggested the governmental loan policy should be reversed, with higher commercial rates charged to the big industrialists and lower rates to the small owners.

(Difficulties in getting bank loans were probably one factor in 1978 attacks on banks, although other factors were more often mentioned.)

Tax holidays of various kinds have been given to encourage foreign investors, or investors in certain regions. Although this policy was publicized as a way to decentralize industry out of the Tehran region, by offering tax inducements to factories built at least 120 km from Tehran, it was found that the concentration of industry in the Central Province where Tehran is located in fact increased after the policy was enunciated, with a kind of ring of industries built about 120 km from Tehran.

Although legally a company did not need a license in order to operate, any sizable company did need one to import, export, deal with the government, etc. Government licenses were given out only to a few companies in each field, and their main theoretical rationale was to keep the field from getting so overcrowded that plants overproduced and could not operate to capacity. In fact, the need to get and keep a license, like many other government rules, required that at least one top person in the company spend much time in Tehran cultivating one or more leading personages in order to insure the receipt of a license or other needed favorable treatment. Regarding licenses and other matters, stories circulate of Iranians of the highest status who took, say, 10 per cent of a new company's stock gratis in return for using their influence to deliver a license. Such practices, along with most of the industrial practices listed above, and with other forms of corruption, significantly increased the sale price of Iranian goods, thus limiting their domestic and ultimately needed foreign market. They also further skewed income distribution. (Corruption, often stressed in discussions of Iran, is probably most important as one more mechanism that pushes wealth up [and out], far more than it trickles down.)

As to foreign capital, although foreigners may legally own only a minority share in Iranian industries, they are subject to few other restrictions and they may repatriate profits freely. Brochures for foreign investors proclaimed that profits on capital of 30 per cent were normal in Iran. Economists who know the country often speak of 50 per cent, and profits in trade and industry of 100–200 per cent are not unknown. Hence it is not surprising that the 'traditional' Middle Eastern reluctance to invest in 'unprofitable' industry gave way to an industrial boom, but it was a boom aimed largely at a restricted, relatively wealthy market, which carried within it major problems.

It is within the context of industrial policies favoring large profits by a few capital-intensive industries that the occasional campaigns against 'profiteers,' or in favor of shareholding by factory workers, which were given more publicity than the above policies, must be evaluated. Such measures were at best palliatives taken in face of rising profits, income inequalities, high inflation, and a failure to meet government promises of greater economic and social equity. Along with certain other policies they were also designed to allay the discontent of the class that evinced, through fairly frequent, illegal, and unreported strikes, its continued discontent – the factory workers. Partly through government favoring of factory workers by shareholding and other measures, which were, however, less dramatic than their announcements would make it seem, and partly through rising wages for qualified workers, workers in factories and in certain trades became a relatively favored group in the mid-70s. One cannot, however, take reports regarding categories of workers whose wages say, tripled in a few years, as typical of the popular classes as a whole. As for the jailed or exiled 'profiteers,' they were more often disfavored bazaar merchants or members of minorities than rich modern Muslim businessmen.

The above remarks do not mean that the government's industrial policy since 1961 produced only negative results. The rate of industrial growth was one of the highest in the world, and rose further with the impact of huge oil revenues since 1974. What can be strongly questioned is the continuation of preferential policies toward Western-style industries; the disfavoring of small crafts and industries, which contribute to production, to employment, and to greater income equality; the favoring of foreign investments and the kind of production to which foreigners must contribute heavily; and the underwriting of heavy consumer durables which contribute to the overcentralization of the national market in Tehran, and to the development of a kind of consumer demand which has meant that 'import substitution' has led to a rise in imports of food, capital goods, and even many consumer goods. Thus, many of the problems that were frequently noted by Iran's own governmental planners – such as overcentralization in Tehran and a few large cities, too many automobiles and luxury imports, too much dependence on foreigners, and above all the constantly growing gap in income distribution – were fed by the government's industrial policies.[10]

THE AGRARIAN SCENE

Many of the same points can be made about the government's agricultural policies, which, like industrial policies, were largely supported by oil income. Since the launching of Land Reform in two major stages since 1962, Iran's agrarian policies have generally been discussed in terms of Land Reform, but it is increasingly clear that this important reform was only one part of a more general agricultural policy, which should be discussed as a totality. As Land Reform was the first phase of this policy, it will be dealt with first.

Only since World War II has there been serious governmental consideration of Land Reform, and the Mossadeq reforms noted above and the Shah's sale of the majority of his father's (disputed) crown lands to their peasants may be regarded as preliminary, but not comprehensive, reform measures. A more serious reform bill in 1960 was eviscerated by the majlis, and a time when the majlis had been dissolved, and a reformist government under prime minister Ali Amini and agricultural minister Hassan Arsanjani was in power, was chosen for a new land reform pushed by Arsanjani. The first phase of the reform, passed in 1962, sold to peasants on the basis of the (generally low) tax evaluations of their landlords all villages above one village or its (inflated) equivalent, owned by the larger landlords. Only peasants with a cultivating right got land, thus eliminating landless laborers. In the subsequent second and third phases of reform, applied from 1965 and 1969 respectively, much more conservative means were used to settle lands of landlords with one village or less. A small majority of the peasants with cultivating rights on these lands finally became owners of some land, but far less than they had cultivated and needed for subsistence. Orchards, plantations, certain pastures, and mechanized lands were exempted in both phases. All new landholders were supposed to become members of newly formed cooperative credit societies. For all the weaknesses of the reform – many landlords succeeded in giving lands to family or friends, a few had enough influence to escape reform, many lands were declared 'mechanized' and hence unreformable on slight evidence, and peasant shares varied greatly even within one village, from zero for those with no cultivation rights to high quantities to a few – the reform in its first phase may be regarded as progressive and having a potential for success. To become a real success, however, it would have been necessary to give more land to most peasants, to increase government aid and inputs, and also to encourage peasant self-management of expanding multi-purpose cooperatives. None of these things was done.[11]

Instead, one finds in agriculture a close parallel of the policies followed in industry, with the greatest amount of government economic and technical aid and encouragement going into very large agricultural units while the small and middle peasant, to say nothing of the impoverished agricultural laborer, were increasingly starved of government help and actively discouraged from effectively managing their own affairs on a comprehensive cooperative basis.

The government bias toward big units was manifested within a few years of agrarian reform especially through two policies, embodied in two major laws and programs. One was the law for the creation of Farm Corporations. In these large units one, or usually more, villages were combined into a corporation, with peasants 'persuaded' to turn over their recently received lands to their corporation, in return for which they got one or more shares in the corporation, according to how much they gave in. Their wages were based on a combination of land and labor, but since Farm Corporations use modern machinery not all shareholders could be employed, while the former farm laborers could hardly ever be employed, and these groups contributed to the massive migration to overcrowded cities. Farm corporations were run by government specialists sent out from Tehran, and require a large expenditure for machinery, and for salaries, housing, and other buildings for the non-farmers, etc. Farm corporation directors and others often claim that their enterprises are profitable, but their basis of calculation does not include all these initial and overhead expenses by the government, and the claim of current profitability is not credible. It is clear that in the early phases at least peasants generally dislike the farm corporation, but I have seen no studies of their attitudes ten years after joining. It would seem surprising, however, if a peasant would put as much productive effort into a farm corporation as he would on his own farm. The number of farm corporations is about 100, and they were scheduled to continue a steady increase.

The other form of large production that has been favored, at least until very recently, has been huge agribusinesses, usually owned and operated by multinational corporations. These farms of tens of thousands of acres have generally been built below new dams, especially in Khuzistan. Despite their supposed concentration on 'new' land, they too have cleared off many small peasants, and those who did not become agricultural laborers joined the rural exodus. Agribusinesses have generally farmed only a small part of the land they held, and their relative contribution to the Iranian economy has been considered dangerously small by Iranian experts – well below that of the middle peasants. Before 1978 some of the largest agribusinesses, especially in Khuzistan, were taken over by the government in part because of poor performance, but it is unclear what policies will be adopted toward their lands. Both agribusinesses and farm corporations have been proven to be far less productive than middle peasants[12] but one may suspect that the former were favored both by foreign farm equipment manufacturers and Iranian special interests.

Government policy also favored smaller private mechanized farming. Toward the reformed villages, however, the government did little in terms of economic or technical aid, or aid in forming multi-purpose cooperative societies. In certain spheres, there was progress in a minority of villages as in the military service literacy corps, supplemented to a small degree by health and development corps. In the more direct problems of production, however, the government did little. Few of the technical benefits of the 'green revolution' were diffused; there were scarcely any efforts to pool resources for machinery; and extension services, and technical teaching are extremely inadequate. The cooperatives remain mostly purely credit societies, instead of giving the aid in marketing and other economic needs that a multi-purpose society could give. The cooperatives' loan policies favor the wealthier peasants, some of whom borrow and relend at high rates, and many cooperatives retain the rule that loans go only to landholding peasants for agricultural purposes, so that the large army of village carpet weavers (mostly women and girls) and other craftspeople, among others, are denied access to low-interest loans despite their credit-worthiness. In addition, studies show that cooperative loans cover only a small share of peasant credit needs, the rest of which must be met at the old usurious rates. Cooperative loan policy thus favors a growing income gap within the village, which is also favored by the much-touted digging of deep wells for the first time in many villages. By drawing off the water that once fed the more democratically divided underground channel, the owner of a well can monopolize and sell a precious resource; not to mention the problem of a constantly lowered water table, already found in some regions.

The Iranian government, in favoring a policy of mechanized extensive farming and disfavoring the small and medium peasant, despite the latter's proven higher productivity per person within Iran itself, has adopted a policy that might be economically rational in a country with large cultivable territories and a shortage of labor. In Iran, however, the present cultivable surface is too small for a heavily underemployed rural labor force, and to push ahead with large mechanized farms rather than more intensive techniques operated by peasants with a personal stake in their own lands has been counterproductive. The productive record of agribusiness has been bad; farm corporations have contributed less than would the same amount of government capital and effort spread over reformed villages; and increases in agricultural production have been low. Although official statistics on the annual rise in agricultural production state that it was ca. 4 per cent a year, this figure is almost universally considered unreliable and based on the need to mask the shocking reality that agricultural production rose more slowly than the population. A more reasonable estimate is that agricultural production rose ca. 2–2.5 per cent a year (and population 3 per cent). With rising mechanization, the unemployment or very low income of agricultural laborers, and the rise in rural population, there was a rapid stream of rural migrants into the cities, especially Tehran – cities that have not the housing, amenities, or even jobs to cope with them. The agrarian situation plus a growth in food consumption meant a rapid rise in agricultural imports, which once more will create a major problem when oil income begins to run out. Government policies also impoverished many nomads and forced them to settle, thus reducing sheep production, and forcing growing imports of meat and wool.

If the government favored the big over the small in both city and countryside, it also favored the cities – already wealthier and more powerful – over the countryside. This is shown particularly in price controls on basic food products, which for a time kept down the vocal discontent of the more volatile urban masses. Although to some degree supported by direct government subsidies, these controls were also based on fixed low prices paid to producers for certain agricultural products – prices which further depressed agricultural incomes relative to urban ones.

INCOME DISTRIBUTION

With what has been said, it is not surprising that income gaps widened in the 1960s and 1970s. Although no good income surveys exist, there are regular family expenditure surveys, and on the basis of these both Iranian and foreign economists have done studies with similar conclusions. Briefly, since the 1960s, income inequalities in Iran, which were already great on a world scale, have increased, and this increase has been particularly dramatic since 1974, when oil income shot up after the great price rise. The size and increase in Iran's distribution gap is notable whether the top decile or two are compared with the bottom decile or two, or whether one takes the GINI coefficient, which measures deviation from the norm all along a normal distribution scale. In addition, an important recent Iranian study shows increases in income inequality in all different major dimensions: between the top and the bottom; between the cities and the countryside; within the cities; and within the countryside.[13] All this took place despite a repeatedly expressed government determination to reduce income inequalities. However, as noted briefly above, overall it is the rich who are subsidized by oil and other governmental money, and the poor much less.

This should not be taken to mean that 'the poor are getting poorer' since, on the whole, this was not the case. Given the huge increase in G.N.P. per capita noted above, the rich could get much richer and many of the poor still get slightly richer. The Iranian popular classes started from such a low income level, however, that even doubling or tripling their effective income would not bring them to anything like European working class standards. Also, they witnessed the conspicuous consumption of the higher classes all around them, and this was bound to give rise to increasingly vocal discontents. The consumption patterns encouraged by the current distribution along with the dizzy growth of recent years based on oil created a host of national problems: constantly increasing spending on imports; orientation of the economy toward dependence on foreigners and toward consumer durables whose market centers are in Tehran and a few other cities; the continued flow of the population towards the overcrowded cities; the lack of urban low-cost housing and the skyrocketing of housing prices, partly caused by the growing presence of foreigners encouraged by arms expenditures and the consumer economy, etc. A more equitable income distribution could be aided by, and could contribute to, a serious policy of economic decentralization and dispersion of the population, and could create a market for goods with greater Iranian inputs. A policy favoring peasants and artisans could boost production, add to employment, and encourage population dispersion (especially if crafts and small industries were developed in or near villages).

OIL INCOME AND GOVERNMENT POWER

One of the key features of oil income in Iran as in many other countries is that it long enabled the government significantly to add to its domestic and foreign power. It is impossible to separate oil income from other government income, but since oil income provides the great majority of government income, such a separation is scarcely necessary.

Mohammad Reza Shah's 25 years of strong control was based on a number of factors. In the early stages U.S. support, itself partly based on oil interests and seconded by the British and others, was of importance. It was the Americans who transferred FBI training methods to Iran, later seconded by the Israelis. Many Iranians were apt pupils in intelligence and secret police methods, and this aptitude had some basis in money, which in turn had its base in oil. Both the large size of the various Iranian police, intelligence, and secret police organizations, and their and the government's ability to 'persuade' (and not only by terror) owed something to the money at the government's disposal.

The wide-ranging attraction of Western-trained and often Western-based intellectuals and technocrats into government and university service was based partly on a desire to go home, partly on a belief that they could be useful there, but also on the handsome salaries and working conditions they were often offered, and here the change in emoluments from days when Iran had rather little oil income on which to base such a policy is notable.

The international side of the power coin is also important. The press has often noted the unprecedented purchases of the world's most sophisticated arms by Iran, and it goes without saying that these are based on oil money. Many of these arms were too advanced for many Iranians to learn to use before they became obsolete; nonetheless, there was such a variety of them that even with all the inevitable waste Iran appeared as a power to be reckoned with in the Persian Gulf and the Middle East, where Iran's foreign policy initiatives, whether regarding Iraq, the Dhofar rebels, or Tumbs and Abu Musa usually succeeded. Arms purchases, however, increased inflation, imports, shortages of crucial building and other materials and man-power, and the overcrowding of ports and access roads.

THE OPPOSITION

Despite the size and effectiveness of the police, secret police, army, and gendarmerie in enforcing the Shah's policy of disallowing opposition movements, due partly to the support and sophisticated training of these forces via oil income, opposition groups continued to exist and sometimes to manifest activity even before 1978. Among three border nationalities there have been nationalist movements in the past ten years. Some Kurds in the late 1960s and some Baluchis in the 1970s engaged in armed struggle, but in both cases the movements were far from gaining widespread active support, and were put down after many months by the Iranian armed forces. Both movements were more based on ties to nationalist movements among the related ethnic group beyond the border (although Barzani in Iraq was not favorable, as he was hoping for Iranian aid against Iraq, which he later got) than on the Sunnism of these groups. There is also a movement among the Arabs of the oil province, Khuzistan, calling for independence of that province, which they call Arabistan. This movement has had outside Arab support, particularly from Iraq until the Irano-Iraqi agreement of 1975. Those who support it say that Arabistan (as it was officially called before Reza Shah) was independent until Reza Khan moved in militarily and overthrew the tribal Shaikh Khaz'al in 1924. In fact, Khuzistan was recognized as within the borders of Iran for the whole Qajar period although, like many distant tribal areas, it was mostly ruled internally by its tribal leaders. Before and during World War I the British supported Shaikh Kaz'al financially and militarily, and he was encouraged to think of independence of Reza Khan and to hope for British support in this, but the area was never legally independent and the British did not support him. The current demand for independence is a dream, unless the world situation should change drastically, since the majority of the population of Khuzistan is now non-Arab, and the oil wells on which Iran's growth and prosperity is based are in Khuzistan. So far Arab nationalist feeling in Khuzistan has not caused the government much trouble, but nationalism everywhere is so volatile that this may not always be the case.

By far the largest national minority, the Azerbaijani Turks, have not recently been involved in an active nationalist movement, although any aware visitor to the province can see that cultural nationalism at least is strong. The Iranian practice of teaching and publishing almost exclusively in Persian may have to give way to some recognition of Iran's multinationalism. Tribal groups whose native language is not Persian, like the Turkic Qashqai and Sunni Turcomans may also push demands, as they have in the past.

Aside from national opposition, there were even before 1978 opposition trends among different classes and social groups. Among these are factory workers, who engaged in growing numbers of strikes in the 1970s. Although only government-approved, which means government-controlled, trade unions were legal, and strikes were illegal, there were numerous strikes, including some in oil and other major industries. These were usually put down by the police or armed forces, with official threats of dismissal and/or punishment if the strikers did not go back to work, some of which were carried out. On the other hand, salary and other demands were often partially granted, indicating the government's concern to keep workers in large industry relatively satisfied, as did, in another way, the Shah's schemes for profit sharing and stock purchase by workers. There appear to have been no non-official workers' organizations beyond the bounds of one local industry, but it would probably have been almost impossible to form such a group.

Another frequently oppositional group were the students, who often staged strikes with a variety of demands – strikes that like the workers' strikes were unreported in the Iranian press and usually in the West. Their strikes, evidently considered less serious for the state and economy than workers' ones, often lasted for some time, although the usual carrot and stick methods were used to suppress them. As in some Western countries student demonstrations were partly in favor of general political, economic, and social demands, and partly for university-related aims.

The bazaar middle classes have often been oppositional, but until 1978 their opposition often took a rather indirect form, often expressed in semi-religious gatherings or processions. Very important have been intellectuals and professionals. Writers and poets have continued to express in indirect terms that might avoid the strict censorship in Iran their opposition to the way things are and their pessimism or hostility to the Iranian environment. One of the most popular essays of the 60s, *Gharbzadegi* (Westoxication) by the late Al-e Ahmad, criticized superficial aping of the West in a way not at all profound, but it struck a responsive chord as much for what it suggested and could not say as for what it said.

President Carter's stand on human rights was for a few months taken somewhat seriously in Iran. On the one hand the government released some political prisoners and in principle adopted some more normal international standards for trial conduct, and on the other hand three important petitions were presented to the government by mid-1977 asking for a better human rights policy. One of these featured formerly prominent members of the National Front, another writers and intellectuals, and another lawyers. Several signers had previously been jailed, and it is striking that no similar petitions are known for many years before 1977, and if they had been signed it is likely that many of their signers would have been jailed. Although the persons who signed showed great courage, their action suggested an easing up on human rights issues.

Aside from ethnic and class groups, the opposition may be discussed in terms of ideologically based groups and parties. Among these is the Tudeh or Community Party, formed in the 1940s, and now following a line so moderate and pro-Soviet that many leftists hold it in contempt. An offshoot is pro-Chinese, but once Iran and China set up relations, the Chinese became even more pro-Shah than the Soviets (the Chinese liked the Shah because they found him basically anti-Soviet), and this offshoot group is not in a much more radical position than the Tudeh. Various groups even before 1978 identified with Mossadeq and the National Front, but the latter never had a single ideology, and these groups also varied, with some religious and some secular nationalism. The National Front, as in the past, represents especially modern middle class and professional groups.

Quite important have been Iran-based guerilla organizations— the Fedaiyyin, which appeals to Marxism, and the Mojahedin to Islam and sometimes Marxism. They conceived of themselves as vanguards of a growing guerilla movement, but until 1978 their activities centered largely on assassinations of Iranian politicians and U.S. advisers. It seems likely that these activities encouraged the crackdown experienced in Iran since the late 1960s, although they probably also kept alive the idea of active opposition to the government.

Finally, the religious opposition, which overlaps some of the above groups, should be stressed. Twelver Shi'ism has long been more independent of the state than Sunnism, and Shi'i leaders, or mujtahids, are considered superior to the shahs in temporal as well as religious rulings. Religious leaders were active in politics in the Qajar period, and provided political leadership in the constitutional revolution in 1905–11. Although kept from politics under Reza Shah, religious leaders reentered politics from 1941. Ayatollah Kashani and some other religious leaders were for a time in Mossadeq's coalition. The more extremist Fedaiyyin-e Islam assassinated leaders considered pro-Western or anti-religious, and attempted to kill one of Mossadeq's liberal ministers, Fatemi. Many conservative ulama, as well as the Fedaiyyin, opposed Mossadeq.

The ulama have long been divided between those with government ties or appointment and the majority who are more independent of the government, who are more trusted. Since the residence there of the last single head of the Shi'i faith, Ayatollah Borujerdi, Qom has replaced the Iraqi shrine cities as the center of Iranian Shi'ism. After Borujerdi's death in 1961 the independent ulama revived their oppositional role. This opposition saw the government as tyrannical and many of its measures as anti-Islamic. Although there is dispute over whether most of the oppositional ulama opposed land reform, as the Shah claimed without documents, some of them clearly did, and most of the religious opposition were against votes for women. Ulama opposition in 1963–4 may have involved the above issues, but was also based on issues the government did not mention: Iran's relations with Israel, including supplying oil; the restoration of extraterritorial rights to U.S. soldiers and their families, a U.S. military loan, and governmental tyranny. In June 1963 there were large ulama-led anti-government riots, tied to the arrest of the main oppositional mujtahid, Ayatollah Khomeini, which were bloodily suppressed. Khomeini continued for years to publish from Iraq. His writings then showed him to be a fundamentalist on some things, such as the Family Protection Law of 1967 that went far toward equalizing women's family rights. On other matters he innovates, as in his argument that Islam opposes monarchy – a stronger point than those of his Shi'i predecessors, but one which finds support both in the elective Sunni caliphate and the Twelver Shi'i belief in the absence of legitimate rule pending the return of the 'hidden' Twelfth imam.[14]

Recent study shows that religious centers like Qom remained centers of opposition to the government by both the ulama and religious students, sometimes, as in 1975, breaking into large demonstrations, which like other demonstrations got no press coverage. Many secularly educated students and intellectuals have also shown an increasingly religious orientation. This is partly because with the expansion in the number of students more are now coming from petty bourgeois religious backgrounds. But the phenomenon is also in part oppositional, with many students finding the Islamic opposition the most effective and appealing.

The association of the government's oppression with its ties to the West, and of current evils with Westernization, make many students and some intellectuals idealize Islam as an alternative, and seek in it a basis for a more just and independent state.

The tendency for religion to be class-divided has not been overcome by the above counter-tendency. Most of the modernized middle and upper classes, even if they call themselves Muslim, till 1979 flouted Islamic rules, never went to a mosque, and followed a Western life style. The bazaar classes and the masses remain overwhelmingly Islamic, and there is a conflict in life styles. In these classes the women wear the *chador*, marriages are arranged, major religious rules are followed, and religious leaders are influential.

The Shah's regime tried to some degree to identify with Islam; finding complaisant ulama, and teaching a monarchist version of Islam in the schools. It also made not very successful attempts to create a 'religious corps' to teach religion in the villages.

Also important are lay intellectuals who attack the secularization and Westernization of Iran and call for the reestablishment of an Islamic society as they interpret it. These men, associated with reformist mosques and schools that opened in the 1960s, but were soon closed by the government, in addition to opposing the government tried to lay the basis for a reformed Islamic society, based on their interpretations of Islam. Although the leaders of this trend have sometimes been jailed, the writings of one, Ali Shariati (d. 1977), were also used in a newspaper by the government, probably because of their anti-communist content. Basically, however, Shariati's interpretation of Islam was progressive and reformist, and he helped attract new groups to the religious opposition.[15] There thus exist several competing interpretations of Shi'i Islam, but since the mujtahids have often differed in their views, this is not an entirely new situation.

A POLICY FOR THE FUTURE

Desirable policies may be summarized as: reduce or end the high subsidies to the rich, and increase subsidies to productive activities by the poor. Iran, however, faces the problem that if wages are raised rapidly Iran's products will become even less competitive on international markets. It seems reasonable to concentrate not so much on wages as on other desperate needs: (1) education, which remains poor both quantitatively and qualitatively, and includes scarcely any decent vocational education; (2) housing, the lack of which has reached emergency proportions qualitatively, quantitatively, and in price, especially in the cities; (3) health care, which is still concentrated almost entirely in Tehran and the cities, although a few paramedical programs have been started; (4) supplementary occupations for villages, where underemployed men and women abound, and where crafts and small industries could be promoted; (5) loans and technical support for productive activities by the poor and middle income groups should be greatly expanded and those to the rich decreased; such support could include low-interest loans to peasants, craftspeople, and small businesses; more production and marketing cooperatives among craftspeople and carpet weavers; a great expansion in capital and range of activities of rural cooperatives; and technical aid and education for villagers; (6) encouragement of people to enter the low-paid and badly trained teaching profession primarily through greatly increased housing, insurance, health and other amenities, and also upgrading of training of new and in-service teachers, including encouragement of greater initiative by teachers and pupils.

The impression of most who lived in or visited the main cities in the 1970s has been negative; in Tehran especially, unbearable traffic and pollution, transport difficulties for those with or without private automobiles, repeated shortages of food items, housing shortages with incredible prices for both rich and poor, and a sense of tension among the population lead to a widespread characterization of the city as 'unlivable.' Governmental and private strategies and policies to 1978 created not only progress but also major problems that require basically new strategies for their solution.

POSTSCRIPT, MARCH 1979

The problems and forces outlined above, along with hatred for royal dictatorship and elite corruption, contributed to the Iranian Revolution of 1978–79. It is too early to predict much about Iran's future, but it may be said that the groups now in power have made economic criticisms of the old regime that are somewhat similar to those outlined above. On the other hand, the wave of Islamic fundamentalism creates dangers for human rights, especially women's and minority rights, while demands by groups whose first language is not Persian create a difficult challenge for Iran.

NOTES

1. On the ulama and other social groups under the Qajars see Chapters 2 and 5 of this volume; H. Algar, *Religion and State in Iran 1785–1906*, Berkeley 1969; N. Keddie, 'The Roots of the Ulama's Power in Modern Iran,' in *Scholars, Saints, and Sufis*, ed. N. R. Keddie, Berkeley, 1972; *Religion and Rebellion in Iran: The Tobacco Protest of 1891–92*, London, Frank Cass, 1966; 'The Iranian Power Structure and Social Change 1800–1969: An Overview,' *International Journal of Middle East Studies*, 2, 1971, 3–20; Charles Issawi, ed., *The Economic History of Iran 1800–1914*, Chicago, 1971; A. Ashraf and H. Hekmat, 'The State of the Traditional Bourgeoisie in Nineteenth Century Iran,' volume on Middle Eastern economic history, ed. A. Udovitch, Princeton, Darwin Press, 1979.

2. This point was well made by Gad Gilba in his paper and discussion at the conference on nineteenth century Iran and Turkey, Babolsar, Iran, 1978.

3. See Chapter 8 of N. Keddie, *The Middle East and Beyond*, London, Frank Cass, forthcoming.

4. On British and Russian relations with Iran and Iranians see F. Kazemzadeh, *Russia and Britain in Persia 1864–1914*, New Haven, 1968; N. Keddie, 'British Policy and the Iranian Opposition: 1901–1907,' *Journal of Modern History*, 39, 3, September, 1967, 266–282; N. Keddie, 'Iranian Politics 1900–1905: Background to Revolution,' three parts, *Middle Eastern Studies*, 1969.

5. On the period of revolt see Algar, *op. cit.* and the relevant books and articles by Keddie cited in note I. See also Chapter 1, and N. Keddie, *Sayyid Jamal ad-Din 'al-Afghani': A Political Biography*, Berkeley, 1972; *An Islamic Response to Imperialism*, Berkeley, 1968; Chapter 2 of *The Middle East and Beyond*, London, Frank Cass, forthcoming; Homa Pakdaman, *Djamal-ed-Din Assad Abadi dit Afghani*, Paris, 1969; and the Persian sources cited in all the above. See also the books on the revolution by E. G. Browne, Morgan Shuster, and R. McDaniel, and the articles and forthcoming book that discuss aspects of it by E. Abrahamian.

6. The best-documented account, which rests on the basis of the diary of the head of the British forces in Iran, Gen. Ironside, and British F.O. documents, including the handwritten minutes by Foreign Secretary Curzon and others, is in R. Ulmann, *The Anglo-Soviet Accord: Anglo-Soviet Relations 1917–1921*, Princeton, 1972, pp. 388 ff.

7. The case of the U.S. Ambassador to Italy, Clare Booth Luce, became public years later when the U.S. Senate discussed her nomination as ambassador to Brazil; it was clarified to me earlier, as were other aspects of U.S. policy when the late Max Thornburg kindly allowed me to use a series of his private papers, including correspondence with Luce and a record of a conversation with Dean Acheson in which Thornburg proposed U.S. aid in the overthrow of Mossadeq. A few of these documents are quoted in my dissertation, 'The Impact of the West on Modern Iranian Social History,' Berkeley. The oil boycott against Iran is discussed, among other places, in Anthony Sampson's brilliant and readable *The Seven Sisters: The Great Oil Companies and the World They Shaped*, Bantam paperback, 1976.

8. This point is made in several works. The most interesting discussion is G. B. Baldwin, *Planning and Development in Iran*, Baltimore, 1967.

9. *Ibid.*, p. 196.

10. Much of this analysis is based on private conversations or on semi-confidential reports by Iranian and international organizations. Among the most useful published works are R. Looney, *The Economic Development of Iran*, New York, 1973; I.L.O., *Employment and Income Policies for Iran*, Geneva, 1973; David Housego, 'Quiet thee Now and Rest,' *The Economist*, August 28, 1976; and Robert Graham, *Iran: The Illusion of Power*, London, 1978.

11. On land reform see the works cited in note 7, and Chapter 7 of this volume and the sources cited therein, including especially the works of A. Lambton. See also Paul Vieille, *La féodalité et l'Etat en Iran*, Paris, 1975. E. Hooglund's important dissertation, 'The Effects of the Land Reform Program on Rural Iran 1962–1972' (Baltimore, Johns Hopkins University, 1975) is unfortunately not generally available. A. K. S. Lambton, *The Persian Land Reform, 1962–1966* is the standard book on the subject.

12. M. A. Katouzian, 'Oil versus Agriculture: A Case of Dual Resource Depletion in Iran,' *The Journal of Peasant Studies*, V, 3 (April 1978), 347–369, and the forthcoming Oxford University dissertation by Fatemeh Etemad Moghadam.

13. M. H. Pesaran and F. Gahvary, 'Growth and Income Distribution in Iran,' in press. Pesaran has done a series of outstanding studies on income distribution, as has F. Mehran; most of the latter are distributed in mimeo by the I.L.O. On income distribution see also Looney, *op cit.* and his *Income Distribution Policies and Economic Growth in Semiindustrialized Countries*, New York, 1975, and I.L.O., *op cit.*

14. Secular opposition groups are surveyed by Fred Halliday, *Iran: Dictatorship and Development*, Harmondsworth, 1979; and the religious opposition is discussed by H. Algar in N. Keddie, ed., *Scholars, Saints and Sufis*, and by N. Keddie in 'Religion and Politics in Contemporary Iran,' *Le Monde Diplomatique*, August 1977, and in Chapter 4 of this volume. Numerous works by Khomeini, Shariati, and others are available in Persian.

15. See especially Mangol Bayat-Philipp's paper in M. Bonine and N. Keddie, eds, *Modern Iran: Continuity and Change*, (Albany, State University of New York Press, 1981), and the sources cited therein.

Bibliography of author's works

(in chronological order within divisions excluding articles in this
volume or incorporated in *Sayyid Jamal ad-Din 'al-Afghani')*

I. Books

Religion and Rebellion in Iran: The Tobacco Protest of 1891–92, London, Frank
    Cass, 1966 (U.S. Humanities Press). Persian trans., Amir Kabir, Tehran,
    1977.

*An Islamic Response to Imperialism: Political and Religious Writings of Sayyid
    Jamal ad-Din 'al-Afghani'* (with translations from Persian, Arabic, and
    French writings), Berkeley, University of California Press, 1968.

Sayyid Jamal ad-Din 'al-Afghani': A Political Biography, Berkeley, UC Press,
    1972.

Scholars, Saints, and Sufis: Muslim Religious Institutions since 1500, ed., intro,
    and article, Berkeley, UC Press, 1972, paperback 1978.

Women in the Muslim World, co-ed, with Lois Beck, intro., Cambridge, Mass,
    Harvard University Press, 1978.

Iran: Religion, Politics and Society, London, Frank Cass, 1980.

The Middle East and Beyond, London, Frank Cass, 1980.

Iran: Roots of Revolution, with Y. Richard, New Haven, Yale University Press,
    1980.

Modern Iran: Continuity and Change, co.ed. with M. Bonine, Albany, S.U.N.Y.
    Press, 1981.

II. Contributions to Books

Historical Obstacles to Agrarian Change in Iran (short monograph), Claremont,
    Cal., 1960.

Co-author, 'Fida'iyyan-i Islam,' *Encyclopedia of Islam*, 1964.

'The Iranian Constitutional Revolution of 1905–1911: A Brief Assessment,' *Iran Society Silver Jubilee Souvenir*, Calcutta, 1970.

'Sayyid Jamal ad-Din al-Afghani: A case of Posthumous Charisma?' *Philosophers and Kings*, ed. D. Rustow, New York, Braziller, 1970.

'Iran', chapter in Fischer Weltgeschichte, *Der Islam*, II, ed. G. E. von Grunebaum, Frankfurt, 1971, 160–217. Also in Italian and Spanish editions, with French and English to come.

'The Assassination of the Amin as-Sultan (Atabak-i A'zam),' *Iran and Islam*, ed. C. E. Bosworth, Edinburgh, Edinburgh U. Press, 1971.

Co-author 'Namads,' author of many long explanatory captions and 19 photos, *A Survey of Persian Handicraft*, ed. J. and S. Gluck, Tehran, 1977 (Persian translation Tehran, 1977).

'Class Structure and Political Power in Iran since 1796,' ed. A. Banani as a special issue of *Iranian Studies, State and Society in Iran*, 1979.

'Socio-Economic Change in the Middle East since 1800: A Comparative Analysis,' in the volume of selected papers from the Princeton University conference on the economic history of the Middle East, ed. A. Udovitch, Princeton, the Darwin Press, 1980.

Chapter, 'Iran 1852–1922,' *Cambridge History of Iran*, vol. VII, forthcoming.

'Social Structure and Social Change in the Middle East before 1800,' in *The Middle East and Beyond*, Frank Cass, London, 1980.

'Material Culture: A Neglected Aspect of Middle East History,' in *The Middle East and Beyond*, Frank Cass, London, 1980.

'The Islamic Middle East,' bibliographical article in *The Past Before Us*, ed. M. Kammen, Ithaca, Cornell University Press, 1980.

'Islam and Revolution in Iran,' to be published in a volume of papers on the Iranian revolution edited from a conference held by the Friedrich Ebert Foundation, Bonn, March 1980.

'History and Economic Development,' in *The Social Sciences and Economic Development*, ed. K. Farmanfarmaian, Princeton, 1976.

III. Articles, etc.

'Western Rules versus Western Values: Suggestions for a Comparative Study of Asian Intellectual History,' *Diogenes*, 26, 1959 (also published in French and Arabic).

Trans. and Annotation, Sayyed Hasan Taqizadeh, 'The Background of the Constitutional Movement in Azerbaijan,' *Middle East Journal*, XIV, 4, 1960, 456–65.

'Symbol and Sincerity in Islam,' *Studia Islamica*, XIX, 1963, 27–63.

'British Policy and the Iranian Opposition, 1901–1907,' *Journal of Modern History*, 39, 3, 1967, 266–82.

'Islamic Philosophy and Islamic Modernism,' *Iran: Journal of the British Institute of Persian Studies*, VI, 1968, 53–6.

'The Iranian Village before and After Land Reform,' *Journal of Contemporary History*, III, 3, 1968, 69–91. Reprinted in H. Bernstein, ed., *Development and Underdevelopment*, Penguin Books, England, 1974.

'Iranian Politics 1900–1905: Background to Revolution,' *Middle Eastern Studies*, V, 1, Jan. 1969, 3–31; 2, May 1969, 151–67; 3, Oct. 1969, 234–50.

'Pan-Islam as Proto-Nationalism,' *Journal of Modern History*, 41, March 1969, 31–53.

'The Roots of the Ulama's Power in Modern Iran,' *Studia Islamica*, XXIX, 1969, 31–53.

'The Iranian Power Structure and Social Change 1800–1969: An Overview,' *International Journal of Middle East Studies*, II, 1, Jan. 1971, 3–20.

'The Persian Land Reform 1962–1966, by A. K. S. Lambton,' Review Article, *Middle Eastern Studies*, VII, 3, 1971, 373–8.

'Intellectuals in the Middle East: A Brief Historical Consideration,' *Daedalus*, Summer 1972, 39–57.

'Is there a Middle East?' *International Journal of Middle East Studies*, IV, 3, 1973, 255–71.

'An Assessment of American, British, and French Works since 1940 on Modern Iranian History,' *Iranian Studies*, VI, 2–3, 1972, 255–71.

4 articles, with photos, on Iranian crafts and carpets, *Kayhan International*, Tehran, spring 1974.

4 articles, with photos, on the restoration of Persepolis and Isfahan and its attendant scholarly findings, *Kayhan International*, spring 1974.

'Islam et politique en Iran,' *Le Monde Diplomatique*, August 1977.

'The Midas Touch,' *Iranian Studies*, X, 4, Autumn 1977. (The article was in fact completed in late 1978 and the issue appeared in 1979.)

'Roots of Revolution,' *The Gazelle Review*, Spring 1979.

'Oil, Economic Policy and Social Conflict,' *Race and Class*, Spring 1979.

'Problems in the Study of Middle Eastern Women,' *International Journal of Middle East Studies*, X, 2, 1979, 225–40.

'Iran: Is "Modernization" the Message?' *Middle East Review*, XI, 3, 1979, 55–6.

'Islam and Politics: New Factors in the Equation,' *Los Angeles Times*, Opinion lead, 2 Dec. 1979.

'Khomaini's Fundamentalism is as Revolutionary as His Politics,' *Los Angeles Times*, Opinion first page, 13 Jan. 1980.

'Iran: Change in Islam; Islam and Change,' *International Journal of Middle East Studies*, XI, Nov. 1960; revised version to appear in a volume on modern Islam and politics, ed. J. Esposito.

IV. Publications Near Completion

Louis Beck and I have a contract with U.S. publisher to do a book with colour and black and white photos on the Qashqai tribe of Iran, which is her specialty. For the last two summers I spent most of my time with the tribe, studying and taking photographs.